D1268707

# The Interpretation of Financial Statements

Steven M. Bragg

For more information about AccountingTools® products, visit our Web site at www.accountingtools.com.


ISBN-13: 978-1-938910-53-1


Printed in the United States of America

# Table of Contents

# Preface

When someone asks for information about a business, they are likely to receive its financial statements. These statements quantify the results, financial position, and cash flows of a business. However, these documents only provide information at quite a high level, and so may obscure more than they reveal. *The Interpretation of Financial Statements* is designed to cut through this obscurity, describing a number of tools for dissecting financial statements, as well as a wealth of additional insights into the reasons for the presence of or changes in certain numbers.

The bulk of the book covers three topics, which are the interpretation of the balance sheet, income statement, and cash flows. Eight chapters address the various parts of the balance sheet, another four chapters cover the income statement, and a separate chapter examines the statement of cash flows. There is also a lengthy chapter pertaining to the contents and interpretation of additional public company information. In these chapters, we describe the accounts that make up the various line items in the financial statements, demonstrate the use of applicable analysis tools, and also discuss specific operational and financial issues that may be causing certain results to appear in the financial statements.

You can find the answers to many questions about the interpretation of financial statements in the following chapters, including:

- What are the circumstances under which a business can report a cash balance of exactly zero?
- What policy decisions can lead to an increase in the amount of accounts receivable?
- What might cause a spike in the cost of goods sold just prior to the end of the year?
- Are there any valid reasons for a decline in the proportion of depreciation to fixed assets?
- What is the implication of accounts payable being converted into debt?
- What are the circumstances under which a business might elect to buy back shares?
- What techniques can be used to evaluate the quality of sales?
- How can the capitalization limit impact the supplies expense?
- What are the possible reasons for an unusually large dividend?
- Which discussion topics in the Form 10-K can be used to evaluate the compensation of the management team?

*The Interpretation of Financial Statements* is designed for someone reviewing the financial statements of a business from the outside. This may be a lender, supplier, investor, or financial analyst. It can also be used by students to gain a deeper understanding of how to examine financial statements.

Centennial, Colorado
February 2015

# About the Author

**Steven Bragg, CPA,** has been the chief financial officer or controller of four companies, as well as a consulting manager at Ernst & Young. He received a master's degree in finance from Bentley College, an MBA from Babson College, and a Bachelor's degree in Economics from the University of Maine. He has been a two-time president of the Colorado Mountain Club, and is an avid alpine skier, mountain biker, and certified master diver. Mr. Bragg resides in Centennial, Colorado. He has written the following books and courses:

Accountants' Guidebook
Accounting Controls Guidebook
Accounting for Derivatives and Hedges
Accounting for Inventory
Accounting for Investments
Accounting for Managers
Accounting Procedures Guidebook
Bookkeeping Guidebook
Budgeting
Business Combinations and Consolidations
Business Ratios
CFO Guidebook
Closing the Books
Constraint Management
Corporate Cash Management
Corporate Finance
Cost Accounting Fundamentals
Cost Management Guidebook
Credit & Collection Guidebook

Financial Analysis
Fixed Asset Accounting
GAAP Guidebook
Hospitality Accounting
Human Resources Guidebook
IFRS Guidebook
Interpretation of Financial Statements
Inventory Management
Investor Relations Guidebook
Lean Accounting Guidebook
Mergers & Acquisitions
New Controller Guidebook
Nonprofit Accounting
Payables Management
Payroll Management
Project Accounting
Public Company Accounting
Revenue Recognition

# On-Line Resources by Steven Bragg

Steven maintains the accountingtools.com web site, which contains continuing professional education courses, the Accounting Best Practices podcast, and over a thousand articles on accounting subjects.

*The Interpretation of Financial Statements* is also available as a continuing professional education (CPE) course. You can purchase the course (and many other courses) and take an on-line exam at:

www.accountingtools.com/cpe

# Chapter 1
## Overview of the Financial Statements

## Introduction

A person who wants to learn about a business usually begins by inspecting its financial statements. The financial statements include three documents, which are the balance sheet, income statement, and statement of cash flows, as well as a set of accompanying footnotes. These documents describe the financial results, position, and cash flows of an organization.

Someone reading financial statements may need to make a critical decision, such as whether to invest in or lend money to an organization. If so, it is essential to extract as much information as possible from the financial statements to aid in making the decision. The entire point of this book is how to do so. We begin in this chapter with brief discussions of where the information in the financial statements comes from, the general layout of each of the financial statements, and the types of tools that will be used in the following chapters to analyze them.

## The General Ledger

The source of the financial statements is the general ledger. A general ledger is the master set of accounts in which is summarized all transactions occurring within a business during a specific period of time. An account is a record of accounting transactions. An example of a general ledger at a highly summary level is as follows:

### Sample General Ledger

| Account Number | Account Description | Debit | Credit |
|---|---|---|---|
| 1000 | Cash | $60,000 | |
| 1500 | Accounts receivable | 180,000 | |
| 2000 | Inventory | 300,000 | |
| 3000 | Fixed assets | 210,000 | |
| 4000 | Accounts payable | | $90,000 |
| 4500 | Accrued liabilities | | 50,000 |
| 4700 | Notes payable | | 420,000 |
| 5000 | Equity | | 350,000 |
| 6000 | Revenue | | 400,000 |
| 7200 | Cost of goods sold | 290,000 | |
| 7300 | Salaries expense | 200,000 | |
| 7400 | Payroll tax expense | 20,000 | |
| 7500 | Rent expense | 35,000 | |
| 7600 | Other expenses | 15,000 | |
| | Totals | $1,310,000 | $1,310,000 |

The information stored in the general ledger is transferred directly into the financial statements, which are described in the following sections.

> **Note:** Explanations for the account names listed in the general ledger are stated in the following chapters.

Before delving into the layouts and content of the financial statements, we will briefly diverge to address the topics of the accrual basis of accounting, costs, and expenses, which are integral to the formulation of the information in the statements.

## The Accrual Basis of Accounting

A key concept that drives the content of the financial statements is the accrual basis of accounting. This is the concept of recording revenues when earned and expenses as incurred. It differs from the cash basis of accounting, under which revenues are recorded when cash is received, and expenses are recorded when cash is paid. For example, a company operating under the accrual basis of accounting will record a sale as soon as it issues an invoice to a customer, while a cash basis company would instead wait to be paid before it records the sale. Similarly, an accrual basis company will record an expense as incurred, while a cash basis company would instead wait to pay its supplier before recording the expense.

The accrual basis of accounting is advocated under the major accounting frameworks, such as generally accepted accounting principles (GAAP) and international financial reporting standards (IFRS). These frameworks provide guidance regarding how to account for revenue and expense transactions in the absence of the cash receipts or payments that would trigger the recordation of a transaction under the cash basis of accounting.

The accrual basis tends to provide more even recognition of revenues and expenses over time than the cash basis, and so is considered to be the most valid accounting system for ascertaining the results of operations, financial position, and cash flows of a business. In particular, it supports the matching principle, under which revenues and all related expenses are to be recorded within the same reporting period; by doing so, it should be possible to see the full extent of the profits and losses associated with specific business transactions within a single reporting period.

The accrual basis requires the use of estimated reserves in certain areas. For example, a company should recognize an expense for estimated bad debts that have not yet been incurred. By doing so, all expenses related to a revenue transaction are recorded at the same time as the revenue, which results in an income statement that fully reflects the results of operations. Similarly, the estimated amounts of product returns, sales allowances, and obsolete inventory may be recorded in reserve accounts. These estimates may not be entirely accurate, and so can lead to materially inaccurate financial statements. Consequently, a considerable amount of care must be used when estimating reserves.

The use of reserves brings up the concept of the *contra account*, which appears in the balance sheet. A contra account offsets the balance in another, related account

2

with which it is paired. For example, the balance sheet contains an asset line item for accounts receivable. It is typically paired with a contra asset account called the allowance for doubtful accounts, after which a net balance is shown that states the residual receivables balance once the two line items are combined. A sample presentation in the balance sheet is:

| | | |
|---|---|---|
| Accounts receivable | $1,000,000 | |
| Allowance for doubtful accounts | -50,000 | |
| | | $950,000 |

As another example, an allowance for obsolete inventory may be paired with the inventory line item in the balance sheet, to show the net amount of the inventory asset. A sample presentation in the balance sheet is:

| | | |
|---|---|---|
| Inventory | $600,000 | |
| Allowance for obsolete inventory | -20,000 | |
| | | $580,000 |

A small business may elect to avoid using the accrual basis of accounting, since it requires a certain amount of accounting expertise. Also, a small business owner may choose to manipulate the timing of cash inflows and outflows to create a smaller amount of taxable income under the cash basis of accounting, which can result in the deferral of income tax payments.

A significant failing of the accrual basis is that it can indicate the presence of profits, even though the associated cash inflows have not yet occurred. The result can be a supposedly profitable entity that is starved for cash, and which may therefore go bankrupt despite its reported level of profitability.

## Costs versus Expenses

The concepts of cost and expense appear throughout the following chapters. These terms are not the same. The difference between cost and expense is that cost identifies an expenditure, while expense refers to the consumption of the item acquired. These concepts are expanded upon below.

Cost most closely equates to the term *expenditure*, so it means that you have expended resources in order to acquire something, transport it to your location, and set it up. However, it does not mean that the acquired item has yet been consumed. Thus, an item for which you have expended resources should be classified as an asset until it has been consumed. Examples of asset classifications into which purchased items are recorded are prepaid expenses, inventory, and fixed assets.

For example, the cost of an automobile may be $40,000 (since that is what you paid for it) and the cost of a product you built is $25 (because that is the sum total of the expenditures you made to build it). The cost of the automobile likely includes sales taxes and a delivery charge, while the cost of the product probably includes the cost of materials, labor, and manufacturing overhead. In both cases, funds were expended to acquire the automobile and the product, but neither one has yet been

3

consumed. Accordingly, the first expenditure is classified as a fixed asset, while the second one is classified as inventory; both are considered to be assets. Similarly, an advance paid to an employee is classified as a prepaid expense, which is an asset.

Expense is a cost whose utility has been used up; it has been consumed. For example, the $40,000 automobile you purchased will eventually be charged to expense through depreciation over a period of several years, and the $25 product will be charged to the cost of goods sold when it is eventually sold. Thus, in both cases, we have converted a cost that was treated as an asset into an expense as the underlying asset was consumed. The automobile asset is being consumed gradually, so we are using depreciation to eventually convert it to expense. The inventory item is consumed during a single sale transaction, so we convert it to expense as soon as the sale occurs.

A key reason why a cost is, in practice, frequently treated exactly as an expense is that most expenditures are consumed at once, so they immediately convert from a cost to an expense. This situation arises with any expenditure related to a specific period, such as the monthly utility bill, administrative salaries, rent, office supplies, and so forth.

## The Balance Sheet

A balance sheet (also known as a statement of financial position) presents information about an entity's assets, liabilities, and shareholders' equity, where the compiled result must match this formula, which is called the *accounting equation*:

$$\text{Total assets} = \text{Total liabilities} + \text{Equity}$$

This equation drives the name of the document, where the total of all assets must *balance* the total amount of liabilities and equity. This balancing concept is necessary, since the ownership of an asset can only occur if an organization either pays for it with an obligation (such as a loan) or with the funds invested by shareholders or the ongoing profits of the business (which is equity).

In essence, a balance sheet describes what a business owns, what it owes, and what residual amount net of the first two items is left over for its shareholders. It is used to assess an entity's liquidity and ability to pay its debts.

The balance sheet reports the aggregate effect of transactions as of a specific date. For example, if a balance sheet has been produced as part of a package of financial statements for the month of April, the information contained within the balance sheet is as of April 30, which is the last day of the month. Thus, it essentially represents a snapshot of the financial condition of a business as of a moment in time.

The basic format of a balance sheet is noted in the following exhibit. It contains a header, which describes the name of the entity whose financial information is being reported on, the name of the report, and the date as of which the report was constructed. In the following line items, we have noted how each one adds up into the various subtotals and totals in the document.

## Sample Balance Sheet Format

Lowry Locomotion
Balance Sheet
As of December 31, 20X1

| ASSETS | |
|---|---|
| **Current assets** | |
| Cash | A |
| Investments | B |
| Accounts receivable | C |
| Inventory | D |
| Prepaid expenses | E |
| **Total current assets** | A + B + C + D + E = F |
| | |
| **Non-current assets** | |
| Fixed assets | G |
| Goodwill | H |
| Other assets | I |
| **Total non-current assets** | G + H + I = J |
| | |
| **Total assets** | F + J |
| | |
| **LIABILITIES AND EQUITY** | |
| **Current liabilities** | |
| Accounts payable | K |
| Other payables | L |
| Accrued liabilities | M |
| Unearned revenues | N |
| **Total current liabilities** | K + L + M + N = O |
| | |
| **Noncurrent liabilities** | |
| Long-term debt | P |
| Bonds payable | Q |
| **Total noncurrent liabilities** | P + Q = R |
| | |
| **Total liabilities** | O + R = S |
| | |
| **Shareholders' equity** | |
| Common stock | T |
| Preferred stock | U |
| Additional paid-in capital | V |
| Retained earnings | W |
| Treasury stock | X |
| **Total shareholders' equity** | T + U + V + W + X = Y |
| **Total liabilities and shareholders' equity** | S + Y |

To see how these calculations are used in a balance sheet, the following example replaces the line item computations with numbers taken from the general ledger of a business.

## Sample Balance Sheet with Numeric Presentation

Lowry Locomotion
Balance Sheet
As of December 31, 20X1

| ASSETS | |
|---|---|
| **Current assets** | |
| Cash | $45,000 |
| Investments | 80,000 |
| Accounts receivable | 425,000 |
| Inventory | 415,000 |
| Prepaid expenses | 15,000 |
| **Total current assets** | $980,000 |
| | |
| **Non-current assets** | |
| Fixed assets | 800,000 |
| Goodwill | 200,000 |
| Other assets | 20,000 |
| **Total non-current assets** | $1,020,000 |
| | |
| **Total assets** | $2,000,000 |
| | |
| **LIABILITIES AND EQUITY** | |
| **Current liabilities** | |
| Accounts payable | $215,000 |
| Other payables | 30,000 |
| Accrued liabilities | 28,000 |
| Unearned revenues | 12,000 |
| **Total current liabilities** | $285,000 |
| | |
| **Noncurrent liabilities** | |
| Long-term debt | 200,000 |
| Bonds payable | 350,000 |
| **Total noncurrent liabilities** | 550,000 |
| | |
| **Total liabilities** | $835,000 |
| | |
| **Shareholders' equity** | |
| Common stock | 10,000 |
| Preferred stock | 50,000 |
| Additional paid-in capital | 320,000 |
| Retained earnings | 825,000 |
| Treasury stock | -40,000 |
| **Total shareholders' equity** | $1,165,000 |
| **Total liabilities and shareholders' equity** | $2,000,000 |

The line items appearing in the preceding balance sheet example are stated in a particular order, which is derived from a concept called the *order of liquidity*. This refers to the presentation of assets in the balance sheet in the order of the amount of time it would usually take to convert them into cash. Thus, cash is always presented first, followed by investments, then accounts receivable, then inventory, and then fixed assets. Goodwill is listed last. The approximate amount of time required to convert each type of asset into cash is noted below:

1. *Cash*. No conversion is needed.
2. *Investments*. A few days may be required to convert to cash in most cases.
3. *Accounts receivable*. Will convert to cash in accordance with the company's normal credit terms.
4. *Inventory*. Could require multiple months to convert to cash, depending on turnover levels and the proportion of inventory items for which there is not a ready resale market.
5. *Fixed assets*. Conversion to cash depends entirely on the presence of an active after-market for these items.
6. *Goodwill*. This can only be converted to cash upon the sale of the business for an adequate price.

In short, the order of liquidity concept results in a logical sort sequence for the assets listed in the balance sheet. The same concept applies to the liabilities section of the balance sheet, where those obligations most likely to be paid off first are listed first.

## The Income Statement

The income statement contains the results of an organization's operations for a specific period of time, showing revenues and expenses and the resulting profit or loss. The typical period covered by an income statement is for a month, quarter, or year, though it could cover just a few days.

An income statement is used to measure the ability of an organization to achieve sales, and its efficiency in servicing customers. If a business does well in both respects, then it earns a profit. A profit is the amount by which sales exceed expenses. Instead, if expenses exceed sales, then the entity generates a loss. The cumulative amount of this profit or loss, net of any dividends paid to investors, appears in the retained earnings line item in the balance sheet.

The basic format of an income statement is noted in the following exhibit. It contains a header, which describes the name of the entity whose financial information is being reported on, the name of the report, and the date range for which information is being presented. In the following line items, we have noted how each one adds up into the various subtotals and totals in the document. The flow of information in the statement is to begin at the top with sales, subtract out expenses directly related to sales, then subtract all other expenses to arrive at before-tax income, and then subtract income taxes to arrive at the net income figure.

## Sample Income Statement Format

Laid Back Corporation
Income Statement
For the month ended December 31, 20X1

| | |
|---|---|
| Net sales | A |
| Cost of goods sold | B |
| Gross margin | $A - B = C$ |
| | |
| Operating expenses | |
| Advertising | D |
| Depreciation | E |
| Rent | F |
| Payroll taxes | G |
| Salaries and wages | H |
| Supplies | I |
| Travel and entertainment | J |
| Total operating expenses | $D + E + F + G + H + I + J = K$ |
| | |
| Other income | L |
| Total income before taxes | $C - K + L = M$ |
| Income taxes | N |
| | |
| Net income | $\underline{M - N}$ |

To see how these calculations are used in an income statement, the following example replaces the line item computations with numbers taken from the general ledger of a business.

**Sample Income Statement with Numeric Presentation**

Laid Back Corporation
Income Statement
For the month ended December 31, 20X1

| | |
|---|---:|
| Net sales | $1,000,000 |
| Cost of goods sold | 480,000 |
| Gross margin | $520,000 |
| | |
| Operating expenses | |
| Advertising | 10,000 |
| Depreciation | 8,000 |
| Rent | 32,000 |
| Payroll taxes | 25,000 |
| Salaries and wages | 359,000 |
| Supplies | 5,000 |
| Travel and entertainment | 11,000 |
| Total operating expenses | $450,000 |
| | |
| Other income | 10,000 |
| Total income before taxes | $80,000 |
| Income taxes | 30,000 |
| | |
| Net income | $50,000 |

In short, the balance sheet provides a point-in-time picture of a business, while the income statement provides a report card on its results in between these point-in-time snapshots.

# The Statement of Cash Flows

The statement of cash flows is used to identify the different types of cash payments made by a business to third parties (cash outflows), as well as payments made to a business by third parties (cash inflows). Though less frequently used than the balance sheet and income statement, this additional report provides valuable information about the cash status of a business.

This statement is needed, because the information in the income statement does not exactly correspond to cash flows. Instead, an accrual-basis income statement may record revenues and expenses for which cash flows have not yet occurred. In addition, there is no information in the income statement regarding the cash required to support investments in receivables, fixed assets, inventory, and other assets, nor is there any information about cash flows related to the sale of stock, obtaining or paying back loans, and similar matters.

The basic format of a statement of cash flows is noted in the following exhibit. It contains a header, which describes the name of the entity whose financial information is being reported on, the name of the report, and the date range for which information is being presented. In the following line items, we have noted how each one adds up into the various subtotals and totals in the document. The flow of information in the statement is to begin with a derivation of cash flows generated by the operations of a business, followed by the cash flows associated with investing activities and financing activities, which results in a net change in cash for the period. Cash flows are separated into the operating, investing, and financing activities classifications in order to give the reader more information about how cash is generated and used.

## Sample Statement of Cash Flows Format

Newton Enterprises
Statement of Cash Flows
For the year ended 12/31/20X1

| | | |
|---|---|---|
| **Cash flows from operating activities** | | |
| Net income | | A |
| Adjustments for: | | |
| Depreciation and amortization | B | |
| Provision for losses on accounts receivable | C | |
| Gain/loss on sale of assets | D | |
| | | $B + C + D = E$ |
| Increase/decrease in accounts receivables | F | |
| Increase/decrease in inventories | G | |
| Increase/decrease in trade payables | H | |
| | | $F + G + H = I$ |
| Cash generated from/used in operations | | $A + E + I = J$ |
| | | |
| **Cash flows from investing activities** | | |
| Purchase of fixed assets | K | |
| Proceeds from sale of equipment | L | |
| Net cash generated from/used in investing activities | | $K + L = M$ |
| | | |
| **Cash flows from financing activities** | | |
| Proceeds from issuance of common stock | N | |
| Proceeds from issuance of long-term debt | O | |
| Dividends paid | P | |
| Net cash generated from/used in financing activities | | $N + O + P = Q$ |
| | | |
| Net increase/decrease in cash and cash equivalents | | $J + M + Q = R$ |
| Cash and cash equivalents at beginning of period | | S |
| Cash and cash equivalents at end of period | | $R + S$ |

To see how these calculations are used in a statement of cash flows, the following example replaces the line item computations with numbers taken from the general ledger of a business.

**Sample Statement of Cash Flows with Numeric Presentation**

Newton Enterprises
Statement of Cash Flows
For the year ended 12/31/20X1

| Cash flows from operating activities | | |
|---|---|---|
| Net income | | $100,000 |
| Adjustments for: | | |
| Depreciation and amortization | 12,000 | |
| Provision for losses on accounts receivable | 18,000 | |
| Gain on sale of assets | -10,000 | |
| | | 20,000 |
| Increase in accounts receivables | -80,000 | |
| Decrease in inventories | 30,000 | |
| Decrease in trade payables | -16,000 | |
| | | -66,000 |
| | | |
| Cash generated from operations | | 54,000 |
| | | |
| **Cash flows from investing activities** | | |
| Purchase of fixed assets | -80,000 | |
| Proceeds from sale of equipment | 24,000 | |
| Net cash used in investing activities | | -56,000 |
| | | |
| **Cash flows from financing activities** | | |
| Proceeds from issuance of common stock | 120,000 | |
| Proceeds from issuance of long-term debt | 57,000 | |
| Dividends paid | -32,000 | |
| Cash generated from financing activities | | 145,000 |
| | | |
| Net increase in cash and cash equivalents | | 143,000 |
| Cash and cash equivalents at beginning of period | | 230,000 |
| Cash and cash equivalents at end of period | | $373,000 |

Some elements of the statement of cash flows are derived from the other financial statements. The net income figure comes from the income statement, along with several of the net income adjustment items. The cash balances at the bottom of the report are taken from the balance sheet, while the increases and decreases in the various assets and liabilities are derived by calculating the differences between the line items in the most recent balance sheet and the same line items in the balance sheet pertaining to the end of the immediately preceding reporting period. For example, the change in accounts receivable noted in the statement of cash flows is derived by calculating the difference in the accounts receivable line items in the last two balance sheets.

## Interactions between the Financial Statements

When a business transaction is recorded in the accounting records, it may impact several of the financial statements at the same time. In this section, we describe a number of these interactions. The intent is to point out how someone reading the financial statements can see how information flows through and is represented in the balance sheet, income statement, and statement of cash flows. Key interactions are as follows:

- *Sales on credit*. When sales are made on credit, the amount appears as both a sale in the income statement and an increase in accounts receivable in the balance sheet. If goods are sold, then this also reduces the inventory line item in the balance sheet by an amount that appears in the cost of goods sold in the income statement.
- *Cash receipts*. When cash is received from a customer in payment of an invoice, this reduces the accounts receivable balance and increases the amount of cash, both of which are located in the balance sheet. This also appears within the operating activities section of the statement of cash flows, since it impacts cash.
- *Buy inventory on credit*. When merchandise and raw materials are acquired from suppliers on credit, the amount appears as both an increase in the inventory and accounts payable line items, which are located on opposite sides of the balance sheet.
- *Receive expenses invoice*. When an invoice is received from a supplier for goods or services that are consumed at once, the amount appears as an expense in the income statement and an increase in the accounts payable liability in the balance sheet.
- *Pay suppliers*. When an invoice is paid, this reduces both the cash and accounts payable line items, which are located on opposite sides of the balance sheet. This also appears within the operating activities section of the statement of cash flows, since it impacts cash.
- *Sell shares*. When cash is received from investors when they buy shares from a business, this increases both the cash balance and the amount of shareholders' equity; these line items are located on opposite sides of the balance sheet. This also appears within the financing activities section of the statement of cash flows, since it impacts cash.
- *Acquire debt*. When cash is received from a lender under the terms of a loan, this increases both the cash and debt liability line items, which are located on opposite sides of the balance sheet. This also appears within the financing activities section of the statement of cash flows, since it impacts cash.

## Financial Statement Footnotes

Financial statement disclosures are explanatory and supplemental notes that accompany the financial statements issued by a business. The exact nature of these footnotes varies, depending on the type of business and how it records information.

Financial statement disclosures are an integral part of the financial statements, so they should be issued alongside the statements.

There are an enormous number of detailed disclosures that may be provided, depending upon the types of business transactions that a company engages in, and the industry in which it does business. Even more extensive footnotes are required by the Securities and Exchange Commission of any publicly-held company when they issue their annual financial statements on the Form 10-K and quarterly financial statements on the Form 10-Q. Selections of these footnotes are discussed in the Additional Public Company Information chapter.

In this section, we provide a sampling of the types of disclosures that may be appended to the financial statements. The following list touches upon the more common footnotes, and is by no means even remotely comprehensive. If a company is in a specialized industry, there may be a number of additional disclosures required that are specific to that industry. A representative set of financial statement disclosures include:

- *Accounting policies.* Describes significant accounting principles followed.
- *Bad debts.* Notes the method used to derive bad debt reserves, and the reserve amount as of the balance sheet date.
- *Business combinations.* Describes the type of combination, the reason for the acquisition, the payment price, liabilities assumed, goodwill incurred, acquisition-related costs, and many other factors.
- *Cash.* Notes any uninsured cash balances or restrictions on the use of cash.
- *Contingencies and commitments.* Describes the nature of any reasonably possible losses, and any guarantees, including maximum liabilities.
- *Customers.* States whether any customers comprise a significant proportion of the company's total business, and the amount of that proportion.
- *Debt.* Describes loans payable, interest rates, and maturities occurring over the next five years.
- *Endowments.* Notes the total amount of any deficiencies in donor-restricted endowment funds, where the fair value is less than the amount required by donors or the law.
- *Fixed assets.* Notes the investments in various types of fixed assets, methods of depreciation used, the amount of capitalized interest, and impairments.
- *Goodwill and intangibles.* Reconciles any changes in goodwill during the period, and any impairment losses.
- *Hedging.* States the objective and strategies for using a hedging instrument, as well as the risks being hedged.
- *Impairments.* Describes any assets that have been impaired and the amounts of the impairments.
- *Inventories.* Describes any cost flow assumptions used, as well as any write-downs.
- *Investments.* Notes the fair value and unrealized gains and losses on investments.
- *Leases.* Itemizes future minimum lease payments.

- *Liabilities.* Describes any larger accrued liabilities.
- *Pensions.* Reconciles various elements of the company pension plan during the period, and describes investment policies.
- *Receivables.* Notes the carrying amount of any financial instruments that are used as collateral for borrowings, and concentrations of credit risk.
- *Related parties.* States the nature of the relationship with a related party, and the amounts due to or from the other party.
- *Revenue recognition.* Notes the company's revenue recognition policies.
- *Risks and uncertainties.* Notes the use of significant estimates in accounting transactions, as well as various business vulnerabilities.
- *Segment data.* Identifies company segments and the operational results of each one.
- *Stockholders' equity.* Describes any changes in equity during the period, as well as the terms of any convertible equity and dividends in arrears.
- *Subsequent events.* Discloses the nature of subsequent events and estimates their financial effect.

When interpreting the information in the financial statements, it can be quite helpful to review the footnotes for related information. In many cases, the footnotes provide detailed schedules of information and/or explanatory comments that clarify the presentation in the financial statements.

## Interpretation Tools

The financial statements are a quantification of the operations of a business. Since these are essentially summary documents, they only provide an overview. To obtain a more detailed understanding from the financial statements, we must sift through the information in a variety of ways. By doing so, it is possible to answer questions for which solutions might not otherwise be immediately apparent, such as:
- What is the ability of an organization to take on and pay back debt?
- Is an entity improving, or is it in a state of decline?
- Would a business be a good investment opportunity?
- Is a company suffering from competitive pressure?

This sifting process can be accomplished with several tools, which are noted in the following sub-sections.

### Ratio Analysis

Ratio analysis is the comparison of line items in the financial statements of a business. Ratio analysis is used to evaluate a number of issues with an entity, such as its liquidity, efficiency of operations, and profitability. This type of analysis is particularly useful to analysts outside of a business, since their primary source of information about an organization is its financial statements; they do not have access to more detailed management reports. Ratio analysis is particularly useful when employed in the following ways:

- *Trend line*. Calculate each ratio over a large number of reporting periods, to see if there is a trend in the results. The trend can indicate financial difficulties that would not otherwise be apparent if ratios were being examined for a single period. Trend lines can also be used to estimate the direction of future ratio performance.
- *Industry comparison*. Calculate the same ratios for competitors in the same industry, and compare the results across all of the companies reviewed. Since these businesses likely operate with similar fixed asset investments and have similar capital structures, the results of a ratio analysis should be similar. If this is not the case, it can indicate a potential issue, or the reverse - the ability of a business to generate a profit that is notably higher than the rest of the industry. The industry comparison approach is used for sector analysis, to determine which businesses within an industry are the most (and least) valuable.

Ratio analysis is a useful tool. However, there are a number of limitations of ratio analysis to be aware of. They are:

- *Historical*. All of the information used in ratio analysis is derived from actual historical results. This does not mean that the same results will carry forward into the future.
- *Aggregation*. The information in a financial statement line item being used for a ratio analysis may have been aggregated differently in the past, so that running the ratio analysis on a trend line does not compare the same information through the entire trend period.
- *Operational changes*. A company may change its underlying operational structure to such an extent that a ratio calculated several years ago and compared to the same ratio today would yield a misleading conclusion. For example, if a just-in-time production system was implemented, this might lead to a reduced investment in fixed assets, whereas a ratio analysis might conclude that the company is letting its fixed asset base become too old.
- *Accounting policies*. Different companies may have different policies for recording the same accounting transaction. This means that comparing the ratio results of different companies may be like comparing apples and oranges. For example, one company might use accelerated depreciation while another company uses straight line depreciation, or one company records a sale at gross while the other company does so at net.
- *Business conditions*. Place ratio analysis in the context of the general business environment. For example, 60 days of sales outstanding might be considered poor in a period of rapidly growing sales, but might be excellent during an economic contraction when customers are in severe financial condition and unable to pay their bills.
- *Interpretation*. It can be quite difficult to ascertain the reason for the results of a ratio. For example, a current ratio of 2:1 might appear to be excellent,

15

until you realize that the company just sold a large amount of its stock to bolster its cash position. A more detailed analysis might reveal that the current ratio will only temporarily be at that level, and will probably decline in the near future.

- *Company strategy*. It can be dangerous to conduct a ratio analysis comparison between two firms that are pursuing different strategies. For example, one company may be following a low-cost strategy, and so is willing to accept a lower gross margin in exchange for more market share. Conversely, a company in the same industry is focusing on a high customer service strategy where its prices are higher and gross margins are higher, but it will never attain the revenue levels of the first company.
- *Point in time*. Some ratios extract information from the balance sheet. Be aware that the information on the balance sheet is only as of the last day of the reporting period. If there was an unusual spike or decline in the account balance on the last day of the reporting period, this can impact the outcome of the ratio analysis.

In short, ratio analysis has a variety of limitations. However, as long as you are aware of these problems and use alternative and supplemental methods to collect and interpret information, ratio analysis is still useful.

## Horizontal Analysis

Horizontal analysis is the comparison of historical financial information over a series of reporting periods, or of the ratios derived from this information. The analysis is most commonly a simple grouping of information that is sorted by period, but the numbers in each succeeding period can also be expressed as a percentage of the amount in the baseline year, with the baseline amount being listed as 100%.

When conducting a horizontal analysis, it is useful to do so for all of the financial statements at the same time, so that you can see the complete impact of operational results on the company's financial condition over the review period. For example, as noted in the next two illustrations, the income statement analysis shows a company having an excellent second year, but the related balance sheet analysis shows that it is having trouble funding growth, given the decline in cash, increase in accounts payable, and increase in debt.

Horizontal analysis of the income statement is usually in a two-year format such as the one shown below, with a variance also reported that states the difference between the two years for each line item. An alternative format is to simply add as many years as will fit on the page, without showing a variance, so you can see general changes by account over multiple years.

| | 20X1 | 20X2 | Variance |
|---|---|---|---|
| Sales | $1,000,000 | $1,500,000 | $500,000 |
| Cost of goods sold | 400,000 | 600,000 | -200,000 |
| Gross margin | 600,000 | 900,000 | 300,000 |
| | | | |
| Salaries and wages | 250,000 | 375,000 | -125,000 |
| Office rent | 50,000 | 80,000 | -30,000 |
| Supplies | 10,000 | 20,000 | -10,000 |
| Utilities | 20,000 | 30,000 | -10,000 |
| Other expenses | 90,000 | 110,000 | -20,000 |
| Total expenses | 420,000 | 615,000 | -195,000 |
| Net profit | $180,000 | $285,000 | $105,000 |

Horizontal analysis of the balance sheet is also usually in a two-year format, such as the one shown next, with a variance stating the difference between the two years for each line item. An alternative format is to add as many years as will fit on the page, without showing a variance, in order to see general changes by line item over multiple years.

| | 20X1 | 20X2 | Variance |
|---|---|---|---|
| Cash | $100,000 | $80,000 | -$20,000 |
| Accounts receivable | 350,000 | 525,000 | 175,000 |
| Inventory | 150,000 | 275,000 | 125,000 |
| Total current assets | 600,000 | 880,000 | 280,000 |
| | | | |
| Fixed assets | 400,000 | 800,000 | 400,000 |
| Total assets | $1,000,000 | $1,680,000 | $680,000 |
| | | | |
| Accounts payable | $180,000 | $300,000 | $120,000 |
| Accrued liabilities | 70,000 | 120,000 | 50,000 |
| Total current liabilities | 250,000 | 420,000 | 170,000 |
| | | | |
| Notes payable | 300,000 | 525,000 | 225,000 |
| Total liabilities | 550,000 | 945,000 | 395,000 |
| | | | |
| Common stock | 200,000 | 200,000 | 0 |
| Retained earnings | 250,000 | 535,000 | 285,000 |
| Total equity | 450,000 | 735,000 | 285,000 |
| | | | |
| Total liabilities and equity | $1,000,000 | $1,680,000 | $680,000 |

We generally refer to horizontal analysis in the following chapters as the construction of a trend line. An example that uses horizontal analysis is provided in the Interpretation of Operating Expenses chapter; the chapter discusses a part of the income statement that can yield particularly fine insights when reviewed on a trend line basis.

**Experience**

A substantial part of the interpretational advice in the following chapters is not based on ratio analysis or horizontal analysis, but rather on years of experience in reading financial statements. There are many subtleties that may not be immediately apparent to a novice user of financial statements, but which appear downright glaring once a few hundred financial statements have been perused. Here are several examples, which are expanded upon in the following chapters:

- Smaller companies have a habit of not recording depreciation expense at all until the end of the year, which tends to overstate their profits until the final month.
- The balance in the prepaid expenses account tends to be overstated until the end of the year, when the books are cleaned up prior to the arrival of the auditors, resulting in a large charge to expense in the last month of the year.
- The accounts receivable line item may decline not due to better collection efforts, but because the oldest receivables have been converted into loans and now reside in a different line item in the balance sheet.
- Watching the trend of sales returns can provide advance warning of product problems that may trigger a product recall.
- An increase in the fixed asset account and a decrease in the compensation expense may mean that management is recording software development costs as an asset.

There are always new permutations on the techniques used to interpret financial statements, which are intended to discern the accounting vagaries of different industries, special types of business transactions, and especially the desire of management to make a company look better than it really is. In the following chapters, we will address how to develop a more accurate picture of an organization, using just its financial statements.

## Summary

This chapter has provided an overview of the layout of the financial statements and how they interact. In the following chapters, we will examine the individual line items contained within each of these statements, and note the different types of information that can be extracted from them, as well as the conclusions that can be reached about a business.

The information in this and the following chapters is entirely focused on the information buried within the financial statements. It is not intended to give the reader a comprehensive grounding in the principles of accounting, which would require a much larger text. For more background information, consider the author's *Bookkeeping Guidebook* or *Accountants' Guidebook*.

# Chapter 2
# Interpretation of Cash and Investments

## Introduction

The cash and investments line items on the balance sheet denote the current cash balance and all excess cash invested in financial instruments. In essence, these are the immediate sources of liquidity for a business. There are some issues related to these line items that can be useful for obtaining a broader perspective on whether an entity has a sufficient amount of cash on hand, which are addressed in this chapter.

## The Interpretation of Cash and Investments

The cash and investment line items appear within the current assets section of the balance sheet. Cash and investments are obviously the most liquid of the different categories of current assets, so they are positioned at the top of this cluster of accounts. A sample presentation showing where cash and investments are located on the balance sheet is noted in the following exhibit.

**Sample Presentation of Cash and Investments**

| Current Assets | |
|---|---:|
| **Cash** | **$84,000** |
| **Investments** | **109,000** |
| Accounts receivable | 342,000 |
| Inventory | 280,000 |
| Total current assets | $815,000 |

These two line items contain a great deal of information. They are comprised of several general ledger accounts that are usually clustered together in the balance sheet. These accounts are as follows:

- *Checking account.* Contains the cash balances being made available for immediate use to pay for ongoing expenditures, such as supplier invoices and taxes. Payments may be made from this account by check or electronic payment.
- *Payroll account.* Contains the cash balances used to pay for ongoing wage and salary payments to employees. In a smaller organization, this account may be eliminated, with all payroll payments originating from the checking account.
- *Petty cash.* Contains quite a small balance that indicates the amount of cash held in petty cash boxes around the company, for use in paying for incidental items.

- *Investments*. Contains the funds used to buy various types of investments, such as certificates of deposit, commercial paper, bonds, and equity securities. If the amount of funds invested is large, this account may be broken down into several accounts, with each one storing information about different types of investments.

An additional account that may sometimes be listed in the general ledger is the savings account, but we have assumed that a business is more likely to simply park all excess cash in separate investments than to use a low-interest savings account.

Thus, the underlying detail of the cash and investments line items noted in the last example could be broken down into the structure that appears in the following sample presentation.

**Sample Detailed Presentation of Cash and Investments**

| Current Assets | | |
|---|---|---|
| **Checking account** | **$23,700** | |
| **Payroll account** | **10,000** | |
| **Petty cash** | **300** | |
| Investments | 50,000 | |
| Cash | | $84,000 |
| Investments | | 109,000 |
| Accounts receivable | | 342,000 |
| Inventory | | 280,000 |
| Total current assets | | $815,000 |

This further breakdown of the information in the cash and investments line items brings up a number of issues, which are noted in the following sub-sections.

**Natural Cash Balance**

The treasurer of a business may find that there is a certain amount of cash that must be kept on hand at all times, in order to meet obligations for payments to suppliers and employees, as well as to continue to invest in fixed assets. All cash balances above this natural cash balance are excess, and so can be paid back to shareholders or used in some other way, such as for an acquisition or to maintain a reserve.

From an analysis perspective, this means that the cash line item should constitute a certain minimum percentage of assets. Over time, this percentage may increase above the natural level, but should not drop below it. If the cash balance were to drop below the natural level, this would indicate that the company is having difficulty generating sufficient cash to meet its obligations, and should be considered a warning sign of impending financial trouble.

---

**EXAMPLE**

Luminescence Corporation has been in business for many years. Recently, this manufacturer of floodlights has entered the business of producing LED lights, which is a different market and involves different production techniques. An analyst compiles a few line items from its preceding annual balance sheets, and notes the following changes:

| (000s) | 20X1 | 20X2 | 20X3 | 20X4 | 20X5 | 20X6 |
|---|---|---|---|---|---|---|
| Cash | $5,600 | $6,050 | $5,700 | $6,830 | $5,800 | $4,340 |
| Total assets | 112,000 | 114,150 | 116,300 | 119,820 | 120,900 | 135,700 |
| Cash percentage | 5.0% | 5.3% | 4.9% | 5.7% | 4.8% | 3.2% |

These year-end results indicate that Luminescence requires a cash balance of about 5% of total assets in order to conduct its operations. Consequently, the sudden drop of cash to 3.2% of assets in the most recent year is troubling. It could only indicate that fixed asset expenditures were made from operating cash, but could also indicate that the business is having trouble paying its bills.

## Relevance of a Low Cash Figure

The cash line item might contain an extremely low number, perhaps one that is even negative or exactly zero. What is the significance of these low cash figures, and can they be of concern? The following bullet points clarify what a low cash figure could imply:

- *Low cash coupled with a line of credit.* If the liabilities section of the balance sheet contains a line item for a line of credit, it is quite possible that a business is simply drawing down cash from its line of credit in order to pay its bills. Once its cash reserves are depleted, it accesses the line of credit for more cash and pays its bills again. This arrangement may not be an issue if a company has a highly seasonal business, where it uses up cash during part of the year and pays off its debt when sales peak. The best way to learn if this is the case is to obtain monthly financial statements and track the amount of line of credit usage by month, as well as sales levels.
- *Zero cash.* When the cash balance is exactly zero, this probably means that a business cut checks in advance of having the cash to do so. Thus, it has no money with which to pay its bills. At year end, the auditors force the company to create a journal entry that reverses a sufficient amount of these payables to bring the cash balance up to zero.
- *Negative cash.* As just noted, a negative cash balance means that an entity has paid out more check payments than it can cover with its available cash. While the auditors will force a business to alter its books to show a cash balance of zero, this may not happen during the preparation of the intervening monthly financial statements, resulting in negative balances.

In short, the danger posed by a low cash balance depends on the situation. It could simply be part of the normal operations for a seasonal business, or it could indicate that an organization is teetering on the edge of bankruptcy.

**Restricted Cash**

In rare cases, there may be a line item in the balance sheet that is labeled "Restricted cash." If the amount is actually restricted, it could cause liquidity problems, since the accounting staff may not have enough cash to meet ongoing payables obligations. However, this is not always the case. In some instances, the board of directors may have declared that a certain amount of cash is being set aside, perhaps for a long-term strategic requirement, such as a building program. While there may be an internal injunction on use of this cash, it is quite likely that management will authorize its use if there is a pressing need.

The situation is different if the restriction is being imposed by an outside entity. For example, a company's bank may have restricted access to a certain amount of funds, because it is being set aside to pay for future obligations under a letter of credit. In this case, there is no way to access the cash.

The latter situation is clearly much more critical than the former, so it helps to peruse the footnotes accompanying the financial statements to see if there is any further clarification of the nature of a cash restriction.

**Events Triggering Changes in Cash**

Even in a well-run, closely budgeted business, there will be continual changes in the ending cash balance. A reviewer of the financial statements can discern the reasons for these changes by examining other parts of the financial statements. Here are several events that can trigger changes in cash:

- *Fixed asset expenditures.* If a business is in an industry where a large investment in equipment and facilities is needed, then compare the cash line item to the fixed assets line item in the balance sheet. A sudden drop in cash may correspond to an offsetting increase in fixed assets.
- *Dividends.* If the board of directors declares a dividend, this is first recorded as a dividend payable, and will then be extracted from the retained earnings account in equity. Thus, a dividend can be detected in two places in the balance sheet.
- *Stock buybacks.* The board of directors may authorize a program of stock buybacks, which may extend over a period of time. If so, a press release may signal this program, as will the appearance of a treasury stock account that offsets the equity section of the balance sheet.
- *Expense spikes.* There may occasionally be quite large spikes in the expenses appearing in the income statement that correspond to cash reductions. For example, there may be a large payout related to a lawsuit or a product recall. These payouts may be buried within the income statement if the line items are highly aggregated, but could appear in the accompanying footnotes.
- *Working capital changes.* One of the most common reasons for a change in cash is that it is being used to fund more working capital. Working capital is current assets minus current liabilities. For example, if goods are sold to a customer on long credit terms, this uses cash until payment is received. As

another example, if the payment on a payable is accelerated at the request of a supplier, the cash balance will decline. The interaction of these differing effects has a significant impact on cash.

The changes noted here can also be spotted in the statement of cash flows at an aggregate level. A perusal of the financial statement footnotes may also locate discussions of the preceding items.

## Sources of Cash

An analyst might look at a robust cash balance, conclude that a business is in excellent financial condition, and stop reviewing the financial statements for further information. This would be a mistake. Instead, review the balance sheet for the past few quarters or years to see if there has been a recent increase in the amount of outstanding debt or equity. Alternatively, look at the statement of cash flows to see if any debt has been obtained or shares sold. If so, it is likely that these financing activities have created a one-time bump in the cash balance, which will now be reduced if the business does not also generate enough cash internally to pay for its ongoing obligations.

If a hefty cash balance has indeed come from financing activities, then it is useful to estimate the *burn rate* of the cash. Burn rate is the amount of cash being used up per reporting period. This can be derived by going back through the balance sheets since the financing was arranged, to derive the approximate rate at which the business appears to be using up the cash. This figure can then be extrapolated into the future to estimate when the business will run out of cash.

---

## EXAMPLE

Monique Ponto, a start-up maker of high-end women's watches, sold shares one year ago for a total of $2,000,000. At that time, its cash balance was $150,000, so the stock sale resulted in an initial cash balance of $2,150,000. Since then, the company's balance sheets have reported the following cash balances:

| | 4th Quarter 20X1 | 1st Quarter 20X2 | 2nd Quarter 20X2 | 3rd Quarter 20X2 | 4th Quarter 20X2 |
|---|---|---|---|---|---|
| Cash balance | $2,150,000 | $1,750,000 | $1,400,000 | $1,090,000 | $830,000 |
| Cash used | -- | 400,000 | 350,000 | 310,000 | 260,000 |
| Rate of decline in cash usage | -- | -- | 50,000 | 40,000 | 50,000 |

The decline in cash usage over time indicates that the business may eventually stop burning through cash. At the moment, the rate of decline in cash usage appears to be about $50,000 per quarter. If this trend continues, one might expect that the entity will stop drawing down its cash reserves by the end of the first quarter of 20X4. The analysis follows:

| | 4th Quarter 20X2 | 1st Quarter 20X3 | 2nd Quarter 20X3 | 3rd Quarter 20X3 | 4th Quarter 20X3 | 1st Quarter 20X4 |
|---|---|---|---|---|---|---|
| Beginning cash balance | $-- | $830,000 | $620,000 | $460,000 | $350,000 | $290,000 |
| Projected cash usage | -- | 210,000 | 160,000 | 110,000 | 60,000 | 10,000 |
| Ending cash balance | 830,000 | 620,000 | 460,000 | 350,000 | 290,000 | 280,000 |

## The Impact of Sales Growth on Cash

When reviewing the cash balance, a key consideration is the rate of growth of the business. When a business is growing rapidly, its ability to generate cash from operations will probably not be sufficient to fund the expenditures needed to invest in fixed assets, extend credit to new customers, or pay for increased amounts of inventory. For example, when a retail chain expands to a new location, it must pay for the new store and all of the inventory that is needed in the new location. If management is attempting to expand at a high rate of speed, then all of the on-hand cash will undoubtedly be used up in short order, requiring that external financing be obtained to continue the growth. In this situation, the analyst should estimate the cash burn rate (as noted earlier) and judge the extent to which management can continue to procure cash in order to replenish the bank account at regular intervals.

Conversely, if management is engaged in an orderly shutdown of certain aspects of a business, one may find that the company will soon be awash in cash. This condition can arise when facilities are sold off, receivables are collected, and inventory is liquidated.

---

**Tip:** The margins that a business earns on its sales are a significant driver of its ability to grow. For example, a software company experiences extremely high profit levels, and so generates so much cash that it can afford to grow rapidly without requiring any additional cash infusions. Conversely, an oil refiner must make massive capital investments to open a new facility, and so cannot grow as quickly.

---

## Sufficiency of the Cash and Investment Balance

A conservative analyst might want to obtain assurance that a business can pay for its current liabilities with just its cash and investments. This view assumes that it will take too long to convert receivables and inventory into cash. To obtain this information, divide cash and investments by current liabilities, which is a modified version of the cash ratio. A variation that may be slightly more accurate is to exclude accrued expenses from the current liabilities in the denominator, since it may not be necessary to pay for these items in the near term. The calculation is:

$$\frac{\text{Cash} + \text{Investments}}{\text{Current liabilities}}$$

A 1:1 ratio would show that management likes to keep significant cash reserves on hand to deal with liabilities, which reduces the short-term risk of not being able to pay bills.

However, the ratio only measures cash balances as of a specific point in time, which may vary considerably on a daily basis, as receivables are collected and suppliers are paid. Further, the ratio essentially assumes that the cash on hand now will be used to pay for all accounts payable, when in reality the cash from an ongoing series of receivable payments will also be used. Also, the measurement assumes that investments can be converted into cash at once, which is not necessarily the case. Consequently, there are some issues with relying too much on this measurement to estimate the liquidity of a business.

---

**EXAMPLE**

Quest Adventure Gear has $100,000 of cash and $400,000 of investments on its balance sheet at the end of May. On that date, its current liabilities are $1,000,000. Its modified cash ratio is:

$$\frac{\$100,000\ Cash + \$400,000\ Investments}{\$1,000,000\ Current\ liabilities}$$

$$= 0.5:1\ Modified\ cash\ ratio$$

---

### The Liquidity of Investments

When estimating the sufficiency of cash to pay for current liabilities, it is not always accurate to include the investments balance in the comparison. The problem is that some investments may be in illiquid investments from which cash cannot be extracted for a long time. The nature of these investments will not be apparent just by looking at the balance sheet, but a description of the types of investments might be included in one of the footnotes that accompany the financial statements. If so, it could make sense to assume that investments cannot be readily convertible into cash, and exclude this line item from consideration when determining the ability to pay for current liabilities.

### The Return on Investment

It is possible to compare the interest income or investment income line item on the income statement to the amount appearing in the investments line item on the balance sheet in order to obtain a general idea of the return on investment that a business is achieving. The result will only be approximate, since the calculation would be based on the ending investments asset balance, which may not be representative of the average investment balance over the course of the reporting period.

Even if the resulting income percentage *is* accurate, a high return on investment is not necessarily a cause for rejoicing. The objective of cash management for a corporation is to preserve all cash and ensure that investments are as liquid as possible, after which return on investment comes in a distant third place. Consequently, a high return on investment could indicate that management is investing its cash in high-risk investments and/or ones that cannot be easily converted back into cash.

## Analysis Conclusions

The analysis of cash and investments focuses on the short-term liquidity of a business. In essence, is there enough cash on hand to meet the immediate obligations of the organization? When analyzing cash and investments, we suggest the following order of priority:

1. *Estimate the natural cash balance.* Review the history of cash balances that the business has reported, and estimate the normal proportion of cash that appears to be necessary for operations. Drops below this level are significant warning flags.

2. *Review the statement of cash flows.* See if there are any financing events listed on the statement of cash flows indicating that cash was raised by obtaining debt or selling stock. Also note the presence of any major fixed asset expenditures or dividend payments. These all indicate how cash has been sourced and used.

3. *Compare cash to the growth rate.* If a business declares in its press release that it wishes to expand at a rapid rate, try to estimate the rate at which the organization will need to add more cash in order to support the declared rate of growth. The outcome of this analysis may very well indicate that the entity will be in financial difficulty soon, or will at least need to obtain outside funding.

The cash and investment balance tends to represent the outcome of many other issues within a business, such as decisions to grow or contract, to invest in new assets, or to pay a dividend. As such, changes in these line items can be considered a prime indicator of issues elsewhere in a company.

# Chapter 3
## Interpretation of Receivables

## Introduction

The accounts receivable line item on the balance sheet summarizes the amounts owed to a company by its customers in exchange for providing them with goods and services. Receivables are the result of extending credit to customers, which is a required part of doing business in many industries. This is an important area to examine, because it represents cash that a business has not yet collected, and which could become uncollectible.

## The Interpretation of Accounts Receivable

The accounts receivable line item appears within the current assets section of the balance sheet. Accounts receivable is considered to be more easily convertible into cash than inventory, but less so than investments, and so is usually positioned between these two line items. A sample presentation showing where accounts receivable is located in the balance sheet is noted in the following exhibit.

### Sample Presentation of Accounts Receivable

| Current Assets | |
| --- | --- |
| Cash | $84,000 |
| Investments | 109,000 |
| **Accounts receivable** | **342,000** |
| Inventory | 280,000 |
| Total current assets | $815,000 |

This single line item is comprised of several general ledger accounts that are usually clustered together in the balance sheet. These accounts are as follows:

- *Accounts receivable – trade*. Contains amounts billed by a business to its customers when it delivers goods or services to them in the ordinary course of business. The balance in this account comprises the bulk of the number that appears on the balance sheet.
- *Accounts receivable – other*. Contains amounts due for payment to an entity other than its normal customer invoices for goods shipped or services performed. Examples of these other receivables are amounts owed to a company by its employees for loans or wage advances, tax refunds owed to it by taxing authorities, or insurance claims owed to it by an insurance company.
- *Allowance for doubtful accounts*. Contains a reserve for the expected amount of accounts receivable that will not be collected. This reserve is an

estimate that is usually based on the historical experience of a company with bad debt. This is a contra account, and is specifically paired with the accounts receivable – trade account. The reserve is funded by charging the expected future amount of bad debts to the bad debt expense account in the current period, for which the offset is an increase in the balance in the allowance for doubtful accounts.

Thus, the underlying detail of the accounts receivable line item noted in the last example could be broken down into the structure that appears in the following sample presentation.

**Sample Detailed Presentation of Accounts Receivable**

| Current Assets | | |
|---|---:|---:|
| Cash | | $84,000 |
| Investments | | 109,000 |
| **Accounts receivable – trade** | **335,000** | |
| **Accounts receivable – other** | **28,000** | |
| **Allowance for doubtful accounts** | **-21,000** | |
| **Accounts receivable** | | **342,000** |
| Inventory | | 280,000 |
| Total current assets | | $815,000 |

This further breakdown of the information in the accounts receivable line item brings up a number of issues, which are noted in the following sub-sections.

## Inherent Profit Margin

Before delving into the accounts receivable area, it is useful to understand how important this area may be to a business – or not. The key concern is the contribution margin associated with the average product sale. Contribution margin is sales minus all variable expenses, and can be calculated from the income statement. In the following portion of a sample income statement, we extract the costs of materials and labor from the cost of goods sold, and subtract them from sales to arrive at the average contribution margin. The relevant portions of the income statement are noted in bold.

**Sample Derivation of Contribution Margin**

| Sales | | $1,000,000 |
|---|---|---|
| Cost of goods sold: | | |
| Direct materials | $250,000 | |
| Direct labor | 80,000 | |
| Factory overhead | 190,000 | |
| Total cost of goods sold | | $520,000 |
| | | |
| Contribution margin | 670,000 | |
| Contribution margin percentage | 67% | |
| Gross margin | | $480,000 |
| Gross margin percentage | | 48% |

Because factory overhead is a fixed cost, we exclude it from the contribution margin calculation. The result is typically quite a high contribution margin percentage. This is of some importance when matched with the amount of accounts receivable outstanding, for it indicates the proportion of cash that a business actually has invested in its accounts receivable.

For example, if a business has a high average contribution margin, it generates a high profit margin with each sale, and so has little cash invested in each receivable. This means it can afford to extend quite generous payment terms to its customers without investing much cash in the resulting receivables. For this type of business, a relatively high bad debt percentage may be inconsequential, since the bad debt can be easily offset by the large profits, and the company loses little cash when a receivable is written off.

The situation is entirely different when the contribution margin is quite small. In this case, a business cannot afford to have any bad debt, and so will tightly restrict the extension of credit to only its best customers. If a receivable cannot be collected, then nearly the entire amount of the receivable represents lost cash that the business cannot recover. In this latter case, all of the analyses provided through the remainder of this chapter are particularly important.

## Age of the Trade Receivables

The key issue when reviewing receivables is estimating whether the amount outstanding is reasonable. This is impossible to judge without comparing it to the overall activity of the business. Accordingly, we compare receivables to sales, using the days sales outstanding (DSO) measurement. This proportion is expressed as the average number of days over which receivables are outstanding before they are paid.

Days sales outstanding is most useful when compared to the standard number of days that customers are allowed before payment is due. Thus, a DSO figure of 40 days might initially appear excellent, until you realize that the standard payment terms are only five days. A combination of prudent credit granting and robust collections activity is the likely cause when the DSO figure is only a few days longer than the standard payment terms.

To calculate DSO, divide 365 days into the amount of annual credit sales to arrive at credit sales per day, and then divide this figure into the average accounts receivable for the measurement period. Thus, the formula is:

$$\frac{\text{Average accounts receivable}}{\text{Annual sales} \div 365 \text{ days}}$$

---

**EXAMPLE**

An analyst examining the financial statements of Oberlin Acoustics, maker of the famous Rhino brand of electric guitars, wants to derive the days sales outstanding for the company for the April reporting period. In April, the beginning and ending accounts receivable balances were $420,000 and $540,000, respectively. The total credit sales for the 12 months ended April 30 were $4,000,000. The analyst derives the following DSO calculation from this information:

$$\frac{(\$420{,}000 \text{ Beginning receivables} + \$540{,}000 \text{ Ending receivables}) \div 2}{\$4{,}000{,}000 \text{ Credit sales} \div 365 \text{ Days}}$$

$$=$$

$$\frac{\$480{,}000 \text{ Average accounts receivable}}{\$10{,}959 \text{ Credit sales per day}}$$

$$= 43.8 \text{ Days}$$

---

The DSO measurement is best used when plotted on a trend line, so that gradual changes in the ability of a business to collect receivables become more obvious. The following sample table shows a trend line analysis by quarter for an 18-month period. Note the sudden jump in DSO during the holiday season, which could have been triggered by a loosening of credit policy to boost sales to more questionable customers.

**Sample DSO Trend Line Analysis**

| (000s) | Quarter 1 20X4 | Quarter 2 20X4 | Quarter 3 20X4 | Quarter 4 20X4 | Quarter 1 20X5 | Quarter 2 20X5 |
|---|---|---|---|---|---|---|
| Annual sales* | $13,500 | $13,900 | $13,400 | $16,900 | $16,200 | $15,700 |
| Average sales per day | $37.0 | $38.1 | $36.7 | $46.3 | $44.4 | $43.0 |
| Average receivables | $1,554 | $1,562 | $1,468 | $2,315 | $2,131 | $2,021 |
| DSO | 42 days | 41 days | 40 days | 50 days | 48 days | 47 days |

* Annual sales are computed on a trailing 12-month basis

The correlation between the annual sales figure used in the calculation and the average accounts receivable figure may not be close, resulting in a misleading DSO number. For example, if a company has seasonal sales, the average receivable figure may be unusually high or low on the measurement date, depending on where the company is in its seasonal billings. Thus, if receivables are unusually low when the measurement is taken, the DSO days will appear unusually low, and vice versa if the receivables are unusually high. There are two ways to eliminate this problem:

- *Annualize receivables*. Generate an average accounts receivable figure that spans the entire, full-year measurement period.
- *Measure a shorter period*. Adopt a rolling quarterly DSO calculation, so that sales for the past three months are compared to average receivables for the past three months. This approach is most useful when sales are highly variable throughout the year.

If a company is not changing its policy for granting credit and is expending a consistent amount of effort on its collection activities, then the DSO figure should not change much from period to period. However, what factors could underlie a change in DSO? The causes of a decline or increase in DSO are as follows:

## Decline in DSO

The general trend in DSO is for it to increase, not decrease. This is because the managers of a business usually want to increase sales on an ongoing basis, and so will eventually offer credit to more marginal customers. It takes longer to collect from these more questionable customers. Thus, a declining DSO is uncommon. If it does occur, the reason could be one of the following:

- *Invoices written off*. Perhaps the most likely reason for a DSO reduction is simply that a number of old invoices have been written off as uncollectible. Doing so reduces the total amount of trade receivables outstanding, and so reduces DSO. If large write-downs of this type continue to happen over time, it may mean that a business has a flawed credit granting policy that is allowing large credit sales to low-quality customers.
- *Conversion to loans*. It is possible that some customers are so unable to pay within terms that the company has been forced to convert these receivables into loans, which will be paid off over a number of months. There are several indicators of this problem, such as loans receivable appearing on the balance sheet and/or interest income appearing on the income statement.
- *Tighter credit policy*. Management might decide to tighten the credit policy of the business, which means that the amount of credit granted to customers is reduced and/or that the number of days before payment is expected is reduced. Management could do this because it expects a downturn in the economy, and anticipates that customers will be less able to pay. Another reason is that the company has little cash on hand, and wants to stop funding receivables. An indicator of the latter situation is that the days of payables outstanding also increases, which indicates that suppliers are not being paid on time.

- *Improved collections.* The company controller may have decided to improve the technological capabilities of the collections staff, or invested more funds in adding to or training the collections staff. The outcome should be a certain amount of reduction in the DSO figure.
- *Large invoice collected.* It is possible that the business had quite a large invoice outstanding, for which payment has just been received. This is more likely for a smaller business that deals with a small number of customers, where receivables are more likely to be "lumpy".
- *Business ramping down.* Perhaps the least likely reason for a decline in DSO is that management is intentionally winding down a business. In this case, old receivables are being collected and not being replaced with new credit sales.

### Increase in DSO

To some extent, the reasons for an increase in DSO are a reverse of the reasons for a decline in DSO, as noted in the following bullet points:

- *Looser credit policy.* A startup business usually has a tight credit policy, since it has little cash to invest in accounts receivable. When management wants to increase sales, one way to do so is a greater willingness to offer looser credit terms. Thus, growing sales frequently involves accepting a larger DSO figure.
- *Unwilling to write off invoices.* The controller may not want to write off old accounts receivable as a matter of policy, or perhaps because a massive write-down would have an excessively negative impact on profits. If there is a surge in bad debt expense early in the year, it could indicate that management delayed writing off invoices in the preceding year in order to artificially boost profits.
- *Budget cuts in collections.* Management may have imposed cost cuts on the collections department, so that fewer personnel are now handling collections for the same number of customers. Given the lower level of attention to overdue receivables, the DSO figure is bound to increase.
- *Product problems.* If a business has just launched a new product line and DSO then increases, it could mean that the products have so many problems that customers are refusing to pay for them. An indicator of this could be a sudden flattening or decline in sales shortly after the new products are launched.

### Age of the Other Accounts Receivable

Accounts receivable are expected to be collectible within 12 months. If not, then they should be reclassified as long-term assets. However, the items in the other accounts receivable account are not reviewed anywhere near as closely to ensure that this is the case. Indeed, if the account contains loans due from employees, it is quite likely that a notable portion of the account balance is not a current asset at all. If so, this means that the reported amount of current assets is too high.

**No Allowance for Doubtful Accounts**

A common problem with the accounting methods used by smaller businesses is that they have no allowance for doubtful accounts at all. Instead, they use the *direct method*, where they only write off bad debts when a specific invoice is clearly uncollectible. The problem with the direct method is that bad debt expense recognition is delayed to a point usually several months after an invoice was initially recognized as revenue. For example, a business records a sale of $10,000 in December, and then writes it off as a bad debt in the following April. This means that the revenue is too high in one period, and the later expense recognition depresses profits in a later period. In general, this means that a business using the direct method is reporting somewhat higher profits than is really the case.

If accounts receivable is listed as one aggregated line item in the balance sheet, it can be difficult to ascertain whether a business is using an allowance for doubtful accounts or the direct method. One clue is in the label used for this line item. If the line is described as "Accounts receivable, net" The "net" part of the label indicates that receivables are being netted against an allowance for doubtful accounts. If there is no "net" term in the label, it is more likely that the direct method is being used.

**Reliability of the Allowance for Doubtful Accounts**

When there is an allowance for doubtful accounts listed in the balance sheet, this does not necessarily mean that an excessive amount of faith can be placed in the amount presented. The allowance is simply an estimate of the expected amount of bad debts that are contained within the total amount of accounts receivable presented. This estimate is usually based on the historical proportion of bad debts to sales, which is generally considered reasonable. However, the allowance can be wrong under several circumstances, which are:

- *New products.* If a business has entered a new industry or launched a significantly new product line, there is no way to be certain of the amount of bad debt that will arise from these sales. The actual amount could be substantially lower or higher than what the company has experienced in the past, and only the passage of time will reveal what the allowance percentage should have been.
- *New customers.* If a company has added a large number of new customers, it has no credit history for them, and so cannot realistically model the extent of any bad debt losses that will be incurred from sales to this group.
- *Change in credit policy.* If management decides to restrict credit to just the best customers, the allowance could justifiably drop to near zero. Conversely (and more likely), if credit is made available to anyone who asks for it, the existing bad debt percentage on which the allowance is based will certainly be too low.
- *Economic conditions.* The amount of bad debt incurred will change along with general economic conditions. For example, if there is a recession and management has not already restricted credit, one can reasonably expect that the bad debt percentage will increase – perhaps substantially.

- *Fraud.* Management may want to present the best possible results in the income statement, and so intentionally does little to increase the balance in the allowance for doubtful accounts. This situation can arise when management will be paid bonuses if a certain profit figure is achieved.

## No Allowance for Other Accounts Receivable

The preceding list of accounts that roll up into the balance sheet line item does not include an allowance for doubtful accounts for the accounts receivable – other account. There is no reserve, because there is no general accounting practice for doing so. Instead, the reserve is only used for trade receivables. This can be a problem, for businesses rarely spend much time reviewing the contents of this "other" account, which means that the account may contain receivables that will not be collected. Consequently, if the accounts receivable line item contains a large amount of "other" receivables, view their collectability with concern.

## Amount of Bad Debts Recognized

The end result of the credit and collection process is the proportion of accounts receivable that cannot be collected – the bad debt percentage. Ultimately, the bad debt percentage, combined with days sales outstanding, are the core receivable-related measurements that can be extracted from the financial statements.

The bad debt percentage is a simple calculation, just the bad debt expense for the year divided by credit sales. However, be aware that the reported amount can be "adjusted," sometimes by a significant amount. Under the accrual basis of accounting, bad debts are estimated and charged to the allowance for doubtful accounts. If the collections manager wants to present a somewhat lower bad debt percentage at the end of the year, he or she can simply underestimate the amount of bad debts expected to be incurred, and reduce the size of the allowance for doubtful accounts. This issue can be mitigated by adopting a standard procedure for calculating the amount of the allowance, and rigidly adhering to that procedure.

---

### EXAMPLE

Quest Adventure Gear, maker of rugged travel clothing, has been experiencing increasing difficulty in collecting from its retailer base of customers over the past few years despite growing sales. A prospective lender is interested in the risk posed by these bad debts, and compiles the following analysis from Quest's financial statements:

| | 20X1 | 20X2 | 20X3 | 20X5 | 20X6 |
|---|---|---|---|---|---|
| Bad debt expense | $35,000 | $47,000 | $68,000 | $130,000 | $176,000 |
| Credit sales | 2,900,000 | 3,100,000 | 3,250,000 | 3,500,000 | 3,900,000 |
| Bad debt percentage | 1.2% | 1.5% | 2.1% | 3.7% | 4.5% |

The analysis indicates that Quest is losing a substantial amount of cash from its aggressive pursuit of more retailers.

---

## Analysis Conclusions

The interpretation of accounts receivable is one of the most important topics for an analyst, since it gives insights into so many aspects of a business – sales growth strategy, credit policy, collections funding, and the state of the economy. Much more information can be obtained if the subject business is willing to present an expanded balance sheet that reveals all of the line items associated with accounts receivable. When analyzing receivables, we suggest the following order of priority:

1. *Measure contribution margin.* Determine the proportion of cash that has been tied up in receivables by calculating the average contribution margin. If this margin is low, a business must maintain tight control over its receivables in order to generate a profit.
2. *Measure the age of the trade receivables.* A central issue is how long it is taking a company to collect its receivables, and especially how this measurement is trending. The analyst may find that a sharp jump in DSO is driving a steep decline in the amount of available cash.
3. *Measure the bad debt percentage.* Though the bad debt percentage can be manipulated, examine it on a trend line to see if a business is experiencing collection issues in relation to the historical trend.
4. *Compare bad debts to receivables.* If there is a continuing pattern of the bad debt expense bumping up in an irregular manner as receivables decline, it is likely that management is using the direct method to record bad debts, rather than an allowance method. If so, the reported amount of profits is too high by the amount of bad debts that are being recognized on a delayed basis.
5. *Look for new sales line items.* If there are entirely new line items for sales listed on the income statement, it is likely that a company has no bad debt experience in these areas. If so, the amount of bad debt recognized could be unreliable.

The only situation in which the analyst will be able to extract little new information from the accounts receivable line is when a business has steady sales and product margins, has not altered its credit policy, and has maintained approximately the same group of customers. This level of consistency is rare, so expect to see some issues with accounts receivable.

# Chapter 4
## Interpretation of Inventory

## Introduction

The inventory line item on the balance sheet aggregates the different types of inventory that a business owns. Inventory is needed by a manufacturer for its production process, before it completes goods and sells them. A retailer or wholesaler may maintain significant stocks of inventory in order to fulfill customer orders. Consequently, the inventory asset is a key requirement for doing business in some industries.

The management of this asset is also a concern, since there may be reduced demand for inventory that is retained for too long, or it may spoil. Given the aging problem with inventory, it can present a notable risk of loss to a business, if not monitored closely.

## The Interpretation of Inventory

The inventory line item appears within the current assets section of the balance sheet. Of the current assets, inventory is considered to be the least convertible into cash, and so is listed last within the current assets section of the balance sheet, after accounts receivable. A sample presentation showing where inventory is located in the balance sheet is noted in the following exhibit.

### Sample Presentation of Inventory

| | |
|---|---|
| Current Assets | |
| Cash | $84,000 |
| Investments | 109,000 |
| Accounts receivable | 342,000 |
| **Inventory** | **280,000** |
| Total current assets | $815,000 |

This line item is comprised of several general ledger accounts that are usually clustered together in the balance sheet. These accounts are as follows:

- *Raw materials inventory*. Contains materials obtained from suppliers that must be transformed through a production process into finished goods. This account is only used by manufacturers, so do not expect to see it in the accounts of a retailer or wholesaler.
- *Work-in-process inventory*. Contains the cost of goods that are currently in the midst of the production process. The amount in this account can be quite small, especially if the production process is a rapid one.

- *Finished goods inventory*. Contains all goods that have passed through the manufacturing process and are ready for sale to customers. A potentially confusing point is that purchased merchandise could also be recorded in this account (see the next account description).
- *Merchandise*. A retailer or wholesaler does not manufacture goods – it simply buys them in completed form from suppliers, and records them in this account. As just noted, goods that have been acquired in this manner could also be recorded within the finished goods account.
- *Reserve for obsolete inventory*. Contains a reserve for the expected amount of inventory that will be declared obsolete. This reserve is an estimate that may be based on a company's history with obsolete inventory, or perhaps on a periodic review of the inventory. This is a contra account, and is specifically paired with the cluster of inventory accounts. The reserve is funded by charging the expected future amount of obsolete inventory to the cost of goods sold expense in the current period, for which the offset is an increase in the balance in the reserve for obsolete inventory. Many companies do not have a reserve set up for obsolete inventory. If there is one, it indicates a more advanced level of accounting awareness.

Thus, the underlying detail of the inventory line item noted in the last example could be broken down into the structure that appears in the following sample presentation.

**Sample Detailed Presentation of Inventory**

| Current Assets | | |
|---|---|---|
| Cash | | $84,000 |
| Investments | | 109,000 |
| Accounts receivable | | 342,000 |
| **Raw materials inventory** | 76,000 | |
| **Work-in-process inventory** | 38,000 | |
| **Finished goods inventory** | 141,000 | |
| **Merchandise inventory** | 42,000 | |
| **Reserve for obsolete inventory** | -17,000 | |
| **Inventory** | | **280,000** |
| Total current assets | | $815,000 |

This further breakdown of the information in the inventory line item brings up a number of issues, which are noted in the following sub-sections along with more general concepts.

## Relative Importance of Inventory

In some industries, the proper management of inventory is a key driver of profitability, and so is closely watched by outside analysts. In other industries, inventory is a complete nonevent, since its use has little impact on sales. Given this wide range of outcomes, the analyst should first review the industry within which a business operates, as well as its specific competitive stance, to determine the extent to which inventory is a concern. Here are several examples of how inventory can impact a business:

<u>Industry</u>

- *Services industries.* There are many industries where there is no inventory at all, or where it comprises a vanishingly small proportion of sales. In these industries, the emphasis is more likely to be on the delivery of personal services – for example, to provide consulting, tax advice, or perhaps field service to faulty equipment. If any inventory is kept on hand, it is probably for very specific and high-margin uses, such as maintaining a store of key repair parts for the copier machines of clients.
- *Hospitality industry.* This industry is comprised of hotels, restaurants, spas, casinos, and similar businesses. Their main type of inventory is the ingredients for meals; since this inventory tends to spoil quickly, there is a self-regulating feature that forces a business to use inventory or throw it out, resulting in very high inventory usage rates. There may also be a small amount of merchandise sales, such as workout clothes sold by spas, but the amount of these sales is incidental to operations.
- *Clothing industry.* The customers of clothing designers are fickle in the extreme, so new designs must be brought to market quickly and inventory levels monitored daily to guard against sudden declines in demand. Excess stocks may be unloaded to discounters once demand drops off to a sufficient extent. In this industry, constant inventory monitoring is mandatory.
- *Repair parts.* Customers may require replacement parts for all sorts of equipment, and may continue to require them for many years after the original equipment purchase. Examples are repair parts for vehicles, washers and dryers, and air conditioning units. In the repair business, inventory may be stored for years before it is sold, but can then be sold at very high margins. Consequently, there is an incentive to initially keep fairly high inventory levels, after which a key concern is watching demand over time to decide whether any of the residual inventory levels can be considered obsolete. This can be quite a difficult inventory management environment.

The presented industries are intended to provide examples of the differing impacts of inventory on a business, ranging from none at all in the services business to high turnover levels in the hospitality and clothing industries, to low turnover levels in the repair parts business.

<u>Competitive Stance</u>

- *Low cost model.* A business may choose to compete by keeping the cost of its products low, so that it can pass these savings along to customers through low prices. To do so, it is necessary to minimize unit costs by such means as highly efficient production systems and lengthy production runs. Under this approach, the analyst should look for medium-to-high inventory levels in proportion to sales.

- *High service model.* The reverse of the low cost model is to charge a higher price in return for excellent service. This means keeping extra inventory on hand, so that orders can be filled at once. When this model is being used, it is especially critical to monitor inventory levels, since it is quite possible that too much inventory will be kept in stock, which absorbs cash and can trigger losses due to obsolete inventory.
- *Full product range model.* A marketing-driven company can elect to offer many models of its products, so that every possible customer niche is addressed. While great from a sales perspective, this approach requires a business to maintain inventory for every variation of product that it sells. This model calls for constant attention to inventory balances, since there is a risk of having too much old inventory for which there is no demand.
- *Retail model.* A retailer must maintain adequate stocks of inventory, or else its shelves will appear to be barren, and its customer traffic will decline. Consequently, these operations require significant inventory levels, as well as constant sales monitoring to see if any inventory should be sold off to discounters.
- *Internet store pass-through model.* A common inventory management technique used by some Internet stores is to set rock-bottom prices, take money in advance from customers, and then order the required inventory items from their suppliers. This means that customers wait a long time for delivery, but the store operators maintain essentially no inventory.

Of the competitive models just described, those that bear the most watching are the high service model and the full product range model, where it is easy for a non-observant management team to let inventory levels skyrocket, soaking up excess cash and increasing the risk of inventory write-offs.

## Age of the Inventory

A major issue when reviewing inventory is estimating its age. The estimation task is quite difficult; the inventory may be comprised of different proportions of "hot selling" inventory items and others that have been gathering dust on the shelf – perhaps for years. When only the information in the financial statements is available, the best we can do is to develop an average age for the inventory. This is done using a measure of inventory turnover.

The turnover of inventory is the rate at which inventory is used over a measurement period. This is an important measurement, for many businesses are burdened by an excessively large investment in inventory, which can consume the bulk of available cash. When there is a low rate of inventory turnover, this implies that a business may have a flawed purchasing system that bought too many goods, or that stocks were increased in anticipation of sales that did not occur. In both cases, there is a high risk of inventory aging, in which case it becomes obsolete and has reduced resale value.

When there is a high rate of inventory turnover, this implies that the purchasing function is tightly managed. However, it may also mean that a business does not have the cash reserves to maintain normal inventory levels, and so is turning away prospective sales. The latter scenario is most likely when the amount of debt is high and there are minimal cash reserves.

To calculate inventory turnover, divide the ending inventory figure into the annualized cost of sales. If the ending inventory figure is not a representative number, then use an average figure instead. The formula is:

$$\frac{\text{Annual cost of goods sold}}{\text{Inventory}}$$

The result of this calculation can be divided into 365 days to arrive at days of inventory on hand. Thus, a turnover rate of 4.0 becomes 91 days of inventory.

---

**EXAMPLE**

An analyst is reviewing the inventory situation at the Hegemony Toy Company. The business incurred $8,150,000 of cost of goods sold in the past year, and has ending inventory of $1,630,000. Total inventory turnover is calculated as:

$$\frac{\$8,150,000 \text{ Cost of goods sold}}{\$1,630,000 \text{ Inventory}}$$

$$= 5 \text{ Turns per year}$$

The five turns figure is then divided into 365 days to arrive at 73 days of inventory on hand.

---

The inventory measurement is best used when plotted on a trend line, so that gradual changes in the ability of a business to maintain modest inventory levels become more obvious. The following sample table shows a trend line analysis by quarter for an 18-month period. Note the sudden jump in inventory turnover immediately following the holiday season, which indicates a significant amount of seasonal sales; the business has clearly flushed out its inventory.

**Sample Inventory Turnover Trend Line Analysis**

| (000s) | Quarter 1 20X4 | Quarter 2 20X4 | Quarter 3 20X4 | Quarter 4 20X4 | Quarter 1 20X5 | Quarter 2 20X5 |
|---|---|---|---|---|---|---|
| Annual cost of goods sold* | $17,930 | $18,105 | $18,260 | $20,725 | $19,400 | $19,605 |
| Ending inventory | 980 | 2,235 | 4,454 | 568 | 956 | 2,306 |
| Inventory turnover | 18.3x | 8.1x | 4.1x | 36.5x | 20.3x | 8.5x |
| Inventory days on hand | 20 days | 45 days | 90 days | 10 days | 18 days | 43 days |

* Annual cost of goods sold is computed on a trailing 12-month basis

The correlation between the annual cost of goods sold figure used in the calculation and the average inventory figure may not be close, resulting in a misleading inventory turnover number. For example, if a company has seasonal sales, the average inventory figure may be unusually high or low on the measurement date, depending on where the company is in ramping up inventory for the sales season. Thus, if inventory is unusually low when the measurement is taken, the turnover will appear unusually high, and vice versa if the inventory balance is unusually high. There are two ways to eliminate this problem:

- *Annualize inventory*. Generate an average inventory figure that spans the entire, full-year measurement period.
- *Measure a shorter period*. Adopt a rolling quarterly inventory turnover calculation, so that the cost of goods sold for the past three months is compared to average inventory for the past three months. This approach is most useful when sales are highly variable throughout the year.

A number of factors could underlie a change in inventory turnover. Some of the more common causes of a decline or increase in turnover are as follows:

Decline in Inventory Turnover

A decline in inventory turnover means that there is more inventory on hand in relation to the cost of goods sold. Assuming that the cost of goods sold as a percentage of sales is constant, this implies that more inventory is being required to generate the same amount of sales. The reasons for it may include:

- *Inventory not written off*. A prime reason for a decline in inventory turnover is that management is not allowing the accounting staff to write down the value of the inventory for items that are obsolete. This is a particular problem in smaller businesses whose books are not audited. In these cases, the inventory records may contain an inordinate amount of inventory that can never be sold. If this inventory were to be written off, a business might sustain a massive one-time loss.
- *Excessive raw materials purchases*. If the purchasing process is mishandled, too many raw materials may be purchased in comparison to the production requirements of a business. A common reason for this problem is that the purchasing staff is attracted to volume discounts, and so buys in bulk.
- *Expediting*. A business may engage in expediting, where the most "in demand" customer orders are prioritized through the production area. In this situation, all other production jobs are disrupted and take longer to complete, resulting in a larger investment in work-in-process inventory than is really necessary.
- *Excess finished goods*. The sales department may have been overly optimistic in projecting certain product sales, and authorized the production of far too many products, which are now sitting in the warehouse. This is a particular concern in highly competitive markets where competing products are

constantly being introduced, and especially when product life cycles are short.

Increase in Inventory Turnover

An increase in inventory turnover means that there is less inventory on hand in relation to the cost of goods sold, which generally implies that less inventory is needed to support a given level of sales. The reasons for it may include:

- *Inventory written off.* Management may have decided to write off a portion of the inventory as being unusable. If so, this reduces the inventory balance. This action can be detected by reviewing the cost of goods sold to see if the number increased – this is the account to which the write-off would have been charged.
- *Production outsourced.* The company may have switched to a supplier to manufacture goods on behalf of the company. If so, the supplier may be holding the goods and only shipping them to the company (or directly to its customers) as needed. If so, this can trigger a massive decline in inventory, but could increase the cost of goods sold (since the supplier must earn a profit).
- *Production system changed.* The production management system may have been changed to one that produces based on actual customer orders, rather than to stock. If so, finished goods inventory can be nearly eliminated, possibly on a permanent basis. This system is difficult to install, for it requires a complete revamping of the production process. Companies are usually so pleased with themselves for installing such a system that they issue a press release about it, so this improvement may be readily apparent to the outside observer.
- *Products reformulated.* There are a number of techniques available for reducing the cost of products. If the engineering staff has applied these methods to product designs, the cost of inventory will gradually decline. However, such reductions tend to be modest and will only roll out over a long period of time.

## Reality of the Ending Balance

The reported inventory balance may very well contain estimates of what was actually on hand at the end of the reporting period, and so represents inaccurate information. This can be a major problem, for the ending inventory balance is needed by a business to calculate its cost of goods sold. The calculation used to derive the cost of goods sold is:

Beginning inventory + Purchases – Ending inventory = Cost of goods sold

Thus, if the ending inventory figure is wrong, then the reported cost of goods sold is wrong, which means that the net profit of the business is also incorrect.

It can be quite difficult to derive an accurate ending inventory figure, especially for a smaller business that has a more primitive inventory tracking system in place. There are two types of inventory tracking systems. The more sophisticated method is the *perpetual system*, which maintains a running balance of inventory quantities. The perpetual system requires that each addition to and subtraction from the inventory database be individually recorded in real time. Given the very large number of transactions required to maintain this system, it is easy for a few transactions to be missed, which calls for an ongoing cycle counting program to correct the inventory records. *Cycle counting* is the ongoing daily counting of small amounts of inventory, with the objective of gradually counting all inventory and correcting any issues found.

An alternative system that is much simpler to use is the *periodic system*, which relies upon a physical count of the ending inventory to ensure that the inventory records are correct. No recordation of individual inventory transactions is used. If a business does not conduct a physical count at the end of each month, then the accountant is instead forced to estimate the amount of ending inventory, which could be incorrect.

Both of these systems could yield incorrect results. Though more sophisticated, the perpetual system relies upon closely-followed procedures for recording inventory transactions, as well as an ongoing commitment to cycle counting. The results of a periodic system could also be incorrect, since physical counts may be conducted by inexperienced personnel who mis-count or incorrectly identify inventory items. In short, it is not a given that the inventory figures stated in the balance sheet are correct.

## Type of Costing System Used

The cost of the inventory listed on the balance sheet may be impacted by the cost layering system that has been applied to the inventory. Cost layering refers to the order in which costs are applied to inventory. For example, a business may purchase 10 widgets for $8 each in January, and another 10 widgets for $9 each in February. The business then sells five of these widgets in March. Under the first in, first out (FIFO) cost layering system, the assumption is that the cost of the first widgets purchased will be charged to the cost of goods sold, which would be $40 (calculated as $8 × 5 widgets). Under the last in, first out (LIFO) cost layering system, the cost of the last widgets purchased will be charged to the cost of goods sold, which would be $45 (calculated as $9 × 5 widgets). Under the weighted average cost layering system, the average cost of the widgets purchased will be charged to the cost of goods sold, which would be $42.50 (calculated as $8.50 × 5 units).

How do these cost layering options impact the cost of inventory? The amount of cost left in inventory is based on the amount recognized in the cost of goods sold. Thus, if the FIFO method is used, the costs of the first items in stock are charged to the cost of goods sold, leaving the cost of the last items in stock being used to devise the cost of inventory. Thus, the FIFO method tends to result in inventory costs that closely reflect the replacement cost of inventory.

If the LIFO method is used, the costs of the last items in stock are charged to the cost of goods sold, leaving the cost of the first items in stock being used to devise the cost of inventory. If inventory items have been in stock for a long time and raw materials or merchandise costs have been increasing rapidly since then, this means that the LIFO method tends to result in inventory costs that are lower than the replacement cost of the inventory. If these costs are lower, it makes a business appear to have a lower investment in inventory than is really the case, which also results in an incorrectly high inventory turnover measurement.

## Ownership of the Inventory

It is possible that a business does not even own some or all of the inventory that it presents on its balance sheet. This situation can arise when it is accepting goods on consignment from a third party. Under a consignment arrangement, the owner of the goods sends them to the business, which in turn attempts to sell them to a third party. If a sale is achieved, the business sends payment back to the owner of the goods. The issue that can arise under consignment arrangements is that the business physically holding the goods does not adequately segregate consigned goods from its own goods, and so includes everything in its ending inventory counts.

This issue is not readily detectable at the level of the financial statements. However, if the analyst knows that a business has consignment inventory on hand, be aware that this could cause an over-inflation of the ending inventory balance, which reduces the cost of goods sold and thereby inflates profits.

## Reliability of the Reserve for Obsolete Inventory

In the rare case when there is a reserve for obsolete inventory listed on the balance sheet, do not automatically rely upon the figure presented. The allowance is merely an estimate of what the total amount of obsolete inventory may be, and is usually based on historical write offs of inventory. This historical information can be incorrect for the following reasons:

- *Engineering change orders*. The engineering department periodically issues engineering change orders (ECOs) when it wants to revise the configuration of a product. If the department does so with no preplanning, this means that some raw materials intended for a product are no longer needed, and so can be considered obsolete. This is a significant issue if a business has recently had a product recall, since it indicates the presence of a product that will require an ECO to fix.
- *New product introductions*. When a company introduces a new product, it can only guess at the amount of customer demand, and so may overstock the product. If sales flop, the company will have a large amount of excess finished goods on hand. This issue can be spotted immediately following the roll out of a major new product line, if the finished goods figure jumps to a higher level and then remains there.

- *New competition.* If someone introduces a competing product that takes market share away from the company, this may result in an excess amount of inventory on hand that customers no longer want to purchase.
- *Fraud.* Management may want to present the best possible results in the income statement, and so intentionally does little to increase the balance in the reserve for obsolete inventory. This situation can arise when management will be paid bonuses if a certain profit figure is achieved.

Several of the issues noted in this sub-section cannot be clearly discerned just by examining the inventory number in the balance sheet. Instead, it is also necessary to have a detailed knowledge of the announced product releases of a business, any product recalls, and the types of products being introduced by competitors.

### Amount of Obsolete Inventory and Inventory Adjustments Recognized

When inventory is declared obsolete, it is written off through the cost of goods sold account. Given the volume and dollar amount of the expenses running through this account, it is quite unlikely that an outside observer will be able to spot these write-offs. Similarly, any adjustments to the inventory records are written up or down through the same cost of goods sold account. An active cycle counting program may trigger these changes on a daily basis, so – again – it is not possible to detect the amount of inventory adjustments just from the financial statements.

The one case in which it may be possible to discern write-offs and inventory adjustments is when inventory management systems are relatively poor, so that these records are only updated at the end of the year, just before the annual audit. In this situation, look for a spike in the cost of goods sold expense in the fourth quarter. The amount by which the expense spike exceeds the average cost of goods sold for the preceding three quarters of the year represents a good guess at the aggregate amount of these adjustments.

## Analysis Conclusions

The interpretation of inventory can be critical or completely unimportant, depending on the role that inventory plays within the industry or the competitive stance of a business. If inventory is important, then it probably comprises a large part of the current assets of a business. This investment represents a considerable risk, since it can be difficult to sell off inventory.

We suggest the following order of priority when analyzing inventory, to focus attention on the most important issues:

1. *Establish its importance.* If inventory is rarely used within a business or the investment in it is minimized, there may be no need for further analysis. If the reverse is the case, proceed to the next step.
2. *Measure inventory turnover.* Determine the proportion of inventory to the cost of goods sold, and whether this proportion is changing over time. If inventory turnover is declining, it could mean that a business is using up an

increasing proportion of its available cash to acquire more inventory, which can be risky.

3. *Look for year-end write-offs.* If there is a pattern of increases in the cost of goods sold just prior to the end of the fiscal year, this can indicate that management has been guesstimating inventory levels earlier in the year and/or not writing off obsolete inventory in a timely manner.

4. *Check press releases.* If the company has announced a product recall or increase in warranty claims, expect to see a jump in inventory that is caused by finished goods that customers no longer want to buy. If there is an announcement of an entirely new product line, inventory levels may vary depending on how well management has forecasted demand for the new products. If there has been an announcement of a new production management system, this could trigger a gradual decline in the inventory investment.

If there is evidence of low inventory turnover levels, it could be worthwhile to ask for a more detailed balance sheet that states the balances in raw materials, work-in-process, and finished goods. This additional information might yield insights into where inventory has accumulated, especially when tracked on a trend line. In particular, look for an increase in finished goods over time, which could point toward the accumulation of obsolete goods that customers will not buy.

# Chapter 5
# Interpretation of Fixed Assets

## Introduction

The fixed assets line item on the balance sheet contains the aggregate amount of all fixed assets acquired by a business, less the cumulative amount of depreciation charged against these assets. This line item can represent the largest investment that a business has made. Fixed assets can be hard to liquidate at a reasonable price, so investments in them should be tightly managed. In this chapter, we discuss the concepts available to an analyst who wants to obtain an understanding of the reasonableness of a company's fixed asset investment, how it impacts the reported level of profitability, and the management decisions and accounting methods that can alter the amount of reported fixed assets.

## The Interpretation of Fixed Assets

The fixed assets line item appears just after the current assets section of the balance sheet. Fixed assets may be retained for many years, and so are not considered current assets. A sample presentation showing where fixed assets are located on the balance sheet is noted in the following exhibit.

**Sample Presentation of Fixed Assets**

| Current Assets | |
|---|---|
| Cash | $84,000 |
| Investments | 109,000 |
| Accounts receivable | 342,000 |
| Inventory | 280,000 |
| Total current assets | $815,000 |
| | |
| **Fixed assets** | **$1,635,000** |
| Goodwill | 470,000 |
| Other assets | 80,000 |
| Total assets | $3,000,000 |

This single line item aggregates a large amount of information. It can be comprised of several general ledger accounts that are usually clustered together in the balance sheet. These accounts are as follows:

- *Buildings*. Contains the cost of buildings owned by a business. This is the purchase cost or construction cost of a building.

- *Computer equipment.* Contains the cost of purchased computer equipment. In a service business where the staff is well-equipped with their own computers, this could be the dominant fixed asset account.
- *Computer software.* This account usually contains the cost of major software installations, such as an accounting or production system. Lesser software, such as is found on laptop computers, is more likely to be charged to expense.
- *Equipment.* In a production environment, the cost of manufacturing equipment is likely to be the largest element of fixed assets. This cost includes the costs required to transport equipment to the production facility, the concrete pad on which it is positioned, electrical connections, plumbing, and testing.
- *Furniture and fixtures.* Contains the costs of tables, chairs, couches, conference tables, cubicles, and so forth. This account can have a large balance when there are many white-collar employees, each requiring furnishings.
- *Land.* Contains the purchase cost of land, as well as the cost to demolish buildings situated on the land, and clearing and leveling the land. This asset is considered to last into perpetuity, and so is not depreciated; the only exception is when it is classified as a natural resource and depleted.
- *Land improvements.* Contains the costs of installing drainage, irrigation, fencing, landscaping, parking lots, and walkways. These improvements are expected to have fixed lives, and so are depreciated – unlike the cost of the land itself.
- *Leasehold improvements.* Contains the costs of enhancements made to facilities that are being leased, such as the costs of cabinetry, carpeting, interior walls, ceilings, electrical enhancements, and plumbing additions.
- *Office equipment.* Contains the costs of copiers, video equipment, and so forth. This account is falling into disuse, since most office equipment can also be classified into the computer equipment account.
- *Vehicles.* Contains the costs of all vehicles owned by a business, which may include company cars, delivery vans, forklifts, and so forth.
- *Intangible assets.* Contains the costs of non-physical assets, such as copyrights, patents, licenses, trademarks, Internet domain names, and broadcast rights. This may be the key asset classification for some businesses, such as radio stations.
- *Accumulated depreciation.* Contains the periodic charges made against the fixed asset accounts to gradually charge their balances to expense. Does not include charges for intangible assets. This is a contra account that offsets the balance in the fixed asset accounts.
- *Accumulated amortization.* Contains the periodic charges made against the intangible assets account to gradually charge its balance to expense. This is a contra account that offsets the balance in the intangible assets account.

Thus, the underlying detail of the fixed assets line item noted in the last example could be broken down into the structure that appears in the following sample presentation.

**Sample Detailed Presentation of Fixed Assets**

| | | |
|---|---|---|
| Current Assets | | |
| Cash | | $84,000 |
| Investments | | 109,000 |
| Accounts receivable | | 342,000 |
| Inventory | | 280,000 |
| Total current assets | | $815,000 |
| | | |
| **Buildings** | **$800,000** | |
| **Computer equipment** | **108,000** | |
| **Computer software** | **62,000** | |
| **Equipment** | **201,000** | |
| **Furniture and fixtures** | **49,000** | |
| **Land** | **300,000** | |
| **Land improvements** | **50,000** | |
| **Leasehold improvements** | **20,000** | |
| **Office equipment** | **15,000** | |
| **Vehicles** | **100,000** | |
| **Accumulated depreciation** | **-108,000** | |
| **Intangible assets** | **50,000** | |
| **Accumulated amortization** | **-12,000** | |
| **Total fixed assets** | | **$1,635,000** |
| Goodwill | | 470,000 |
| Other assets | | 80,000 |
| Total assets | | $3,000,000 |

This many line items would clutter up the balance sheet, and so would rarely be found; instead, it is more common to see a total fixed assets line item with an accumulated depreciation offset, followed by an intangible assets line item with an accumulated amortization offset. An example of this presentation is:

**Sample Fixed Asset Presentation in the Balance Sheet**

| | |
|---|---|
| Fixed assets (net of accumulated depreciation of $108,000) | $1,597,000 |
| Intangible assets (net of accumulated amortization of $12,000) | 38,000 |

There are a number of interpretation issues related to fixed assets, which are noted in the following sub-sections.

## Depreciation Method

Depreciation is the gradual charging to expense of an asset's cost over its expected useful life. Thus, a machine that cost $50,000 and is expected to have a useful life of five years could have $10,000 charged against it in each of five years. However, this expense charge could be increased by using one of several available accelerated depreciation methods, such as sum-of-the-years' digits or the double-declining balance (DDB) method. These accelerated methods are designed to charge as much depreciation expense as possible in the earliest years of an asset's use. By doing so, the amount of reported taxable income is reduced, which defers the payment of some income taxes to a later period. The use of an accelerated depreciation method should be included in the footnotes that accompany the financial statements.

From the perspective of interpreting the financial statements, the use of accelerated depreciation makes it appear as though a company's fixed assets are older than is really the case. This is because a high proportion of accumulated depreciation to fixed assets typically implies that the assets have been in use for a long time, over which the accumulated depreciation amount has gradually increased. This could lead to incorrect conclusions regarding the willingness of management to replace fixed assets on a timely basis.

---

**EXAMPLE**

Medusa Medical is a startup company that has developed a concentrated snake oil medicine that can mitigate the effects of rheumatoid arthritis. The company immediately purchases a $100,000 centrifuge, which it assumes will have a five year useful life. Being a startup with little excess cash, the founders want to avoid recognizing taxable income, and so use the double declining balance (DDB) method to recognize depreciation. The DDB method essentially doubles the amount of depreciation recognized in the first year, resulting in a Year One depreciation charge of $40,000. If Medusa had instead used straight-line depreciation, the depreciation recognized would have been $20,000.

If an analyst were reviewing the balance sheet of Medusa after one year, it would be reasonable to assume that the equipment had been in use for two years, rather than the one year that was actually the case, since there is so much more accumulated depreciation. The differences appear in the following comparison table:

|  | Double Declining Balance Method | Straight-Line Method |
|---|---|---|
| Fixed assets | $100,000 | $100,000 |
| Less: Accumulated depreciation | -40,000 | -20,000 |
| Net fixed assets | $60,000 | $80,000 |

The calculation of the straight-line, sum-of-the-years' digits, and DDB methods are described next.

## Straight-Line Method

Under the straight-line method of depreciation, recognize depreciation expense evenly over the estimated useful life of an asset. The straight-line calculation steps are:

1. Subtract the estimated salvage value of the asset from the amount at which it is recorded on the books.
2. Determine the estimated useful life of the asset. It is easiest to use a standard useful life for each class of assets.
3. Divide the estimated useful life (in years) into 1 to arrive at the straight-line depreciation rate.
4. Multiply the depreciation rate by the asset cost (less salvage value).

---

**EXAMPLE**

Pensive Corporation purchases the Procrastinator Deluxe machine for $60,000. It has an estimated salvage value of $10,000 and a useful life of five years. Pensive calculates the annual straight-line depreciation for the machine as:

1. Purchase cost of $60,000 – Estimated salvage value of $10,000 = Depreciable asset cost of $50,000
2. 1 ÷ 5-Year useful life = 20% Depreciation rate per year
3. 20% Depreciation rate × $50,000 Depreciable asset cost = $10,000 Annual depreciation

---

## Sum-of-the-Years' Digits Method

The sum-of-the-years' digits (SYD) method is more appropriate than straight-line depreciation if the asset depreciates more quickly or has greater production capacity in earlier years than it does as it ages. Use the following formula to calculate it:

$$\text{Depreciation percentage} = \frac{\text{Number of estimated years of life as of beginning of the year}}{\text{Sum of the years' digits}}$$

The following table contains examples of the sum-of-the-years' digits noted in the denominator of the preceding formula:

| Total Depreciation Period | Initial Sum of the Years' Digits | Calculation |
|---|---|---|
| 2 years | 3 | 1 + 2 |
| 3 years | 6 | 1 + 2 + 3 |
| 4 years | 10 | 1 + 2 + 3 + 4 |
| 5 years | 15 | 1 + 2 + 3 + 4 + 5 |

The concept is most easily illustrated with the following example.

**EXAMPLE**

Pensive Corporation buys a Procrastinator Elite machine for $100,000. The machine has no estimated salvage value, and a useful life of five years. Pensive calculates the annual SYD depreciation for this machine as follows:

| Year | Number of estimated years of life as of beginning of the year | SYD Calculation | Depreciation Percentage | Annual Depreciation |
|------|------|------|------|------|
| 1 | 5 | 5/15 | 33.33% | $33,333 |
| 2 | 4 | 4/15 | 26.67% | 26,667 |
| 3 | 3 | 3/15 | 20.00% | 20,000 |
| 4 | 2 | 2/15 | 13.33% | 13,333 |
| 5 | 1 | 1/15 | 6.67% | 6,667 |
| Totals | 15 | | 100.00% | $100,000 |

The SYD method is clearly more complex than the straight-line method, which tends to limit its use unless software is employed to automatically track the calculations for each asset.

## Double-Declining Balance (DDB) Method

The DDB method is a form of accelerated depreciation. It may be more appropriate than the straight-line method if an asset experiences an inordinately high level of usage during the first few years of its useful life.

To calculate the double-declining balance depreciation rate, divide the number of years of useful life of an asset into 100 percent, and multiply the result by two. The formula is:

$$(100\%/\text{Years of useful life}) \times 2$$

The DDB calculation proceeds until the asset's salvage value is reached, after which depreciation ends.

**EXAMPLE**

Pensive Corporation purchases a machine for $50,000. It has an estimated salvage value of $5,000 and a useful life of five years. The calculation of the double declining balance depreciation rate is:

$$(100\%/\text{Years of useful life}) \times 2 = 40\%$$

By applying the 40% rate, Pensive arrives at the following table of depreciation charges per year:

| Year | Book Value at Beginning of Year | Depreciation Percentage | DDB Depreciation | Book Value Net of Depreciation |
|------|------|------|------|------|
| 1 | $50,000 | 40% | $20,000 | $30,000 |
| 2 | 30,000 | 40% | 12,000 | 18,000 |
| 3 | 18,000 | 40% | 7,200 | 10,800 |
| 4 | 10,800 | 40% | 4,320 | 6,480 |
| 5 | 6,480 | 40% | 1,480 | 5,000 |
| Total | | | $45,000 | |

Note that the depreciation in the fifth and final year is only for $1,480, rather than the $3,240 that would be indicated by the 40% depreciation rate. The reason for the smaller depreciation charge is that Pensive stops any further depreciation once the remaining book value declines to the amount of the estimated salvage value.

A variation on the DDB method is the 150% declining balance method, which does not recognize depreciation at quite so rapid a rate.

## Existence of Depreciation

When reviewing financial statements, be aware that some organizations only record depreciation once, at the end of the year. They do not bother with a monthly depreciation charge. This situation most commonly arises when reviewing the financial statements of smaller entities, where the accounting records are not maintained at a sufficient level of detail to allow for accurate and ongoing depreciation charges.

The existence of a periodic depreciation charge cannot be ascertained from the balance sheet. Since the balance sheet contains an accumulated depreciation figure that includes depreciation from previous years, one might erroneously conclude that the mere existence of this line item on the balance sheet means that a depreciation charge has been made in the current year. The only way to be certain that depreciation was actually recognized in the current year is to look for this line item in the income statement.

## Sufficiency of Depreciation

From the perspective of long-term competitiveness, a business should be investing roughly the same amount in new fixed assets over time, to replace its old assets as they gradually wear out. It is possible to estimate the amount of this asset replacement by examining the proportion of depreciation to gross fixed assets over time. The proportion should remain roughly the same, especially when the straight-line method of depreciation is being used (since it does not accelerate depreciation charges). The concept is expanded upon in the following example.

**EXAMPLE**

An analyst is reviewing the financial statements of Hodgson Industrial Design, which uses stamping machines to create large numbers of aluminum widgets. The stamping machines wear out after about ten years of continuous use, and must then be replaced. Hodgson's management team has been attempting to aggressively expand the sale of its widgets into the South American market, which has called for a delicate balancing act of investing in more equipment without taking on too much debt. She extracts the following information from Hodgson's balance sheets for the past four years. The expansion began in Year 3.

| (000s) | Year 1 | Year 2 | Year 3 | Year 4 |
|---|---|---|---|---|
| Gross fixed assets | $18,500 | $18,900 | $23,400 | $25,100 |
| Net change in accumulated depreciation | 2,002 | 2,079 | 2,106 | 1,757 |
| Net change in accumulated depreciation as % of gross fixed assets | 11% | 11% | 9% | 7% |

The table reveals that there is an increase in the overall investment in fixed assets, as one would expect to see when sales are increasing rapidly. However, the proportion of depreciation to gross fixed assets has declined, which indicates that Hodgson's management is probably retaining an increasing proportion of old and fully depreciated stamping machines. A likely outcome is that a number of machines will need to be replaced in the near future, when they completely wear out. Another possible outcome is that some machines will fail suddenly, resulting in the company's inability to meet its sales commitments.

There can be valid reasons for a declining proportion of depreciation to gross fixed assets. Here are several possible scenarios:

- *Outsourcing.* A company may have chosen to outsource some or all of its production capabilities to a third party, which allows it to sell off its production assets.
- *Bottleneck focus.* Management may have decided to focus its attention on enhancing the ability of the business to utilize its bottleneck operation. If so, there is less inclination to over-invest in other parts of the business.
- *Life extension.* It is possible to extend the useful life of equipment through the use of preventive maintenance and periodic overhauls. This means the equipment can continue to be used past the point when it has been fully depreciated.

There are also valid reasons for an *increasing* proportion of depreciation to gross fixed assets. Here are several possible scenarios:

- *Bottleneck support.* Management may have decided to invest in more fixed assets upstream from the bottleneck operation in the production area. This is called *sprint capacity*, and is intended to provide a boost in production volume following an unexpected production stoppage. Having extra sprint capacity allows a bottleneck operation to continue operating at full capacity. See the author's *Constraint Management* book for more information.

- *Competitive change*. Management may have decided to increase the investment in certain fixed assets in order to give the company a competitive advantage, perhaps to customize products to the needs of individual customers, or to lower costs. This approach can involve such a large increase in the fixed asset investment that it poses a barrier to entry for potential new competitors.

- *Reduced useful life*. Management may have decided that the existing fixed assets will have a shorter life than was originally anticipated, so the periodic amount of depreciation recognized increases to ensure that it is fully recognized by the end of the shortened useful life.

## What is Being Capitalized

When an expenditure is recorded as a fixed asset, this is called *capitalization*. The decision to engage in capitalization is an important one, because it defers the recognition of a cost to a future period. To some extent, management can decide which expenditures will be capitalized and which will be charged to expense at once, which impacts the reported level of profitability. The following bullet points outline several capitalization issues to be aware of:

- *Capitalization limit*. A company that wants to report the highest possible profits can set its capitalization threshold (known as the capitalization limit) quite low, perhaps at just a few hundred dollars. Doing so allows it to defer the recognition of expenses on a large number of smaller purchases that are expected to be used over a period of at least one year. This issue can be detected if the office supplies expense line item contains quite a low total, since these lesser expenditures would otherwise be charged to that account. Conversely, the capitalization limit might be set high, in order to charge more expenditures to expense at once. This approach can be spotted if the office supplies expense line item is quite large.

- *Interest capitalization*. It is allowable to capitalize the interest expense associated with the funding needed to pay for a constructed asset. This issue can be spotted by comparing the reported amount of debt on the balance sheet to the interest expense on the income statement. If the interest expense is low or nonexistent, it is likely that the expense is being capitalized. This issue usually only appears when large construction projects are in process, such as the construction of a corporate headquarters building or a satellite.

- *Software capitalization*. Under certain circumstances, the cost incurred to develop software for internal use can be capitalized. This can be a major issue, since it could defer the recognition of a large amount of employee salaries and wages, making a company initially appear to be profitable when it is experiencing large negative cash flows. To spot this issue, peruse the capitalization policy noted in the footnotes accompanying the financial statements, and see if there is a large increase in the reported amount of intangible assets.

## What is Being Derecognized

When fixed assets are disposed of, the accounting staff should derecognize them in the accounting records. This means reversing the original fixed asset cost and the associated amount of accumulated depreciation. There may also be a gain or loss to be recognized. Doing so keeps the gross amount of fixed assets and the accumulated depreciation line items in the balance sheet at a reasonable level. If the accounting staff is not attending to its derecognition responsibilities, the result is an ever-increasing amount of fixed assets and accumulated depreciation on the balance sheet. When there is a large amount of accumulated depreciation, this implies that a company's fixed assets are old, which may not really be the case.

There is no sure way to ascertain from the financial statements whether derecognition is taking place, though the complete absence of a decline in the accumulated depreciation balance over time is a possible indicator.

## Proportion of Sales to Fixed Assets

It requires a large amount of fixed assets to compete in some industries, such as computer chips and automobiles. The sales to fixed assets ratio can be used to determine how a company's expenditures for fixed assets compare to those of other companies in the same industry, to see if it is operating in a more lean fashion than the others, or if there may be opportunities to scale back on its fixed asset investment. This is quite useful to track on a trend line, which may show gradual changes in expenditure levels away from the historical trend. The ratio is most useful in asset-intensive industries, and least useful when the required asset base is so small that the ratio would be essentially meaningless.

The ratio can also be misleading in cases when a company must invest in an entire production facility before it can generate any sales; this will initially result in an inordinately low sales to fixed assets ratio, which gradually increases as the company maximizes sales for that facility, and then levels out when it reaches a high level of asset utilization.

To calculate the sales to fixed assets ratio, divide net sales for the past twelve months by the book value of all fixed assets. Book value is the recognized fixed asset cost, minus accumulated depreciation. The formula is:

$$\frac{\text{Trailing 12 months' sales}}{\text{Book value of all fixed assets}}$$

The fixed asset book value listed in the denominator is subject to some variation, depending on what type of depreciation method is used. If an accelerated depreciation method is used, the denominator will be unusually small, and so will yield a higher ratio.

**EXAMPLE**

Mole Industries manufactures trench digging equipment. It has a relatively low sales to fixed assets ratio of 4:1, because a large amount of machining equipment is needed to construct its products. Mole is considering expanding into earth-moving equipment, and calculates the sales to fixed assets ratio for competing companies, based on their financial statements. The ratio is in the vicinity of 3:1 for most competitors, which means that Mole will need to invest heavily in fixed assets in order to enter this new market. Mole estimates that the most likely revenue level it can achieve for earth moving equipment will be $300 million. Based on the 3:1 ratio, this means that Mole may need to invest $100 million in fixed assets in order to achieve its goal.

Mole's CFO concludes that the company does not currently have the financial resources to invest $100 million in the earth moving equipment market, and recommends that the company not enter the field at this time.

## Cash Flow Support of Fixed Assets

Does a company have sufficient cash to pay for its upcoming fixed asset purchases? The cash flow to fixed asset requirements ratio is useful both as a general analysis of a company's future prospects, and also as a means for determining the health of a possible acquisition. The ratio must be greater than 1:1 for a company to have sufficient cash to fund its fixed asset needs. If the ratio is very close to 1:1, then a company is operating near the edge of its available cash flows, and will have issues unless it can obtain additional financing. The ratio is less useful if the company in question has substantial cash reserves, since it can always draw upon these reserves to fund its fixed asset requirements, irrespective of short-term cash flows.

To calculate the cash flow to fixed asset requirements ratio, divide the expected annual cash flow by the total expenditure that has been budgeted for fixed assets for the same period. One can calculate the cash flow figure in the numerator by adding non-cash expenses (such as depreciation and amortization) back to net income, and subtracting out any non-cash sales (such as sales accruals). Also subtract from the numerator any dividends and principal payments on loans. The formula is:

$$\frac{\text{Net income} + \text{Noncash expenses} - \text{Noncash sales} - \text{Dividends} - \text{Principal payments}}{\text{Budgeted fixed asset expenditures}}$$

Some of this information may not be available to the outside analyst. If so, use the "cash generated from operations" line item in the statement of cash flows as the numerator, and the historical trend of fixed asset purchases noted on the statement of cash flows as the denominator.

**EXAMPLE**

An analyst is reviewing a press release issued by Mole Industries, which includes a budget for the upcoming year. The budget includes the following information:

| Budget Line Item | Amount |
|---|---|
| Net income | $4,100,000 |
| Depreciation and amortization | 380,000 |
| Accrued sales | 250,000 |
| Dividend payments | 100,000 |
| Principal payments | 800,000 |
| Budgeted fixed asset expenditures | 3,750,000 |

Based on this information, the analyst calculates the ratio of cash flow to fixed asset requirements as:

$$\frac{\$4,100,000 \text{ Net income} + \$380,000 \text{ Depreciation and amortization} - \$250,000 \text{ Accrued sales} - \$100,000 \text{ Dividends} - \$800,000 \text{ Principal payments}}{\$3,750,000 \text{ Budgeted fixed asset expenditures}}$$

$$=$$

$$\frac{\$3,330,000 \text{ Cash flows}}{\$3,750,000 \text{ Budgeted fixed asset expenditures}}$$

$$= 89\%$$

The ratio is less than one, so the analyst concludes that Mole will need to draw upon its cash reserves to pay for the fixed assets.

## Proportion of Repairs to Fixed Assets

It is useful to review a company's ratio of repair and maintenance expense to fixed assets, especially on a trend line. This comparison is only available to the analyst if there is a separate repairs and maintenance expense line item in the income statement, or if this information is provided in the accompanying financial statement footnotes.

If the ratio of repairs and maintenance expense to fixed assets is increasing over time, there are several ways to interpret it:

- *Old assets.* The business is relying on an aging fixed asset base, since it must spend more to keep them operational. This could mean that the business will eventually be faced with a wholesale replacement of its fixed assets.
- *High utilization.* An entity is experiencing very high asset usage levels, which calls for higher maintenance costs just to keep the machines running fast enough to meet demand. This condition can be spotted by looking for a

high sales to fixed assets ratio (see the prior ratio). A high profit level is also likely.

- *Preparing for sale.* If there is a sudden spike in the ratio in the recent past, it may be because the owner of a company is simply preparing it for sale, and so is either catching up on delayed maintenance or is bringing machinery up to a high standard of performance.
- *Accounting changes.* It is possible that the repairs and maintenance expense has been moved among different accounts, such as from the cost of goods sold account or an overhead cost pool to its own account, which means that there could appear to be a sudden jump in expenses that is not really the case.

This ratio is least useful when the bulk of the repairs and maintenance expense is comprised of salaries paid to a relatively fixed group of repair technicians. In this case, the expense is essentially a fixed cost, and cannot be expected to vary much over time.

A problem that this ratio does *not* reveal is when an acquiree simply lets its machinery decline by not investing in repairs and maintenance; this means that the ratio would remain flat or could even decline over time. In this case, look elsewhere for an indicator, such as declining sales.

To calculate the repairs and maintenance expense to fixed assets ratio, divide the total amount of repairs and maintenance expense by the total amount of fixed assets before depreciation. The amount of accumulated depreciation that may have built up on older assets could otherwise bring the denominator close to zero, so it is better not to use depreciation at all. The formula is:

$$\frac{\text{Total repairs and maintenance expense}}{\text{Total fixed assets before depreciation}}$$

**EXAMPLE**

Mole Industries is investigating the purchase of Grubstake Brothers, a manufacturer of backhoes. Its acquisition analysis team uncovers the following information:

|  | 20X1 | 20X2 | 20X3 | 20X4 |
|---|---|---|---|---|
| Sales | $15,000,000 | $14,500,000 | $13,200,000 | $12,900,000 |
| Profit | $1,000,000 | $200,000 | $(150,000) | $(420,000) |
| Repairs expense | $400,000 | $240,000 | $160,000 | $80,000 |
| Fixed assets | $5,400,000 | $6,000,000 | $6,050,000 | $6,100,000 |
| Repairs to fixed assets ratio | 7% | 4% | 3% | 1% |

The information in the table strongly indicates that the decline in Grubstake's profitability over the past few years has led its management to cut back on repair and maintenance expenditures. Thus, if Mole elects to buy Grubstake, it can expect to invest a considerable amount to replace fixed assets.

## Analysis Conclusions

An outside analyst will have a difficult time gaining detailed insights into the fixed asset base of a company, since so many assets may be aggregated into just a few line items in the balance sheet. The situation is worsened if the accounting staff of a company is not derecognizing fixed assets from the books in a timely manner. Nonetheless, it is possible to obtain a general impression of the adequacy of a company's fixed asset investment. When analyzing fixed assets, we suggest the following order of priority:

1. *Compare fixed assets to sales.* Barring a change in the way a company conducts business, the proportion of fixed assets to sales should remain fairly steady over time. Changes in this ratio could trigger extensive inquiries of management regarding underlying causes.
2. *Compare fixed assets to cash flows.* A business should be generating at least enough cash to pay for its long-term trend of fixed asset purchases. If this is not the case, the competitive position of an entity may be headed for a decline.
3. *Look for interest and software development capitalization.* If either interest expense or the wages associated with software development are being capitalized, there is a significant chance that reported profit levels might actually be masking negative cash flows.
4. *Locate and understand depreciation.* There may be no depreciation listed in the income statement at all, in which case the net income figure is too high. If depreciation is present, determine what type of depreciation method is being employed; the method used could impact profitability.

The balance in the fixed asset line item tends not to change quickly. However, due to the massive amounts of invested funds involved, long-term trends in this line item can portend significant changes in a business. Consequently, it makes sense for the analyst to conduct an ongoing ratio analysis of fixed assets, and to understand the accounting policies that drive the recognition of fixed assets and the calculation of depreciation.

# Chapter 6
# Interpretation of Other Assets

## Introduction

In the preceding chapters, we discussed the major asset classifications – cash, receivables, inventory, and fixed assets. There are other assets listed on the balance sheet that are easier to analyze, and so we have included them both in this chapter. In the following sections, we interpret the prepaid expenses account and the goodwill account. The former is usually quite small, and the latter is more of a theoretical asset, so they require a reduced amount of analysis. Nonetheless, they can both be used as indicators of other issues within a business, as noted in the following sections.

## The Interpretation of Prepaid Expenses

The prepaid expenses line item appears within the current assets section of the balance sheet. Its exact positioning on the balance sheet is subject to interpretation, depending on how liquid the contents of the account are expected to be. Since it could take several months to resolve the items stored in this account, it should probably be considered less liquid than accounts receivable, and perhaps even inventory. In the following exhibit, we place it at the end of the current assets section, as the least liquid line item.

**Sample Presentation of Prepaid Expenses**

| Current Assets | |
|---|---:|
| Cash | $84,000 |
| Investments | 109,000 |
| Accounts receivable | 342,000 |
| Inventory | 260,000 |
| **Prepaid expenses** | **20,000** |
| Total current assets | $815,000 |

The prepaid expenses line item only contains a single account, which has the same name. The account contains expenditures that are paid for in one accounting period, but for which the underlying asset will not be entirely consumed until a future period. Examples of prepaid expenses are:

- Advertising
- Insurance
- Rent

For all of these expenditures, payment is made in advance, and the accounting staff gradually charges them to expense over time as they are consumed. For example, rent is frequently paid prior to the beginning of the month to which the rent applies. This means the rent appears on the balance sheet for one month, is charged to expense in the next month, and is then replaced by another rent prepayment. Or, an ad agency may require prepayment of an advertising campaign, which is then charged to expense as the associated ads are run. In this case, the prepaid amount can be expected to gradually decline over time.

The balance in the prepaid expenses account is generally a small proportion of the total amount of assets. Nonetheless, there are a few issues to be aware of, which are noted in the following sub-sections.

**Nature of the Account Contents**

The balance in the prepaid expenses account is comprised of two elements, which are:

- *Consistent balance items.* Some expense prepayments are replenished every month, and so are consistently present in the prepaid expenses account. For example, medical insurance is prepaid for each month, and is then charged to expense and replaced by the next month's prepayment. This means there is always a minimum balance in the account.
- *Declining balance items.* Some prepayments are charged to expense over a period of time, such as advertising expenditures. These prepayments therefore have a constantly declining balance.

Given the nature of the elements in the account, one can expect the account balance to occasionally spike when a declining balance expenditure is added to the account, but not to decline below a certain level that represents those prepayments that are replenished each month. The concept is shown graphically in the following chart, where the advertising prepayment gradually declines over time, while the medical and rent prepayments hold steady.

**Typical Balance Totals in the Prepaid Expenses Account**

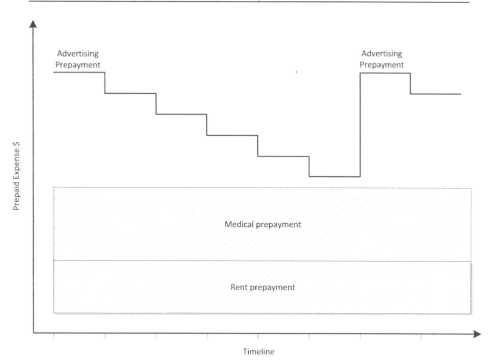

Of the two types of expenses, the issue to focus on is the expenses that maintain a consistent balance in the account. If the amount appearing in the balance sheet suddenly drops and then continues at a lower level, this has four possible implications:

- *Cash basis of accounting.* The company may have switched to the cash basis of accounting, and so only records expenses as they are paid. If so, a number of line items related to accrual accounting will vanish from the balance sheet, so this situation will be fairly obvious.
- *Delayed accounting.* The company is recording expenditures late, which means that it may be informally holding supplier invoices for a period of time before recognizing them. This implies a shortage of available cash to pay suppliers. If this is the case, also look for a higher proportion of accounts payable appearing on the balance sheet.
- *Expense reduction.* The company may have eliminated an expense entirely or at least reduced it, so that the amount reported as a prepaid expense declines. This can be detected by seeing if the associated expense accounts in the income statement contain reduced expense levels.
- *New terms.* The company has negotiated new terms with its suppliers, so that it no longer has to pay in advance. This is quite unlikely for rent and insurance payments, where suppliers want to reduce their risk by obtaining payments in advance.

### The Increasing Account Balance

A key issue with the prepaid expenses account is that the accounting staff may forget to charge items to expense in the correct period. This issue may not be found until the account's contents are investigated, which may not happen until just prior to the year-end audit. At that time, any excess amounts are charged to expense. This situation typically causes expenses to appear slightly low until the end of the fiscal year, when there is a sudden expense jolt that reduces profits. It is possible to spot this issue by examining the income statement for a number of interim periods side-by-side, to see if any expense accounts suddenly drop in a reporting period. If so, it is possible that the expense was never shifted over from the prepaid expenses account.

### The Impact of Sales Growth on Prepaid Expenses

The prepaid expenses line item tends to change in approximate proportion to overall sales. For example, one of the largest components of the account is usually medical insurance prepayments; this amount will vary in direct proportion to company headcount, which typically reflects changes in sales volume.

Rent prepayments are less likely to change in direct proportion to sales levels, since organizations tend to be cautious about entering into new facility lease agreements, which usually run for multiple years. Consequently, a business is more likely to jam its employees into the existing space for as long as possible before finally acquiring more space, for which a rent prepayment will appear in the prepaid expenses line item. This means that an increase in the account that is caused by an additional rent prepayment tends to lag an increase in sales. Similarly, this prepayment will continue past a *decline* in sales, since a business must wait for a lease to expire before it can stop issuing rent prepayments.

## The Interpretation of Goodwill

Goodwill is an asset that arises from the acquisition of another business. In essence, when the acquirer pays the shareholders of the acquiree, the amount paid is allocated to the acquired assets and liabilities. Allocations are based on the fair value of the acquired assets and liabilities. If there is an excess of the amount paid over these allocations, it is recorded as goodwill, which is considered to be the additional value acquired, above and beyond the amount allocated to specific balance sheet items.

---

**EXAMPLE**

Inscrutable Corporation acquires Latham Lumber for $5,000,000. Latham has assets with a fair value of $4,500,000, and liabilities of $250,000. In its accounting for the acquisition, Inscrutable assigns the indicated fair values to these assets and liabilities, leaving a residual of $750,000, which it recognizes as goodwill.

---

If a company routinely acquires other organizations, it may build up quite a substantial goodwill asset, to the point where this becomes the dominant asset on the balance sheet. The goodwill line item appears at or near the bottom of the assets section, as shown in the following exhibit.

**Sample Presentation of Goodwill**

| | |
|---|---|
| Current Assets | |
|     Cash | $84,000 |
|     Investments | 109,000 |
|     Accounts receivable | 342,000 |
|     Inventory | 260,000 |
|     Prepaid assets | 20,000 |
| Total current assets | $815,000 |
| | |
| Fixed assets | $1,635,000 |
| **Goodwill** | **470,000** |
| Other assets | 80,000 |
| Total assets | $3,000,000 |

Given the size of the goodwill asset, it is useful to review it at regular intervals. Several issues are noted in the following sub-sections.

## Goodwill Impairment

A business that has a goodwill asset is required to examine it at intervals of one year or less, to see if the asset has been impaired. Impairment occurs when the fair value of the acquired entity drops below the recognized assets and liabilities derived from the acquisition. When impairment is detected, the organization is required to write off that amount of its goodwill that will bring the recognized cost of the related assets and liabilities down to the fair value of the acquired entity. When these write-offs occur, they tend to be quite large, possibly involving the entire amount of the goodwill asset. This means that a goodwill write-off can easily offset the entire amount of profits recorded by a business.

When an organization records an impairment charge, this means that the entity it acquired is not fairing as well as expected, and can be an indicator of further write-downs of any remaining goodwill. Given this risk, one should closely monitor the disclosures that a business reports regarding the status of its goodwill asset.

## Goodwill Amortization

Non-public companies are allowed to amortize their goodwill assets to expense over a period of not more than ten years. This is a prudent step for a business to take, since it eventually cleans up the balance sheet by eliminating the goodwill asset. This brings up three issues for the analyst:

- *Use of amortization.* If a privately-held business is not taking advantage of the amortization option, why not? It is possible that management is attempting to artificially bolster profits by not using amortization.
- *Reconfigured profits.* If management does choose to use goodwill amortization, the amount of the amortization expense could overwhelm the normal profitability of the business. If so, subtract out the amortization amount from the income statement to gain a better understanding of the actual profitability being reported.
- *Risk of impairment.* If a business chooses to amortize its goodwill asset, the risk of incurring an asset impairment charge declines rapidly, since the goodwill balance is continually declining. If amortization is not taking place, then the full amount of goodwill remains on the books, which means that there is a continuing risk that a large impairment charge will eventually take place.

---

**Related Podcast Episodes:** Episodes 136 and 175 of the Accounting Best Practices Podcast discuss goodwill impairment testing and goodwill amortization, respectively. You can listen to them at: **www.accountingtools.com/podcasts** or **iTunes**

---

## Analysis Conclusions

The prepaid expenses line item tends to be quite small in relation to other asset accounts, and so may be ignored. However, a sudden drop in an expense line item can quite possibly be traced back to this account, so when there is an unexplained expense decline, see if there is a corresponding increase in the prepaid expenses line item. Also, changes in this account tend to follow a consistent pattern over time, so an unexpected change (up or down) could be worth a search of the accompanying footnotes to see if management has listed an explanation.

The goodwill asset cannot be considered a "real" asset, since it cannot be sold for value. Instead, it is more of an indicator of the financial health of any acquired businesses. If an impairment charge is recognized, this means that a portion of a company's operations are not doing as well as expected. A continuing series of impairment charges can indicate that a business is routinely overpaying for its acquisitions, or that it does not know how to manage them.

# Chapter 7
# Interpretation of Current Liabilities

## Introduction

The current liabilities section of the balance sheet contains all recognized obligations of a business that are due for payment within the next year. These obligations may be payable to a variety of parties, including suppliers, employees, lenders, the government, and even customers. When these liabilities are presented at a sufficient level of detail, they can provide numerous insights into the financial condition of a business. In the following sections, we address the presentation, measurement, and specific issues associated with current liabilities.

## The Interpretation of Current Liabilities

The current liabilities section appears at the beginning of the liabilities and equity sections of the balance sheet. A sample presentation showing where current liabilities are located in the balance sheet is noted in the following exhibit.

### Sample Presentation of Current Liabilities

| Current Liabilities | |
|---|---|
| Accounts payable | $360,000 |
| Other payables | 48,000 |
| Accrued liabilities | 22,000 |
| Unearned revenues | 40,000 |
| Total current liabilities | $470,000 |

The line items appearing in the balance sheet are usually derived from the following accounts:

- *Accounts payable.* Contains amounts billed by suppliers to the company. The balance in this account should exactly match the amount in an aged accounts payable report that lists every unpaid supplier invoice and any unused supplier credits.
- *Notes payable.* Contains any debt payable within the next year. This item is dealt with in greater detail in the following chapter, Interpretation of Debt.
- *Sales taxes payable.* If a business is liable for the collection of sales taxes from customers, it bills them for sales taxes and stores the billed amounts in this account until remitted to the applicable government. If a business is liable for sales tax collections in several tax jurisdictions, it is common to set up separate accounts for each one. This can mean that a larger business maintains dozens of sales taxes payable accounts.

- *Dividends payable.* Contains the amount of dividends declared by the board of directors as payable to investors. This account only contains a balance during the period between when a dividend has been declared and not yet paid.
- *Wages payable.* Contains the amount of any wages earned by employees during the reporting period or before, but not yet paid to them. This tends to be a relatively small amount, since employees are usually paid several times each month, leaving only a few days of wages payable at the end of a reporting period. An exception can be in entities that have large numbers of employees who are paid on an hourly basis.
- *Interest payable.* Contains the amount of interest owed on debt but not yet paid. This account is used when the billing from the lender arrives after the end of the reporting period, so an accrued amount is recorded instead. This account is not needed when a company's bank is the lender, and automatically deducts the interest owed from the company's bank account at the end of each month.
- *Income taxes payable.* There is a time lag between when a business recognizes an income tax liability and when it is actually paid to the government (usually at quarterly intervals). The amount of this future payment appears in the income taxes payable account.
- *Warranty liability.* Contains the accrued amount of any liabilities associated with product warranties. This account is only used if ongoing customer warranty claims are material, and it is possible to reliably estimate the amount of this liability.
- *Unearned revenues.* Contains the amount of any customer deposits that a business has not yet earned by producing goods or services. This account is most commonly used in businesses that provide custom products, and so require early customer payments.

Thus, the underlying detail of the current liabilities section noted in the last example could be broken down into the structure that appears in the following sample presentation.

## Sample Detailed Presentation of Current Liabilities

| | | |
|---|---:|---:|
| Current Liabilities | | |
|    Accounts payable | | $360,000 |
|    Other payables | | |
|       Notes payable | $38,000 | |
|       Sales taxes payable | 10,000 | |
|       Dividends payable | -- | |
|    Total other payables | | 48,000 |
| | | |
|    Accrued liabilities | | |
|       Wages payable | 4,000 | |
|       Interest payable | 3,000 | |
|       Income taxes payable | 13,000 | |
|       Warranty liability | 2,000 | |
|    Total accrued liabilities | | 22,000 |
| | | |
|    Unearned revenues | | 40,000 |
| Total current liabilities | | $470,000 |

There are a number of issues with current liabilities, which are noted in the following sub-sections. We begin with a discussion of days payables outstanding, which can then be used to analyze accounts payable.

## Days Payables Outstanding

The accounts payable days formula measures the number of days that a company takes to pay its suppliers. If the number of days increases from one period to the next, this indicates that the company is paying its suppliers more slowly.

To calculate days payables outstanding, summarize all purchases from suppliers during the measurement period, and divide by the average amount of accounts payable during that period. The formula is:

$$\frac{\text{Total supplier purchases}}{(\text{Beginning accounts payable} + \text{Ending accounts payable}) \div 2}$$

This formula reveals the total accounts payable turnover. Then divide the resulting turnover figure into 365 days to arrive at the number of accounts payable days.

The formula can be modified to exclude cash payments to suppliers, since the numerator should include only purchases on credit from suppliers. However, the amount of up-front cash payments to suppliers is normally so small that this modification is not necessary.

As an example, an analyst wants to determine a company's accounts payable days for the past year. In the beginning of this period, the beginning accounts payable balance was $800,000, and the ending balance was $884,000. Purchases for the last 12 months were $7,500,000.

Based on this information, the accounts payable turnover calculation is:

$$\frac{\$7,500,000 \text{ Purchases}}{(\$800,000 \text{ Beginning payables} + \$884,000 \text{ Ending payables}) \div 2}$$

$$=$$

$$\frac{\$7,500,000 \text{ Purchases}}{\$842,000 \text{ Average accounts payable}}$$

$$= 8.9 \text{ Accounts payable turnover}$$

Thus, the company's accounts payable is turning over at a rate of 8.9 times per year. To calculate the turnover in days, divide the 8.9 turns into 365 days, which yields:

$$365 \text{ Days} \div 8.9 \text{ Turns} = 41 \text{ Days}$$

One might measure accounts payable days by only using the cost of goods sold in the numerator. This is incorrect, since there may be a large amount of administrative expenses that should also be included. If only the cost of goods sold is included in the numerator, this creates an excessively small number of payable days.

A significant failing of the days payables outstanding measurement is that it does not factor in all of the short-term liabilities of a business. There may be substantial liabilities related to payroll, interest, and taxes that exceed the size of payables outstanding. This issue can be eliminated by incorporating all short-term liabilities into the days payables outstanding measurement.

## Changes in Payable Days

The number of payable days should be fairly consistent from one period to the next, since it is largely based on the payment terms of suppliers, which change infrequently. There is typically a mix of payment terms among suppliers, such as 30-day terms for raw material suppliers and 10-day terms for freight companies. As long as the mix of these suppliers is consistent, the aggregate payable days should not change. Also, even if the sales volume of a business spikes or drops, the payable days should remain about the same. If there is a change, here are several possibilities for why the change has occurred:

### Decline in Payable Days

- *Tighter credit policy.* Suppliers may have tightened their credit policies, which either allows a company to have less total credit with them or requires them to pay sooner. This circumstance can arise when the economy is contracting, but is more likely if a business has abused its payment terms in the past. The latter scenario is more likely if payable days contracts substantially, since it implies that suppliers are requiring cash on delivery terms.
- *Large invoice paid.* The company may have just paid quite a large invoice amount, which comprises a large part of the total accounts payable. This condition is more likely in a small business that has few suppliers, but could

also arise when a department has been outsourced, and large periodic payments are due to the supplier that has taken over this function.

- *Early payment discounts taken.* If a business has a large store of excess cash on hand, one profitable use for it is to take all possible early payment discounts offered by suppliers, especially since the effective interest rate offered by suppliers is usually quite high. This is likely to be the case when a business has an unusually high cash or investments balance.

Increase in Payable Days

- *Change in payment terms.* An aggressive purchasing department could negotiate for longer payment terms with suppliers. This is most likely to be the case for large companies that make large purchases from suppliers, and so can demand favorable terms. A smaller company does not have the purchasing power to force through longer payment terms, and so could probably only do so in exchange for paying more per unit; if so, the increased cost will appear in the cost of goods sold.
- *Intentionally delayed payments.* The controller may not have sufficient cash to pay supplier invoices on time, and so delays making payments. Evidence of this situation is when the cash balance is persistently low and the available line of credit has been fully accessed.

**Sales Tax Payables Issues**

A significant concern with any business is whether it is withholding and remitting sales taxes at all. If not, and the organization should be, then it may be liable for serious fines, and will be responsible for paying all sales taxes that had not been withheld or remitted in the past. This issue can only be detected if no sales tax line items are separately stated on the balance sheet, and there is no indication that this tax liability has been aggregated into a current liabilities line item.

A rare circumstance that can be detected on a detailed balance sheet is when a company has undergone a sales tax audit and been fined by the taxing authority for unpaid taxes and related penalties. This situation will cause an unusual spike in the sales tax payables line item. The offsetting expense could appear in a number of places on the income statement, and so is less distinguishable on that document.

**Dividends Payable Issues**

The dividends payable line item is usually an unremarkable item that briefly contains a liability for a forthcoming dividend payment, and then declines to a zero balance. A possible issue to watch for is the ability of the issuing entity to pay the dividend. For example, compare the balance in this line item to the amount of cash on hand. Alternatively, see if the amount of debt increases at the same time that the dividend is paid. Either analysis can reveal situations in which a business is digging deep into its cash reserves to make payments to shareholders, which could be a precursor to not being able to pay additional dividends in the future.

## Wages Payable Issues

The balance in the wages payable account is usually not especially large. However, it can spike when a business falls on hard times and defers employee pay. In this case, the accounting staff should accrue the deferred pay, which appears in this line item. The amount could become quite large if a business is unable to pay its employees for a significant period of time. This condition usually corresponds to a steep decline in sales and profits. However, many organizations incorrectly do not record this accrual, even if there is a clear commitment by management to pay employees at a later date.

A more common issue is a sudden spike in the wages payable line item when the financial statements have been released at the end of the fiscal year. This increase is derived from the approval of bonuses, which are usually based on year-end results. If this spike appears, compare it to the amount of cash on hand to see if the business can afford to make the requisite payments.

## Income Taxes Payable Issues

The income taxes liability can be a confusing one. This line item may not even be present, despite the reporting of taxable profits, because a business may be taking advantage of net operating loss carryforwards from prior periods. These carryforwards offset net income, resulting in no tax liability. The presence of these carryforwards may be stated in the footnotes accompanying the financial statements.

## Warranty Liability Issues

When a business has no warranty liability line item and then begins to present it, this could indicate two quite different situations. One possibility is that management is being appropriately conservative in recognizing warranty costs as soon as sales are generated. If so, the liability is likely to be relatively small.

A more worrying alternative is when the liability begins as quite a large figure. In this case, management may be setting up a reserve against the prospect of a major product recall. This situation may be accompanied by press releases regarding a recall. Over time, it is also possible that sales will decline to reflect customer non-acceptance of company products.

## Unearned Revenues

When an organization is in the business of producing custom goods or large capital goods, it probably requires a large customer deposit before beginning work. If so, there should be an unearned revenues account that stores the amount of these deposits that have not yet been earned. This account can also be used for consulting arrangements, where customers may pay more during the course of an engagement than the seller has yet provided in services.

The main issue with this account is whether it even exists. If there is no line item for unearned revenues, it could mean that management is incorrectly recognizing all customer payments as revenue, even if the payments have not yet been earned.

When a company requires up-front payments from customers, the balance in this account tends to be relatively steady, since ongoing deliveries will remove liabilities from this account while new orders replace them. A decline in this account can portend that an entity is clearing out its backlog of customer orders, which can presage a drop in sales. Conversely, an increase in this account can either mean that sales are increasing, or that the business has encountered a bottleneck and is not able to complete work for its customers in a timely manner.

## Analysis Conclusions

We have noted numerous issues that can be relevant to the financial statement analyst. If a detailed balance sheet is provided, the amount of information gleaned can be substantial. When analyzing payables, we suggest the following order of priority:

1. *Measure payable days.* Look in particular for a lengthening of payable days. If coupled with a decline in cash or increase in debt, a business is probably encountering serious liquidity problems.
2. *Check for missing accounts.* If there is no sales taxes payable line item, a business may not be collecting or remitting sales taxes. If there is no un-earned revenues account, revenue may be recognized too soon.
3. *Look for liability spikes.* If there are sudden increases in the sales taxes payable, wages payable, or warranty liability accounts, this could indicate problems elsewhere in a business which may be quite serious.

Unfortunately, the current liabilities section usually only contains a few items, which aggregate so many liability accounts that it is difficult to draw any conclusions from the presented information.

# Chapter 8
# Interpretation of Debt

## Introduction

Debt is one of the key funding sources of a business. When used judiciously, it can bolster cash reserves and be a key support of corporate growth. However, this is an area in which the analyst needs to be extremely watchful, since the ability of a business to support its debt load can change quickly. An excessive amount of debt can be a prime cause of bankruptcy. In the following sections, we address the presentation, measurement, and specific issues associated with debt.

## The Interpretation of Debt

Different elements of debt appear within the current liabilities and noncurrent liabilities sections of the balance sheet. A sample presentation showing where these items are located in the balance sheet is noted in the following exhibit.

### Sample Presentation of Debt

| | |
|---|---|
| Current liabilities | |
| Accounts payable | $360,000 |
| **Notes payable** | **48,000** |
| Accrued liabilities | 22,000 |
| Unearned revenues | 40,000 |
| Total current liabilities | $470,000 |
| | |
| Noncurrent liabilities | |
| **Long-term debt** | **82,000** |
| **Bonds payable** | **100,000** |
| Total liabilities | $652,000 |

The line items appearing in the balance sheet are usually derived from the following accounts:

- *Notes payable.* Contains any debt payable within the next year. This account routinely contains the short-term portion of longer-term debt.
- *Line of credit.* Contains the current balance outstanding on a line of credit. Since this type of debt usually contains an obligation to pay down the entire balance at least once per year, it is considered a current liability.
- *Long-term debt.* Contains that portion of debts payable in more than one year. The portion payable in less than one year is classified into the notes payable account.

- *Bonds payable.* Contains the amount received from investors when they purchased bonds from the issuing entity.

There are a number of issues with the interpretation of these debt accounts, which are noted in the following sub-sections. We begin with a discussion of financial leverage and several ratios, which are used to gain a perspective on the proper amount of supportable debt.

## Financial Leverage

Financial leverage is the amount of debt that an entity uses to buy more assets. This is done to avoid investing an organization's own equity capital in such purchases.

The financial leverage formula is measured as the ratio of total debt to total assets. As the proportion of debt to assets increases, so too does the amount of financial leverage. Financial leverage is favorable when the uses to which debt can be put generate returns greater than the interest expense associated with the debt. Many companies use financial leverage rather than acquiring more equity capital, which could reduce the earnings per share of existing shareholders. Financial leverage has two primary advantages:

- *Enhanced earnings.* Financial leverage may allow an entity to earn a disproportionate amount on its assets.
- *Favorable tax treatment.* In many tax jurisdictions, interest expense is tax deductible, which reduces its net cost to the borrower.

However, financial leverage also presents the possibility of disproportionate losses, since the related amount of interest expense may overwhelm the borrower if it does not earn sufficient returns to offset the interest expense. This is a particular problem when interest rates rise or the returns from assets decline.

Financial leverage is an especially risky approach in a cyclical business, or one in which there are low barriers to entry, since sales and profits are more likely to fluctuate considerably from year to year, increasing the risk of bankruptcy over time. Conversely, financial leverage may be an acceptable alternative when a company is located in an industry with steady revenue levels, large cash reserves, and high barriers to entry, since operating conditions are sufficiently steady to support a large amount of leverage with little downside.

There is usually a natural limitation on the amount of financial leverage, since lenders are less likely to forward additional funds to a borrower that has already borrowed a large amount of debt.

In short, financial leverage can earn outsized returns for shareholders, but also presents the risk of outright bankruptcy if cash flows fall below expectations.

---

### EXAMPLE

Able Company uses $1,000,000 of its own cash to buy a factory, which generates $150,000 of annual profits. The company is not using financial leverage at all, since it incurred no debt to buy the factory.

Baker Company uses $100,000 of its own cash and a loan of $900,000 to buy a similar factory, which also generates a $150,000 annual profit. Baker is using financial leverage to generate a profit of $150,000 on a cash investment of $100,000, which is a 150% return on its investment.

Baker's new factory has a bad year, and generates a loss of $300,000, which is triple the amount of its original investment.

---

## Debt-Equity Ratio

The debt to equity ratio of a business is closely monitored by the lenders and creditors of the company, since it can provide early warning that an organization is so overwhelmed by debt that it is unable to meet its payment obligations. This may also be triggered by a funding issue. For example, the owners of a business may not want to contribute any more cash to the company, so they acquire more debt to address the cash shortfall. Or, a company may use debt to buy back shares, thereby increasing the return on investment to the remaining shareholders.

Whatever the reason for debt usage, the outcome can be catastrophic if corporate cash flows are not sufficient to make ongoing debt payments. This is a concern to lenders, whose loans may not be paid back. Suppliers are also concerned about the ratio for the same reason. A lender can protect its interests by imposing collateral requirements or restrictive covenants; suppliers usually offer credit with less restrictive terms, and so can suffer more if a company is unable to meet its payment obligations to them.

To calculate the debt to equity ratio, simply divide total debt by total equity. In this calculation, the debt figure should also include all lease obligations. The formula is:

$$\frac{\text{Long-term debt} + \text{Short-term debt} + \text{Leases}}{\text{Equity}}$$

---

### EXAMPLE

An analyst is reviewing the credit application of New Centurion Corporation. The company reports a $500,000 line of credit, $1,700,000 in long-term debt, and a $200,000 operating lease. The company has $800,000 of equity. Based on this information, New Centurion's debt to equity ratio is:

$$\frac{\$500,000 \text{ Line of credit} + \$1,700,000 \text{ Debt} + \$200,000 \text{ Lease}}{\$800,000 \text{ Equity}}$$

$$= 3{:}1 \text{ Debt to equity ratio}$$

The debt to equity ratio exceeds the 2:1 ratio threshold above which the analyst is not allowed to grant credit. Consequently, New Centurion is kept on cash in advance payment terms.

---

## Interest Coverage Ratio

The interest coverage ratio measures the ability of a company to pay the interest on its outstanding debt. A high interest coverage ratio indicates that a business can pay for its interest expense several times over, while a low ratio is a strong indicator that an organization may default on its loan payments.

It is useful to track the interest coverage ratio on a trend line, in order to spot situations where a company's results or debt burden are yielding a downward trend in the ratio. An investor would want to sell the equity holdings in a company showing such a downward trend, especially if the ratio drops below 1.5:1, since this indicates a likely problem with meeting debt obligations.

To calculate the interest coverage ratio, divide earnings before interest and taxes (EBIT) by the interest expense for the measurement period. The formula is:

$$\frac{\text{Earnings before interest and taxes}}{\text{Interest expense}}$$

---

**EXAMPLE**

Carpenter Holdings generates $5,000,000 of earnings before interest and taxes in its most recent reporting period. Its interest expense in that period is $2,500,000. Therefore, the company's interest coverage ratio is calculated as:

$$\frac{\$5,000,000 \text{ EBIT}}{\$2,500,000 \text{ Interest expense}}$$

$$= 2:1 \text{ Interest coverage ratio}$$

The ratio indicates that Carpenter's earnings should be sufficient to enable it to pay the interest expense.

---

A company may be accruing an interest expense that is not actually due for payment yet, so the ratio can indicate a debt default that will not really occur, or at least until such time as the interest is due for payment.

## Relative Size of Debt

When can the amount of the debt obligations of a business be considered minor? There is no consistent rule, since fluctuations in any company's business model can cut into its ability to repay debt. Nonetheless, here are several indicators that the relative amount of debt held is not a concern:

- The amount of cash and investments held exceeds the amount of debt. This implies that a company could theoretically pay off its debt from current reserves.

- The amount of reported annual net income could pay off the debt within a few years. This concept assumes that cash flows roughly equate to the reported profitability level, which is not necessarily the case.

## Seasonal Borrowings

A common need for debt is when a business has strongly seasonal sales. In this situation, it needs a short-term loan to pay for the build-up of inventory prior to the main selling season. After the season is over, the business collects all outstanding receivables and pays back the loan. From the perspective of the analyst, this should mean that all short-term obligations are completely paid off at some point during the year. If this is not the case, then an organization is probably under-capitalized or is not generating a sufficient profit. The first scenario can be remedied by replacing any residual debt with the proceeds from a sale of stock. The second scenario is more troubling, and may point toward the eventual demise of the entity, especially if the base level of debt continues to rise over a period of time.

## Line of Credit Usage

When a company is relying upon its line of credit to provide funding during seasonal slow periods, it is quite common for its cash balance to be near zero at some point. Rather than maintaining extra cash reserves, management relies upon the line of credit as its primary source of funding. Despite the extremely low cash balance, this can be an acceptable situation, as long as the lender is reliable in providing funds. In this case, the actual amount of available cash can be considered the remaining available balance on the line of credit, plus any on-hand cash.

---

### EXAMPLE

The Hegemony Toy Company earns the bulk of its revenue during the Christmas season. To prepare for the annual flood of orders from retailers, the company must begin production of its military board games early in the year, which requires the use of its entire cash balance, plus a large proportion of its line of credit. The company's cash and debt balances during the past year were as follows:

| (000s) | Feb. | Apr. | Jun. | Aug. | Oct. | Dec. |
|---|---|---|---|---|---|---|
| Cash balance | $1,200 | $1,000 | $600 | $200 | $0 | $0 |
| Remaining line of credit | 1,000 | 1,000 | 1,000 | 1,000 | 800 | 400 |
| Total available funding | $2,200 | $2,000 | $1,600 | $1,200 | $800 | $400 |

When the cash and line of credit information is combined, it is apparent that Hegemony has a residual buffer of just $400,000 of funding by the end of its selling season. This does not allow much margin for error in forecasting cash usage, so the company should either try to negotiate a larger line of credit or talk to its investors about a capital infusion.

---

## Shifts from Long-term to Short-term Debt

It is customary for long-term debt to periodically be shifted into the shorter-term notes payable line item, as a certain proportion of the long-term debt becomes payable within one year. However, what if *all* of the long-term debt is suddenly shifted into the notes payable line item? This can be triggered when a business no longer meets the covenant requirements associated with a loan. Examples of covenants are maintaining a quick ratio of at least 1:1, and maintaining a cash balance of at least $100,000. When this happens, the lender is entitled to call the loan at any time, which means that the entire amount of the loan is now considered to be payable within one year.

Just because such a reclassification occurs is not necessarily a catastrophic issue for a company, since it is quite possible that the lender will not require immediate repayment. Perhaps more troubling is why the covenants were breached. Covenants are designed to be reasonable, so breaching one may indicate that the financial fundamentals of a business are in decline.

## Conversions from Payables to Debt

When a business is in severe short-term financial difficulties, it may negotiate with its suppliers to convert its accounts payable into notes payable. By doing so, the entity can push its obligations somewhat further out into the future in exchange for the payment of an interest charge. This issue can be spotted when the accounts payable balance suddenly declines and is offset by an increase in the notes payable line item. In addition, the amount of interest expense recognized in the income statement will increase at the same time.

## Conversions from Debt to Equity

When it does not appear possible for a business to ever pay its debt obligations back to lenders, they may instead accept company stock. This transaction will probably be described in the notes that accompany the financial statements. If there are no footnotes, then watch for sudden declines in the line items associated with every type of debt, which are offset by a sudden increase in the equity line items. There will also be a sharp drop in or elimination of interest expense in subsequent reporting periods.

An odd circumstance that arises when there is such a conversion is an improvement in the debt-equity ratio and the interest coverage ratio. In particular, the debt figure in the debt-equity ratio will move from the nominator to the denominator, which makes a business appear to be in quite an excellent financial leverage situation. If this occurs, keep in mind that the cash flow position of the business probably remains quite poor, as can be discerned from the statement of cash flows.

## Debt Forgiveness

When a borrower cannot pay back debt, an alternative to converting the debt into equity is outright forgiveness of some portion of the debt. If so, the accounting standards require that the borrower record this forgiveness as a one-time gain. This gain is a non-cash event, and so does nothing for the cash flows of a business, other than to reduce its ongoing debt payments. The main point is that it generates a one-time spike in profits that can be safely ignored – it does not presage a return to long-term profitability.

## Permanent Debt

A business may seem to always be dealing with a large load of short-term debt. This can be a dangerous position to be in, since this debt must be continually rolled over at the current market rate of interest, which could spike. The reason for the short-term debt could be that no lenders are willing to extend a longer-term loan. If so, a business probably needs to sell shares to investors in order to bolster its equity funding and reduce the amount of debt.

Whenever lenders agree to do so, it makes sense to replace variable-rate short-term debt with fixed-rate long-term debt, if the long-term rate is reasonable. The amount converted to long-term debt should be the amount that a business cannot otherwise pay off within its most recent year of operations.

### EXAMPLE

The balance sheet of the International Mushroom Farmers' Cooperative shows the following amount of short-term debt during the past year:

|  | as of March 31 | as of June 30 | as of September 30 | As of December 31 |
|---|---|---|---|---|
| Short-term notes | $1,350,000 | $1,560,000 | $1,050,000 | $1,210,000 |
| Line of credit | 350,000 | 465,000 | 610,000 | 310,000 |
| Total | $1,700,000 | $2,025,000 | $1,660,000 | $1,520,000 |

The table reveals that the company's short-term debt level never falls below $1,520,000 during the year. This $1,520,000 figure should be converted into long-term debt, thereby allowing the business to flush out its short-term debt at least briefly during the year.

## Offshore Cash

A business may have used permutations in the international tax laws to shift its earnings overseas, thereby avoiding the bulk of its domestic tax liabilities. However, the cash saved in this manner cannot be easily repatriated back into the home country without paying taxes on it. Instead, a business may have to take on debt in the home country in order to meet obligations there, resulting in an odd balance sheet where there is a considerable amount of cash on the books, as well as debt. The reason for this situation may be described in the footnotes that accompany the financial statements.

## Analysis Conclusions

The amount of debt listed on a balance sheet is one of the most closely-watched numbers anywhere in the financial statements, since it can presage a rapid decline in the ability of a company to continue as a going concern. When analyzing debt, we suggest the following order of priority:

1. *Measure interest coverage.* At an absolute minimum, a business must be able to pay back the interest on its debt, which is addressed by this ratio. If it is not able to do so, then a debt restructuring or bankruptcy is imminent.

2. *Note conversions and forgiveness.* See if any sudden declines in debt are offset by increases in equity or the recognition of a gain. If so, a business is having substantial difficulties with its cash flows.

3. *Note seasonal debt changes.* Many entities experience changes in debt levels that correspond to their selling seasons. If this is the case, a periodic spike in debt is no cause for alarm.

The first two analysis points noted here are designed to focus attention on critical end-of-life debt crises. At this point, a business may not have long to live. The real trick is in spotting these issues earlier, before they become major issues. The best approach is to examine debt levels on a trend line, to see if there is a long-running pattern of debt expansion and an inability to repay loans.

# Chapter 9
# Interpretation of Equity

## Introduction

Shareholders' equity is the residual amount left in a business after all liabilities are subtracted from all assets. This part of the balance sheet represents all investments made in a business by investors, plus cumulative profits, minus dividends. It tends to receive less attention than the asset and liability sections of the balance sheet. Nonetheless, the discussions in this chapter reveal several points of interest.

## The Interpretation of Equity

All line items related to equity are aggregated into the shareholders' equity section of the balance sheet. A sample presentation showing where equity items are located on the balance sheet is noted in the following exhibit.

**Sample Presentation of Equity**

| | |
|---|---:|
| Total liabilities | $652,000 |
| | |
| Shareholders' equity | |
| Common stock | $10,000 |
| Preferred stock | 80,000 |
| Additional paid-in capital | 190,000 |
| Retained earnings | 2,100,000 |
| Treasury stock | -32,000 |
| Total shareholders' equity | 2,348,000 |
| Total liabilities and shareholders' equity | $3,000,000 |

These balance sheet line items pair up with several general ledger accounts, which are as follows:

- *Common stock.* Contains the par value of stock sold by a corporation to its investors. Par value is the legal capital per share, and is printed on the face of each stock certificate. The amount is usually set quite low, commonly at $0.01. Some states allow entities incorporating under their laws to issue shares with no par value at all.
- *Preferred stock.* Contains the amount of preferred stock sold by a corporation to its investors. These shares have special rights, perhaps including a periodic fixed dividend, the right to convert to common stock, being paid back ahead of common stockholders in the event of a corporate liquidation, and/or the ability to block the sale of the business.

- *Additional paid-in capital.* Contains the amount paid by investors to a company for its shares, less the amount of par value (which is recorded in the common stock account). This account balance tends to be much higher than the balance in the common stock account, since shares are usually sold for much more than their par values.
- *Retained earnings.* Contains the cumulative amount of earnings generated by a business, minus the amount of any distributions paid back to investors in the form of dividends.
- *Treasury stock.* Contains the amount paid to investors to buy back shares from them. This line item is a contra account, and so contains a negative balance.

In general, the entire shareholders' equity section of the balance sheet increases when a business earns a profit or sells shares to investors; it decreases when the business incurs a loss or issues dividends. There are several additional issues regarding equity that the analyst should be aware of, which are noted in the following sub-sections.

## The Book Value Concept

The book value of a business is the amount of assets stated on its balance sheet, minus the liabilities listed on the balance sheet. Or, stated as a formula, book value is:

$$\text{Assets} - \text{Liabilities} = \text{Book value}$$

Book value equals the amount of equity, which is why we bring up the concept in this chapter.

Book value is a commonly-used measure of the value of a business, probably because it is so easily derived from the published balance sheet of a company. The information could be used to estimate the most appropriate price of a company's stock, such as by comparing the market price of the stock to its book value. Or, the book value concept could be one possible basis for deriving the value of a company, when a potential acquirer wants to issue a bid to the owners of the target company. Also, lenders commonly use book value to estimate whether a prospective or current borrower is a good credit risk. In short, book value has many possible uses.

Despite the widespread use of book value, it is a seriously flawed measurement. The problem is that the amounts stated in a company's balance sheet do not necessarily match their current market values. Instead, some are recorded at their original purchase prices, while others are adjusted to their market values as of the balance sheet date. The problem is exacerbated by the Generally Accepted Accounting Principles (GAAP) framework, which enforces the recordation of the most conservative values for assets. The issue is less of a problem if the International Financial Reporting Standards (IFRS) framework is used, since IFRS allows for the upward revaluation of some assets.

A further issue with book value is the incorporation of intangible assets into the balance sheet. An intangible asset is a non-physical asset that has a useful life spanning more than one accounting period. Examples of intangible assets are software developed for internal use, patents, and copyrights. If a company internally generates intangible assets, the business cannot usually record these assets on its balance sheet. In some cases, the value of these assets represents the primary value of an entire business, so the book value calculation may wildly underestimate the value of the organization.

Conversely, an acquirer is allowed to record that portion of the purchase price of an acquiree that can be allocated to the intangible assets of the acquiree. For example, a portion of the purchase price may be allocated to an intangible asset called "customer relationships," which is then amortized over the presumed remaining life of those relationships. In some cases, these intangible assets can be considered specious at best, and yet are included in the book value calculation because they are listed on the balance sheet.

A further problem with acquisitions is that any portion of the purchase price that cannot be allocated to tangible or intangible assets is recorded as "goodwill," which appears in the balance sheet as an asset. In some cases, goodwill can represent a large part of the assets listed on a company's balance sheet, and so can radically skew the calculation of book value (see the Other Assets chapter for more information).

For the reasons enumerated here, we do not recommend using the book value concept for the purposes of assigning a value to an entire business. The value derived would be nearly arbitrary, and could bear little relationship to the actual market value of the entity.

## Tangible Book Value

Another variation on the book value concept is to remove all intangible assets from the book value formula. Doing so eliminates the inflation of asset values caused by the presence of goodwill, as well as other assets created as part of a corporate acquisition. However, some of these intangible assets may have significant value, so anyone using the tangible book value concept should sort through the various intangible assets and determine which are to be eliminated and which ones retained. This can turn into a qualitative exercise, where different analysts arrive at different tangible book values based on their own perceptions of the worth of certain intangible assets. Consequently, if this measurement is to be used, it should be accompanied by a detailed analysis of each intangible asset included in or excluded from the measurement, as well as justifications for the amounts included.

The calculation of tangible net worth is to subtract all liabilities listed on a company's balance sheet from all tangible net assets stated on the balance sheet. By "net assets," we refer to assets from which all contra accounts, such as the allowance for bad debts, depreciation, and amortization, have been subtracted. The formula is:

Tangible net assets – Liabilities = Tangible book value

**EXAMPLE**

Nefarious Industries has engaged in a number of hostile takeovers in the past decade, resulting in a group of subsidiaries for which Nefarious paid a total of $15,000,000 more than could be assigned to the tangible assets of the subsidiaries. The result is the following intangible assets recorded on the consolidated financial statements of the company:

| Intangible Asset Type | Amount |
|---|---|
| Customer lists | $1,500,000 |
| Internet domain names | 500,000 |
| Licensing agreements | 4,000,000 |
| Water rights | 3,500,000 |
| Goodwill | 5,500,000 |
| Total | $15,000,000 |

The consolidated balance sheet of Nefarious reveals a total of $32,000,000 in assets and $8,000,000 in liabilities. A prospective investor is attempting to determine the tangible book value of the company, and concludes that the licensing agreements and water rights listed as intangible assets have actual value. The other intangible assets are discarded. Based on this review, the investor concludes that the adjusted tangible book value of the company is:

$32,000,000 Assets - $7,500,000 Intangible assets with no value - $8,000,000 Liabilities
= $16,500,000 Adjusted tangible book value

## Book Value per Share

The primary user of book value is an outside investor, who wants to compare the market value of shares owned to their book value, and so needs a measurement that is presented on a per-share basis.

The measurement is typically calculated on the basis of just common stock, with the effects of preferred stock eliminated from the calculation. By doing so, the result shows the amount that a common shareholder might receive upon the liquidation of a business.

To calculate book value per share, subtract preferred stock from stockholders' equity and divide by the number of common shares outstanding. Be sure to use the average number of shares in the denominator, since the period-end amount may incorporate a recent stock buyback or issuance, and so could skew the results. The formula is:

(Stockholders' equity – Preferred stock) ÷ Average common shares = Book value per share

**EXAMPLE**

Grissom Granaries has $15,000,000 of stockholders' equity, $3,000,000 of preferred stock, and an average of 2,000,000 shares outstanding during the measurement period. The calculation of its book value per share is:

$$\frac{\$15,000,000 \text{ Stockholders' equity} - \$3,000,000 \text{ Preferred stock}}{2,000,000 \text{ Average common shares outstanding}}$$

$$= \$6.00 \text{ Book value per share}$$

## Changes in Retained Earnings

One might think that an ever-expanding retained earnings balance is a sign of a financially healthy business. This may or may not be the case. Here are several scenarios that can cause upward or downward changes in the retained earnings line item:

- *Capital intensive industry.* A business may require a large and ongoing investment in working capital or fixed assets. So, even if there is a large amount of retained earnings, the owners are unable to extract any money via a dividend. In essence, the nature of the industry demands that all retained earnings be kept within the business.
- *Growth phase company.* A business may be growing at a rapid rate, and needs all of its available cash to support the continuing rollout of its products. Investors are usually agreeable to not being paid dividends, as long as the high growth rate translates into a higher share price.
- *Shrinking company.* If a business is in decline, management may choose not to invest more money in the business. Instead, they may recommend a continuing series of dividends, with the intent of returning retained earnings to investors while they conduct an orderly shutdown of the business.
- *Investor requirements.* Investors may insist on being paid a large dividend each year to fulfill their own personal income requirements. This is most likely in a business that does not require a large amount of continuing investment. If so, the retained earnings balance could be kept at a low level as a matter of policy.
- *Loan covenants.* An organization may have entered into a loan agreement that requires the business not to issue dividends during the term of the loan. A lender may insist on this requirement to keep the entity from taking out a loan and using it to fund a dividend distribution. In this case, the owners may want to reduce the retained earnings balance, but are constrained from doing so.
- *Lender expectations.* Lenders may not be willing to lend additional funds to a business unless its investors are willing to leave a significant part of the retained earnings balance in the company, so that investor money is also at risk.

Consequently, a continuing increase in retained earnings may not be better than a retained earnings level that might initially appear to be anemic – it just depends on the circumstances.

## Negative Retained Earnings

The implication thus far is that the balance in the retained earnings account will always be positive. However, this is only the case when the preceding reporting periods have cumulatively reported a profit. If this is not the case, the balance in the account will be negative. Here are several scenarios that can relate to the presence of negative retained earnings:

- *Startup company.* A startup company may incur significant losses during its first few years as it attempts to gain traction in the marketplace. The amount of these initial losses may require several additional years of profitable operations to overcome.
- *One-time loss.* A business may have suffered from a major one-time loss, such as the destruction of uninsured property or an adverse lawsuit settlement. As long as there is a trend of consistent profitability and there are enough resources to overcome the one-time loss, negative retained earnings may not be an issue.
- *Non-cash expenses.* A business may create large intangible assets as the result of an acquisition, and must then charge them to expense over time. If so, the resulting expenses can overwhelm the normal operational profits of the business, making it appear as though the company is not doing well. It is necessary to back out all amortization expenses from the income statement to discern this issue.
- *Tax planning.* The owners of a business may be actively planning to defer the payment of income taxes, and so aggressively plan to accelerate the recognition of the largest possible amount of expenses. This is fine, as long as the cash flows of the business remain positive.

If one of the preceding scenarios is not the case, then the implications of having negative retained earnings are more serious. If there is an ongoing trend of losses that are increasing the amount of negative retained earnings, it is likely that a business will eventually fail.

## Appropriated Retained Earnings

Appropriated retained earnings are retained earnings that have been set aside by action of the board of directors for a specific use. An appropriation may be for such purposes as:

- Acquisitions
- Debt reduction
- Marketing campaigns
- New construction
- New product development

- Research and development
- Reserve against expected insurance losses
- Reserve against lawsuit settlements
- Restriction imposed by a loan covenant
- Stock buyback

The board of directors can eliminate the appropriation designation at any time. For example, once a scheduled debt reduction has been completed, the appropriation is cancelled and the segregated retained earnings are returned to the main retained earnings account.

---

**EXAMPLE**

The board of directors of ABC International wants to set aside $10 million for the construction of a new distribution facility, which it does by voting to appropriate $10 million of retained earnings for this purpose. The $10 million is segregated in a separate appropriated retained earnings account until the construction has been completed, after which the amount in the account is returned to the main retained earnings account.

---

The intent of retained earnings appropriation is to not make these funds available for payment to shareholders. However, if a company were to liquidate or enter bankruptcy proceedings, the appropriation status of retained earnings would be irrelevant - the retained earnings would be available for payout to creditors and investors. Thus, an appropriation has no legal status.

There is generally no need to appropriate retained earnings, unless management or the board of directors is trying to communicate to investors that it wants to set aside funds for purposes other than to issue them as dividends to investors. Thus, appropriation is typically used to communicate intentions to outside parties, rather than for any internal management need.

**Treasury Stock Usage**

The balance in the treasury stock account offsets the amount of other stockholders' equity, since it represents the amount of money used to buy back shares from investors. When there is a large balance in this line item, it can indicate a number of possible decisions by the board of directors, such as:

- *Going private.* A publicly-held company can take itself private by buying back shares from a number of smaller investors, until the number of share-holders is below the public-company threshold set by the Securities and Exchange Commission.
- *Supporting the stock price.* The board of directors can direct the company to buy back shares whenever the stock price drops below a certain level. This step is only taken by publicly-held companies, who are more mindful of maintaining a reasonable stock price.

- *Greenmail*. A large investor can threaten to take over a number of board seats, unless he is paid off with a high-priced stock repurchase.
- *Tax advantages*. The board of directors may conclude that it is more tax advantageous to investors to buy back their shares, rather than paying them dividends.

All of the preceding actions will likely be clarified through press releases, disclosures in the footnotes accompanying the financial statements, or articles in the business press.

### Number of Shares Authorized and Outstanding

The number of shares authorized and outstanding is usually stated somewhere on the face of the balance sheet. This information tells the analyst how many shares are still available for issuance, in case an organization wants to sell additional shares to the investment community. For example, if 10 million shares have been authorized and 9.5 million have been issued, then 500,000 shares can still be sold. This is not usually an issue, but it can mean that a business may be constrained from a short-term share issuance if it does not have a sufficient number of remaining shares available for issuance. For example, if a company wants to buy another organization with its shares, it may not have sufficient shares available to pay the shareholders of the acquiree.

If a few months are available, the situation can be remedied by having the existing shareholders vote on a motion to increase the number of authorized shares.

## Analysis Conclusions

When reviewing the contents of shareholders' equity, the main point is to monitor changes in retained earnings. There should generally be an upward trend in this line item, reflecting the ongoing profitability of a business. However, if the board of directors has an ongoing pattern of declaring dividends, then this line item will drop by the amount of periodic dividend issuances.

In addition, we advise against depending too deeply on the concept of book value, since there are so many factors that can render this amount invalid. At most, it should only be used as a backup to other analyses that are based upon more relevant information.

In general, the shareholders' equity section of the balance sheet is not a source of detailed insights. Richer sources of information lie in the other parts of the balance sheet, as well as the other financial statements.

# Chapter 10
# Interpretation of Sales

## Introduction

The sales concept refers to an increase in assets or decrease in liabilities caused by the provision of services or products to customers. It is typically calculated by multiplying the selling price by the number of units sold within a reporting period. The result is classified as gross sales, after which sales returns and discounts are deducted to arrive at a net sales figure. The net sales figure in particular is closely watched, since it is considered a prime indicator of the success of an organization in attracting new customers and generating more sales to existing ones. In this chapter, we cover the presentation of sales in the income statement, and the issues to be aware of when interpreting this information.

## The Interpretation of Sales

The sales line items appear at the top of the income statement. This format allows the reader to immediately focus on the gross level of activity generated in a reporting period. A sample presentation showing where sales are located on the income statement is noted in the following exhibit.

### Sample Presentation of Sales

| | |
|---|---:|
| Gross sales | $1,000,000 |
| Less: | |
| Sales discounts | -$32,000 |
| Sales returns | -18,000 |
| | -50,000 |
| Net sales | $950,000 |

These line items are taken from general ledger accounts that have the same names. The accounts are as follows:

- *Gross sales*. Contains the total sales recorded in a reporting period prior to sales discounts and returns. There could be a large number of sales accounts, if management wants to track sales by individual product, product line, region, or type (such as products or services). This account is more commonly called "sales," rather than "gross sales."
- *Sales discounts*. Contains the reduction in the price of a product or service that is offered by the seller, in exchange for early payment by the buyer. For example, if a buyer deducts 2% from its payment of an invoice in exchange for paying the invoice within 10 days of the invoice date, that is recorded as

a sales discount. This is a contra account, so it offsets the gross sales account.

- *Sales returns.* Contains the original sales amount associated with goods returned to the seller by the buyer. This is a contra account, so it offsets the gross sales account.

The net sales figure on the income statement is a calculation that nets together the gross sales, sales discounts, and sales returns line items presented above it; there is no corresponding net sales account in the general ledger.

There are several issues with these sales line items, which are noted in the following sub-sections.

## The Trend of Sales

When a company has just been founded, its percentage growth rate may be astounding, as the entity fills its primary market niche. Once the niche is filled, management will likely resort to a number of strategies to expand sales, but the rate of sales growth will decline. At some point, it is possible that new competition or entirely new product categories will put pressure on price points and reduce customer demand, resulting in a decline in sales. The following table shows a sample of how to determine the ongoing trend of sales.

**Sample Sales Trend Analysis**

| (000s) | Year 1 | Year 2 | Year 3 | Year 4 | Year 5 | Year 6 |
|---|---|---|---|---|---|---|
| Sales | $1,000 | $1,800 | $2,400 | $2,900 | $3,200 | $3,100 |
| Sales $ change | -- | $800 | $600 | $500 | $300 | -$100 |
| **Sales % change*** | | 80% | 33% | 21% | 10% | -3% |

* The calculation is the increase over the past year's sales, divided by the past year's sales

In the sample trend analysis, the initially massive growth rate ends after the second year, with a continually declining growth rate through the fifth year. Sales then begin to decline. The trend is not always this clear, but a pattern can usually be observed.

A variation on sales trend analysis is same-store sales, which is information that a retail business may publish along with its financial statements. Investors like to watch the sales growth in stores that have already been open for at least a year, to see if a company's products, marketing efforts, and price management can continue to attract an increasing growth pattern.

A rapid rate of sales growth will attract the attention of growth-oriented investors, who want to profit from a surging stock price. Once the sales trend backs away from its initial levels, management may change from its initial focus on sales growth and be more focused on cash flow and profitability. At this point, the initial group of growth-oriented investors will be replaced by income-oriented investors who are more interested in the regularity of cash flows provided by ongoing dividend payments. If there is a sales decline, the stock price will likely drop, which will attract the attention of value investors who want to buy shares at a low price, in hopes of a later resurgence in the stock price.

In short, all of the preceding types of investors closely watch the trend of sales, since the rate of growth (or decline) drives their investment strategies.

## The Quality of Sales

There is ongoing pressure on a business to continually increase its sales, in order to expand the return to investors. This can be a problem when a company eventually maximizes its initial target market. At that point, management may take several steps to add on more sales, such as offering credit to new customers who have questionable payment histories, selling add-on accessories or services (such as product warranties), entering entirely new market niches, or selling in new geographic regions. Each of these decisions can result in sales that are of differing levels of quality. Quality can be defined in many ways, but from the viewpoint of analyzing sales, our focus is on the profit margin associated with each incremental sale. Thus, a high-quality sale carries with it a high profit margin.

This issue is a major concern to the outside reviewer, who has no idea if the next tranche of sales will come from a new group of customers, products, or regions. Here are several indicators that the quality of sales may be declining:

- *Bad debt increases*. If the bad debt expense suddenly increases, it may mean that management has decided to grant credit to a new group of lower-quality customers, in a bid to expand sales. This likely means that the bad debt expense is layered on top of the existing product margins, resulting in an overall reduction in the profitability percentage.
- *Commission increase*. When a company opens up a new sales region, it may offer unusually high sales commissions to its sales staff in order to develop the region. This issue can be detected by calculating the commission expense as a percentage of sales on a trend line.
- *Distribution costs increase*. If the cost of distributing products is broken out on the income statement, a jump in this expense may indicate that a company is expanding its warehousing and retail operations into new geographic regions. If these regions have a lower population per square mile than the company's existing sales regions, the result could be an increased distribution cost per sale, which reduces the profitability percentage.
- *Cost of sales increase*. If there is a sharp increase in the cost of goods sold, there is a good chance that management elected to reduce product prices in order to spur sales. If the cost increase only occurs once, it is possible that management conducted a one-time sale to eliminate older items from inventory.

The preceding points do not necessarily mean that a business will begin to incur losses as it pursues more sales – only that some additional costs will be incurred that will reduce the profit percentage that is earned. If losses *are* being incurred as sales increase, then one must question management's ability to identify which tranche of sales is causing the problem, and to correct the issue.

## The Reliability of Sales

Investors tend to place a higher valuation on a business that has highly reliable sales. We define reliability as sales that are highly likely to recur. For example, a business that sells subscriptions to its services (such as cell phone plans) can be considered to have reliable sales. Also, a business that is in a monopoly position (such as a power company) reports reliable sales, since customers have no choice other than to buy its services. It can be quite difficult to discern which types of company sales are more reliable, unless the entity decides to report different types of sales in separate line items in its income statement. It is also possible that types of sales will be broken out in more detail in the accompanying footnotes.

## The Timing of Revenue Recognition

One of the most critical topics in accounting is the timing of when revenue is recognized on the income statement. In brief, revenue is supposed to be recognized as goods and services are transferred to the customer. This means that advance payments from customers should be stored in a liability account until goods or services have been delivered. Also, there may be a percentage of completion system in place for recognizing revenue in pieces as larger multi-period projects are completed on behalf of customers.

From the perspective of an individual trying to interpret the sales figure in the income statement, this might appear to be an esoteric concept that cannot be judged. However, there are some indicators of how well a company's accounting staff is attending to its revenue recognition duties. First, look in the notes accompanying the financial statements for a description of the company's revenue recognition policies. Also, look for a liability account that stores unearned customer payments. The amount in this account should change in every accounting period, as some liabilities are converted into earned sales, and are replaced by new early payments from customers.

These issues are minimal in many industries, such as retailing, wholesaling, and the manufacture of standardized goods, where there are usually rigid procedures in place for recognizing revenue as goods are shipped to customers.

## Revenue at Gross or Net

There are situations where the entity providing goods or services to a customer is actually arranging to have another party provide the goods and services. In this case, the entity is an agent, not the principal party acting as seller.

The following rules are used to differentiate between the two concepts of principal and agent:

| Criterion | Principal | Agent |
|---|---|---|
| Controls the good or service before transfer to customer | Yes | No |
| Obtains legal title just prior to transfer to seller | Either | Either |
| Hires a subcontractor to fulfill some performance obligations | Yes | No |
| Arranges for the provision of goods or services by another party | No | Yes |
| Does not have inventory risk before or after the customer orders goods, including the absence of risk related to product returns | No | Yes |
| Does not have discretion in establishing prices | No | Yes |
| The consideration paid to the selling entity is in the form of a commission | No | Yes |
| There is no exposure to credit risk that the customer will not pay | No | Yes |

The outside observer can frequently guess at the operating characteristics of a business, and so can make a reasonable estimation of whether an organization is acting as a principal or an agent.

The differentiation between principal and agent is of some importance, for a principal recognizes the gross amount of a sale, while an agent only recognizes the fee or commission it earns in exchange for its participation in the transaction. This fee or commission may be the net amount remaining after the agent has paid the principal the amount billed for its goods or services provided to the customer.

---

**EXAMPLE**

High Country Vacations operates a website that puts prospective vacationers in touch with resorts located in ski towns around the world. When a vacationer purchases a hotel room on the website, High Country takes a 15% commission from the resort where the hotel room is located. The resort sets the prices for hotel rooms. High Country is not responsible for the actual provision of hotel rooms to vacationers.

Since High Country does not control the hotel rooms being provided, is arranging for the provision of services by a third party, does not maintain an inventory of rooms, cannot establish prices, and is paid a commission, the company is clearly an agent in these transactions. Consequently, High Country should only recognize revenue in the amount of the commissions paid to it, not the amount paid by vacationers for their hotel rooms.

**EXAMPLE**

Dirt Cheap Tickets sells discounted tickets for cruises with several prominent cruise lines. The company purchases tickets in bulk from cruise lines and must pay for them, irrespective of its ability to re-sell the tickets to the public. Dirt Cheap can alter the prices of the tickets that it purchases, which typically means that the company gradually lowers prices as cruise dates approach, in order to ensure that its excess inventory of tickets is sold. There is no credit risk, since tickets are paid for at the point of purchase. If customers have issues with the cruise lines, Dirt Cheap will intercede on their behalf, but generally encourages them to go directly to the cruise lines with their complaints.

Based on its business model, Dirt Cheap is acting as the principal. It controls the goods being sold, has inventory risk, and actively alters prices. Consequently, Dirt Cheap can recognize revenue in the gross amount of the tickets sold.

---

The recordation of revenue at gross or net has no impact on the net profits reported by a business, since it will incur the same operating expenses under both approaches. The difference is that a business reporting gross revenues will appear to be generating much more sales volume than a business that only reports net revenues. This also means that a business reporting at gross will report a far smaller net profit percentage than one reporting at net. The following presentation illustrates the situation, where a business has $150,000 of operating expenses and $50,000 of net profits, irrespective of the manner in which it reports revenue:

**Sample Results Using Gross and Net Reporting**

|  | Reports Gross Revenue | Reports Net Revenue |
|---|---|---|
| Revenue | $2,000,000 | $200,000 |
| Cost of goods sold | 1,800,000 | -- |
| Gross margin | $200,000 | $200,000 |
| Operating expenses | 150,000 | 150,000 |
| Net profit | $50,000 | $50,000 |
| Net profit % | 2.5% | 25.0% |

**Orders versus Sales**

A company may tout its order volume in the notes accompanying the financial statements or in separate press releases. What is the difference between sales and orders? A customer order is a formal request by a customer to have goods delivered or services provided. The sum total of all orders outstanding is called the order backlog. A large backlog is considered healthy, because it means a business can be assured of generating sales for as long as the backlog lasts. Once an order has been fulfilled, the customer is invoiced and the amount billed is recorded as a sale. In short, the differences between orders and sales and their implications are:
- Customer orders precede sales.

- A large backlog implies future sales, but not until the seller can deliver goods or services.
- If the backlog declines, this either indicates that management has increased capacity to process more orders per period, or that customer orders are declining.
- If the backlog increases, it could mean that customers are demanding more goods and services, but that the company has an internal bottleneck or supply constriction that does not allow it to address the increased order volume.

A major concern is when the order backlog continually declines over a period of time. Once a business processes its entire backlog, the typical outcome is a sharp decline in sales, unless selling activities can rebuild the backlog.

**The Presence of Sales Discounts**

A reasonable question is why a company is offering early payment discounts at all. The interest rates associated with the more common early payment discount deals are quite high, and so should only be offered by those businesses that are desperate for cash.

The term structure used for credit terms is to first state the number of days being given to customers from the invoice date in which to take advantage of the early payment credit terms. For example, if a customer is supposed to pay within 10 days without a discount, the terms are "net 10 days," whereas if the customer must pay within 10 days to qualify for a 2% discount, the terms are "2/10." Or, if the customer must pay within 10 days to obtain a 2% discount or can make a normal payment in 30 days, then the terms are stated as "2/10 net 30."

The table below shows some of the more common credit terms, explains what they mean, and also notes the effective interest rate being offered to customers with each one.

| Credit Terms | Explanation | Effective Interest |
|---|---|---|
| Net 10 | Pay in 10 days | None |
| Net 30 | Pay in 30 days | None |
| Net EOM 10 | Pay within 10 days of month-end | None |
| 1/10 net 30 | Take a 1% discount if pay in 10 days, otherwise pay in 30 days | 18.2% |
| 2/10 net 30 | Take a 2% discount if pay in 10 days, otherwise pay in 30 days | 36.7% |
| 1/10 net 60 | Take a 1% discount if pay in 10 days, otherwise pay in 60 days | 7.3% |
| 2/10 net 60 | Take a 2% discount if pay in 10 days, otherwise pay in 60 days | 14.7% |

The full calculation for the cost of credit is:

$$(\text{Discount \%} \div (1 - \text{Discount \%})) \times (360 \div (\text{Allowed payment days} - \text{Discount days}))$$

In short, almost any other form of debt financing is less expensive than offering early payment discounts to customers. This means that the presence of a sales discounts line item in the income statement should be a cause for concern.

One can assume that the financing situation is even more dire if there is a relatively quiescent history of sales discounts, which has now spiked. The spike can indicate that management has deliberately enriched the early payment discount offer to attract more customers, or is actively contacting customers to make them aware of the existing deal. In either case, the implication is that management is running short of sources of cash.

## The Trend of Sales Returns

The amount stated in the sales returns line item tends to be quite a small percentage of gross sales, and so is usually not a focus of concern. However, it can make sense to track the sales returns on a trend line, and especially as a percentage of sales. If the percentage suddenly increases, it is a strong indicator of product difficulties that could presage a decline in sales and drop in profits.

---

### EXAMPLE

Oberlin Acoustics manufactures the legendary Rhino brand electric guitar. The company's promotional materials note an unconditional one-year returns policy; the extremely high quality of the guitars has resulted in miniscule returns. In the past year, however, the sales returns percentage has jumped, as noted in the following table:

|  | 20X1 | 20X2 | 20X3 | 20X4 | 20X5 |
|---|---|---|---|---|---|
| Gross sales | $28,900,000 | $29,300,000 | $30,700,000 | $31,300,000 | $32,600,000 |
| Sales returns | $28,900 | $58,600 | $30,700 | $62,600 | $619,400 |
| Sales returns % | 0.01% | 0.02% | 0.01% | 0.02% | 1.9% |

The sudden spike in returns sparks questions from the investment community. The company's investor relations officer responds by issuing a press release, stating that the company has been using a sub-standard shipment of rosewood from its main wood products distributor in Mozambique, resulting in cracked necks and bodies on certain of its guitar models.

---

# Analysis Conclusions

The amount of sales reported is considered by some to be the primary indicator of the health of a business. From a purely financial perspective, this is not really the case, since a consistent level of positive cash flow is a much better indicator of the viability of a business. Nonetheless, the reported sales of a business are routinely dissected to discern ongoing patterns. If you choose to do so, we suggest the following order of priority:

1. *Create trend line analysis.* Plot the reported sales level on a trend line, to see how the percentage growth rate has changed over time. This provides clues

regarding how a business is maturing in the normal life cycle of its products and services.

2. *Review sales quality.* Examine other parts of the income statement, such as the bad debt expense, sales returns, and distribution expenses, to see if a business is incurring additional costs as it expands its sales.

3. *Monitor contra account trends.* Review the trends in sales discounts and sales returns to see if there are any changes from ordinary levels. Such changes could indicate financing or product problems.

It is possible to read too much into the sales line items. One should really examine the entire cost of operations in relation to the reported sales level, to see if management is capable of running a business in such a manner that profits can be consistently generated. In short, merely generating sales does not guarantee the long-term viability of a business.

# Chapter 11
## Interpretation of the Cost of Sales and Gross Margin

## Introduction

The cost of sales is a general concept that can refer to both the cost of services provided to customers and the cost of goods sold to customers. The more complex of the two variations is the cost of goods sold, which includes the costs of materials, labor, and overhead. When the cost of sales is subtracted from net sales, it yields the gross margin, which is a subtotal that shows how much money was made prior to additional deductions for operating expenses (which we will address in the next chapter). This chapter discusses the contents of the cost of goods sold, reasons why these expenses can change, and the reasons for and against using the gross margin and contribution margin for analysis purposes.

## The Interpretation of the Cost of Sales and Gross Margin

The cost of sales and gross margin line items appear just below sales in the income statement. A sample presentation showing where these items are located is noted in the following exhibit.

### Sample Presentation of the Cost of Sales and Gross Margin

| | | |
|---|---|---|
| Net sales | | $950,000 |
| Cost of goods sold: | | |
| Direct materials | $185,000 | |
| Direct labor | 80,000 | |
| Factory overhead | 115,000 | |
| | | 380,000 |
| Gross margin | | 570,000 |
| Gross margin percentage | | 60% |

These line items represent possibly the largest transaction volume generated by a business. They are comprised of several general ledger accounts, which are as follows:

- *Direct materials.* Contains the cost of all finished goods sold to customers during the reporting period. This account may also contain the expenses associated with obsolete inventory, scrap, and inventory adjustments, if management does not find it necessary to separately break out this additional information.

- *Merchandise.* Contains the costs of all purchased finished goods that have been sold. This account is used by retailers and distributors instead of the direct materials account, since they do not manufacture their own goods.
- *Obsolete inventory expense.* Contains the amount charged to expense during the period that represents either the actual or estimated amount of obsolete inventory discovered during the month, net of its residual disposal values. May be included in the direct materials account.
- *Scrap expense.* Contains the excess unusable material that is left over after a product has been manufactured. May be included in the direct materials account.
- *Inventory adjustments expense.* If there is an ongoing inventory counting program, it will likely result in a number of adjustments to the book records of on-hand inventory. The changes in costs caused by these adjustments are stored in this account, so that management can gain an understanding of the extent of the costs associated with inaccurate inventory. May be included in the direct materials account.
- *Direct labor.* Contains the cost of the labor associated with the production of goods. In an environment where services are being supplied to customers instead of products, this account contains the labor associated with the hours being billed to customers.
- *Factory overhead.* Contains all costs incurred during the manufacturing process, not including the costs of direct labor and materials. Examples of factory overhead costs are:
  - Equipment depreciation (see the Interpretation of Fixed Assets chapter)
  - Equipment maintenance
  - Equipment setup costs
  - Factory building insurance
  - Factory rent
  - Factory small tools charged to expense
  - Factory supplies
  - Factory utilities
  - Fringe benefits
  - Insurance on production facilities and equipment
  - Materials management salaries
  - Production supervisor salaries
  - Property taxes on production facilities
  - Quality assurance salaries
- *Freight in.* Contains the transportation cost associated with the delivery of goods from a supplier to the receiving entity.

The underlying detail of the cost of sales line items noted in the last example could be broken down into the structure that appears in the following sample presentation. The merchandise account is not included, since it refers to a different situation that only applies to non-manufacturing entities. These additional line items are not usually broken out separately, since their balances tend to be relatively small.

**Sample Detailed Presentation of the Cost of Sales and Gross Margin**

| | | |
|---|---:|---:|
| Net sales | | $950,000 |
| Cost of goods sold: | | |
| Direct materials | $162,000 | |
| Obsolete inventory expense | 8,000 | |
| Scrap expense | 10,000 | |
| Inventory adjustments | 5,000 | |
| Direct labor | 80,000 | |
| Freight in | 7,000 | |
| Factory overhead | 108,000 | |
| | | 380,000 |
| Gross margin | | 570,000 |
| Gross margin percentage | | 60% |

There are a number of issues to be concerned with when reviewing the cost of sales and gross margin, which are noted in the following sub-sections. We begin with margin analysis.

**Gross Margin Analysis**

The gross profit ratio shows the proportion of profits generated by the sale of goods or services, before operating expenses. In essence, it reveals the ability of a business to create sellable products in a cost-effective manner. The ratio is of some importance from an analysis perspective, especially when tracked on a trend line, to see if a business is continuing to provide products to the marketplace for which customers are willing to pay.

The ratio can also be used for comparison to the gross margins of competitors. When a business' gross margin is unusually low, it could mean that management is cutting prices in order to remain competitive. This situation is most likely when the organization is a small one, and is competing against larger national entities that have obvious cost efficiencies.

The gross profit ratio is calculated as sales minus the cost of goods sold, divided by sales. The formula is:

$$\frac{Sales - Cost\ of\ goods\ sold}{Sales}$$

The ratio can vary over time as sales volumes change, since the cost of goods sold contains some fixed cost elements that will not vary with sales volume.

**EXAMPLE**

An analyst is reviewing a credit application from Quest Adventure Gear, which includes financial statements for the past three years. The analyst extracts the following information from the financial statements of Quest:

| | 20X1 | 20X2 | 20X3 |
|---|---|---|---|
| Sales | $12,000,000 | $13,500,000 | $14,800,000 |
| Cost of goods sold | 5,000,000 | 5,100,000 | 4,700,000 |
| Gross profit ratio | 42% | 38% | 32% |

The analysis reveals that Quest is suffering from an ongoing decline in its gross profits, which should certainly be a concern from the perspective of allowing credit.

An organization may be showing signs of trying to improve its gross margin percentage. There are a number of ways to do so, including the following:
- Outsourcing production
- Stripping away excess production capacity
- Upgrading to more efficient production equipment
- Centralizing purchases with a smaller number of suppliers, to gain volume discounts
- Redesigning products to reduce the cost of raw materials and the production process
- Layoffs of production staff
- Raising prices

## Contribution Margin Analysis

The contribution margin ratio is the percentage of a firm's contribution margin to its sales. Contribution margin is a product's price minus its variable costs, resulting in the incremental profit earned for each unit sold. The total contribution margin generated by an entity represents the total earnings available to pay for fixed expenses and generate a profit. The contribution margin should be relatively high, since it must be sufficient to also cover factory overhead and operating expenses. To calculate the contribution margin ratio, divide the contribution margin by sales. The formula is:

$$\frac{Sales - Variable\ expenses}{Sales}$$

A contribution margin income statement is an income statement in which all variable expenses are deducted from sales to arrive at a contribution margin, from which all fixed expenses are then subtracted to arrive at the net profit or loss for the period. This income statement format is a superior form of presentation, because the contribution margin clearly shows the amount available to cover fixed costs and generate a profit (or loss).

In essence, if there are no sales, a contribution margin income statement will have a zero contribution margin, with fixed costs clustered beneath the contribution margin line item. As sales increase, the contribution margin will increase in conjunction with sales, while fixed costs remain approximately the same.

A contribution margin income statement varies from a normal income statement in the following three ways:

- Fixed production costs are aggregated lower in the income statement, after the contribution margin;
- Variable operating expenses are grouped with variable production costs, so that they are a part of the calculation of the contribution margin; and
- The gross margin is replaced in the statement by the contribution margin.

Thus, the format of a contribution margin income statement is:

**Sample Contribution Margin Income Statement**

| + | Revenues |
|---|---|
| - | Variable production expenses (such as materials, supplies, and variable overhead) |
| - | Variable operating expenses |
| = | Contribution margin |
| | |
| - | Fixed production expenses (including most overhead) |
| - | Fixed operating expenses |
| = | Net profit or loss |

In many cases, direct labor is categorized as a fixed expense in the contribution margin income statement format, rather than a variable expense, because this cost does not always change in direct proportion to the amount of revenue generated. Instead, management needs to keep a certain minimum staffing in the production area, which does not vary even if there are lower production volumes.

The key difference between the gross margin and contribution margin is that fixed production costs are included in the cost of goods sold to calculate the gross margin, whereas they are not included in the same calculation for the contribution margin. This means that the contribution margin income statement is sorted based on the variability of the underlying cost information, rather than by the functional areas or expense categories found in a normal income statement.

It is useful to create an income statement in the contribution margin format when you want to determine that proportion of expenses that truly varies directly with revenues. In many businesses, the contribution margin will be substantially higher than the gross margin, because such a large proportion of production costs are fixed and few of its operating expenses are variable.

**The Inventory Build Concept**

If a company operates in a highly seasonal industry (such as snow blowers, ski equipment, or patio furniture), it will likely need to begin the production of goods well before customers begin to place orders. This means that all production costs will be absorbed into inventory during the no-sales months, with no cost of goods sold appearing in the income statement at all until deliveries are sent to customers. During the period when there are no sales, the income statement will present no sales, cost of goods sold, or gross margin. Instead, the inventory line item in the balance sheet will store the production costs incurred during that period.

**Direct Materials Changes**

The cost of direct materials is literally built into the cost of goods sold, since a certain amount of raw materials is designed into each product. However, this does not mean that a company will always report exactly the same proportion of direct materials expense in every period. Such a situation would only arise when a business sells the same mix of products in every period. A more likely situation is that the sales mix constantly changes. Assuming that there are differing proportions of material costs associated with each product, this means that the direct materials expense could fluctuate considerably over time. Here are several additional factors that can impact the situation:

- *Commissions.* The sales staff may have been incentivized to sell more of certain products, perhaps to clear them from stock. If so, this increases the proportion of the targeted items in the sales mix.
- *Customer preferences.* The types of products that customers are willing to purchase will change over time. This is an especially common issue when products are subject to fads, such as clothing – certain items could be hot sellers one week, and unsellable the next.
- *Discounts.* Management may authorize discounts on certain products, which will likely increase their sales volume. If so, these products will comprise a larger percentage of the total mix of sales. In addition, the discount inherently reduces the total amount of the gross margin percentage.
- *Materials shortages.* The costs of some materials may spike when there is an industry shortage, or when a company runs out of them and must place additional orders on short notice.

**Obsolete Inventory Changes**

The cost of obsolete inventory is rarely listed separately on the income statement. If the cost is presented, look for a continuing series of small charges for obsolete items. This indicates a well-managed department that is constantly monitoring (and therefore detecting) obsolete inventory. A more common circumstance is the end-of-year review for obsolete inventory, resulting in a single large write-off. The implication of the latter situation is that the management team is finding obsolete items so late that their value has declined to the point where the business will gain little from a dispositioning process that might have otherwise sold them off for a reasonable price.

## Scrap Changes

As was the case with obsolete inventory, it is unlikely that the cost of scrap will be separately stated on the income statement. If this line item is presented, one might expect that the scrap level would follow a relatively consistent percentage of total expenses over time. However, this may not be the case, for the following reasons:

- *Process failures.* An incorrect setting on production equipment can cause large amounts of goods to be incorrectly manufactured, which must be scrapped. Similarly, in a restaurant environment a meal might be over-cooked, so the ingredients are thrown out.
- *Product redesigns.* Product designs inherently involve a certain amount of scrap. When a product is redesigned or replaced with an entirely new product, the associated amount of scrap may also change.
- *Raw material quality.* A company may have acquired a low-grade batch of raw materials, which produces a much higher scrap rate than usual. This circumstance may arise when the purchasing department acquires lower-quality materials with the intent of saving material costs.
- *Scrap levels by product.* Each product has an inherent amount of scrap built into the design. As the mix of products manufactured changes by month, so too will the amount of scrap generated during the production process.

## Direct Labor Changes

A common misconception with the direct labor cost is that it varies in direct proportion to the number of units produced. This is not usually the case. Instead, a certain minimum amount of staffing is required for a production line, irrespective of the number of units created by that line. This means that the amount of direct labor cost charged to expense can vary over time. In addition, there may be overtime charges that will cause spikes in the expense from time to time.

In the services industry, the amount of direct labor expense can be even more variable. In this case, the types of services demanded by customers will dictate the cost of labor. For example, a consulting client needs to have programming work done for it. For the programmer skill level needed, a consulting firm charges $150 per hour and pays its consulting staff $50 per hour, which translates into a 33% direct labor cost. Alternatively, another consulting client needs to have strategic planning work done for it. This task requires the services of the senior consulting staff, for which the hourly billing rate is $250 per hour and the related employees are paid $100 per hour. This latter situation results in a 40% direct labor cost. Thus, the mix of services required and the cost of the people needed to provide those services will routinely alter the direct labor expense.

## Factory Overhead Changes

Factory overhead costs are largely fixed costs – that is, they do not change much from period to period. This can be a problem when the production volume varies, since it means that a differing amount of overhead will be applied to the number of units produced in each month. If some of these units remain in stock for several subsequent reporting periods, it can impact the amount of factory overhead expense recognized.

---

### EXAMPLE

The amount of factory overhead for Wilberforce Widgets is a steady $100,000 per month. In January, the company manufactures 10,000 widgets, so $10 of factory overhead is applied to each unit produced. These units are all sold in February, so the amount of factory overhead charged to expense in February is $100,000. In April, the amount of factory overhead is still $100,000, but the production volume has declined to 5,000 units as customer demand shrinks. This means that $20 of factory overhead is now applied to each unit produced. Only 3,000 of these units are sold in May, as customer demand continues to erode. This means that only $60,000 of factory overhead will be charged to expense in May, leaving $40,000 of the cost stored in inventory until a later period.

---

The example illustrates two problems. First, the amount of overhead applied to each unit produced will vary if the number of units manufactured varies. And second, the amount of factory overhead eventually charged to expense will vary in each reporting period, depending on the number of units sold.

## Freight In Changes

The freight cost associated with bringing materials into the production facility is usually aggregated into the cost of goods sold line item. If it is instead listed separately and you choose to monitor it, here are some issues that can cause the amount of freight expense to vary:

- *Rate changes.* Freight costs will vary over time, based on the costs incurred by freight operators. In particular, the cost of fuel can move markedly over just a few months.
- *Rush deliveries.* A production facility may have a scheduling or excessive scrap problem, and runs out of certain raw materials. If so, it may need to air freight the required materials on short notice.
- *Supplier locations.* The purchasing staff routinely alters the mix of suppliers from which materials are procured. This will result in different amounts of miles traveled to bring goods from a supplier to the company. For example, a business may elect to switch its sourcing from a local supplier to one located in China. If so, the freight cost will skyrocket, though presumably because the unit cost being acquired is so much lower.

## Analysis Conclusions

A key problem with the interpretation of the cost of sales and gross margin is that so few of the underlying accounts are actually revealed to the reader. Instead, it is common to be faced with a single "cost of sales" or "cost of goods sold" line item, which limits the amount of analysis that can be conducted. Still, and depending on the level of detail provided, we suggest conducting the following analyses:

1. *Calculate contribution margin.* The contribution margin isolates all variable expenses and throws out factory overhead, so the result is a much better view of the true variable cost of sales. This information should definitely be plotted on a trend line and examined for long-term changes.

2. *Compare to inventory.* If the cost of sales appears to be somewhat low, see if the inventory line item in the balance sheet has increased. It is quite possible that some costs have been parked in the inventory account; if these costs are not released from the balance sheet fairly soon, there is either a long-term seasonal inventory build going on, or the company is losing control over its inventory asset.

3. *Watch the direct materials percentage.* If the direct materials expense line item continues to increase as a percentage of sales, it is quite possible that management is dropping prices in order to meet competitive pressures or to expand sales.

Despite the level of reporting aggregation used for the cost of sales, this line item can contain the largest amount of expense listed anywhere on the income statement. Consequently, it bears close examination on an ongoing basis.

# Chapter 12
# Interpretation of Operating Expenses

## Introduction

Operating expenses are those costs incurred to run a business, other than the production area. This classification includes the costs of selling and marketing, accounting, finance, order entry, research and development, risk management, and corporate. Operating expenses are also known as selling, general and administrative, or SG&A. In this chapter, we cover the presentation of operating expenses and a number of pointers regarding how these expenses behave.

## The Interpretation of Operating Expenses

The operating expenses line items appear in the bottom half of the income statement, after sales, the cost of sales, and the gross margin. A sample presentation showing where these items are located on the income statement is noted in the following exhibit.

### Sample Presentation of Operating Expenses

| | |
|---|---|
| Gross margin | $570,000 |
| | |
| Operating expenses | |
| Advertising | $30,000 |
| Depreciation | 20,000 |
| Rent | 40,000 |
| Payroll taxes | 26,000 |
| Salaries and wages | 360,000 |
| Supplies | 14,000 |
| Travel and entertainment | 30,000 |
| Total operating expenses | $520,000 |

A business may instead choose to present its operating expense information by function. This requires a more complex information tracking system, so that all expenses are charged to specific departments. Given the extra complexity, reporting by functional area is usually only performed by somewhat larger entities.

An example of this type of reporting format follows.

| | |
|---|---|
| Gross profit | $570,000 |
| | |
| Accounting and finance department | $35,000 |
| Corporate department | 62,000 |
| Research department | 50,000 |
| Sales and marketing department | 373,000 |
| Total operating expenses | $520,000 |

The line items noted in the first sample presentation may represent the aggregation of a considerable number of general ledger accounts. The more common of these accounts are:

- *Advertising*. Contains the costs associated with television and radio commercials, display advertising, classified advertising, and billboard advertising, as well as the use of coupons, gifts, loyalty programs, point-of-sale displays, and similar programs. This expense can fluctuate substantially if a business gears up for seasonal advertising campaigns, such as is used by diamond retailers prior to Valentine's Day. The nature of some other businesses calls for more consistent expenditure levels throughout the year, such as is used by banks.

- *Bank fees*. Contains the periodic fees charged by a bank, such as for additional check stock and monthly account maintenance. If there is a spike in this account that occurs once a year, it is probably a bank audit fee that a bank mandates when a company has borrowed money from it.

- *Benefits*. Contains the cost of all benefits provided to employees. These are generally variable costs that adjust with the number of employees, such as medical insurance, life insurance, dental insurance, and short-term disability insurance. Other than the effects of headcount, this expense can change suddenly once a year, when annual rate increases are applied and management decides how much cost sharing with employees is required. If there is an expense bump of this type, it is more likely to begin at the start of the calendar year.

- *Commissions*. Contains the commissions earned by employees for their efforts in obtaining sales for a business. This can be considered a cost of goods sold, since the expense is only incurred if a sale is made; as such, it may instead appear within the cost of goods sold classification on the income statement.

- *Depreciation*. This line item is addressed in more detail in the Interpretation of Fixed Assets chapter. In brief, depreciation is a periodic and ongoing charge to reduce the recorded amount of fixed assets.

- *Insurance*. Contains the fees associated with quite a large number of insurance policies, including general liability, directors and officers, and business interruption insurance. This expense tends to increase as a company increases in size, since a risk manager may eventually be hired who is more proactive in ensuring that risks are mitigated with insurance.

- *Legal and audit fees.* Contains the fees charged by the company's auditors for the annual audit, as well as quarterly reviews if the company is publicly held. Legal fees are especially high for a public company, since it must retain securities attorneys to create filing documents. Legal fees can be especially high in those industries where a company's products can potentially injure users.
- *Salaries and wages.* Contains the compensation paid to selling and administrative employees. Depending on the business, compensation levels can be quite high, such as for information technology workers or accountants skilled in public company reporting.
- *Office supplies.* Contains a typically minimal charge for the cost of supplies, which tends to increase when there are a large number of white collar workers. One of the following sub-sections deals with the impact on this account of a high capitalization limit.
- *Rent expense.* Contains the cost of leased facility space. This can be quite a high figure if there are a large number of employees in the selling and administrative area. For example, an insurance company requires a large staff to handle claims.
- *Telephones.* Contains the cost of both land lines and cell phones. This can be a particularly high cost when the staff is located out of the office, as is the case with insurance adjusters and traveling sales people. These individuals may require not only cell phones, but also data plans for other wireless devices.
- *Travel and entertainment.* Contains the costs of airlines, hotels, car rentals, and other travel costs incurred by employees in the operations area. The size of this line item can vary substantially depending on the business plan being used. For example, a company that emphasizes face-to-face sales calls will incur much higher travel costs than one that only sells through a website.
- *Training.* When a company has a strong emphasis on customer service, needs its workforce to be updated on the latest technology, or is subject to changing regulations, expect it to spend a significant amount on employee training. Examples of such businesses are law firms and audit firms.
- *Utilities.* Contains the costs of the plumbing, electrical, and waste disposal charges for each company location, depending on the applicable lease terms. These costs can be reduced if an entity is located in a region that requires a reduced level of heating and cooling.

We have noted in several places among the preceding general ledger accounts that expense levels can vary drastically, depending on the type of industry and how management chooses to operate a business. This means there is no standard proportion of operating expenses to sales – the amounts will differ for a casino, coal mine, candy manufacturer, and so forth. The best way to review these amounts for reasonableness is to compare them to the expense levels reported by other companies in the same industry.

There are a number of other issues that can be detected amongst the many operating expense line items, which are discussed in the following sub-sections.

## Horizontal Analysis

Horizontal analysis compares historical financial information over a series of reporting periods, with the intent of spotting and investigating spikes and drops in specific periods. A prime place in which to use horizontal analysis is operating expenses, because there can be a large number of line items, and because these expenses tend to be fixed – so that a change is readily apparent. In the following example, we present a horizontal analysis for a number of reporting periods.

**Sample Horizontal Analysis for Operating Expenses**

| Operating expenses | Jan. | Feb | Mar. | Apr. | May | Jun. |
|---|---|---|---|---|---|---|
| Advertising | $30,000 | $28,000 | $-- | $53,000 | $31,000 | $25,000 |
| Depreciation | 20,000 | 20,000 | 20,000 | 14,000 | 14,000 | 14,000 |
| Rent | 40,000 | 40,000 | 40,000 | 40,000 | 40,000 | 46,000 |
| Payroll taxes | 26,000 | 22,000 | 22,000 | 23,000 | 23,000 | 19,000 |
| Salaries and wages | 360,000 | 360,000 | 360,000 | 374,000 | 374,000 | 374,000 |
| Supplies | 14,000 | 2,000 | 3,000 | 9,000 | 3,000 | 3,000 |
| Travel and entertainment | 30,000 | 4,000 | 7,000 | 5,000 | 15,000 | 7,000 |
| Total operating expenses | $520,000 | $476,000 | $452,000 | $518,000 | $500,000 | $488,000 |

In the preceding sample analysis, a number of items were listed in bold, to emphasize points that an analyst might discern. They are:

- *Advertising.* It appears that an advertising invoice was not recognized in March, resulting in the recognition of two months of expenses in April.
- *Depreciation.* It is possible that the depreciation on a high-cost asset was completed in March, resulting in a sharp drop in this expense in April. Alternatively, the asset might have been disposed of, in which case a gain or loss might be recognized elsewhere on the income statement.
- *Rent.* It appears that a scheduled rent increase began in June. An alternative explanation could be that the company entered into a lease on additional facilities.
- *Payroll taxes.* A likely explanation for the drop in payroll taxes in February is that the company completed its state unemployment tax obligations in January. There is a further drop in the expense in June, which could indicate that several employees have exceeded their social security wage caps.
- *Salaries and wages.* It appears likely that the company enacts wage increases for all employees in April, which is when a 4% increase appears. Another clue supporting this thought is that there are no other changes in the expense in any other months, as would be the case if pay raises were conducted at all times.

- *Supplies.* There is a large boost in the supplies expense in January and May. This could be tied to a high capitalization rate (see the Interpretation of Fixed Assets chapter), where the costs of lower-cost assets are charged to expense as incurred. For example, the company may have purchased a number of laptop computers in January and May, and charged them to the supplies expense.
- *Travel and entertainment.* There is quite a large expense in January, which could represent a portion of a company's holiday parties. The additional expense spike in May could be tied to a trade show or some similar event.

As the commentary indicates, it is possible to guess at a number of issues within a company by conducting a horizontal analysis of its operating expenses.

## Strategy Impact on Operating Expenses

When management decides to follow the strategy of keeping prices low in order to gain market share, this usually means cutting deeply into operating expenses, too. For example, the marketing budget could be skimpy, while the research and development budget could be ranked among the lowest in the industry. In addition, the corporate structure is more likely to be flat, so that fewer managers are needed. The end result is a set of operating expenses that are decidedly low in relation to those of competitors.

At the opposite end of the spectrum is a business that emphasizes full service and/or customization. In this case, high prices are the norm, which need to be justified with a plush marketing budget, excellent customer service, and a well-funded research staff.

Neither approach presented here can be considered better than the other – they must instead be viewed in terms of the overall competitive stance that management has adopted for the entire business.

From a stock investment perspective, companies that invest large sums in research and development tend to experience large swings in their stock prices, depending on the outcome of their research activities. The investor who is willing to tolerate the riskiness of these price swings could earn a fortune if a major new product is released, or suffer an equally large loss if a new product introduction fails. Thus, the risk-averse investor might want to consider industries in which research and development spending tends to be low.

## Research and Development Costs

As we just noted in the last sub-section, the strategy of a business drives the amount of funding that it is willing to pour into its research and development activities. Other issues are the nature of the products sold and the amount of money being spent by competitors in this area. For example, a business that produces mainframe computers will likely need to spend a great deal on research in order to "stay competitive. Conversely, a company in the candy business will not require much funding to develop new types of hard candy. Also, if competitors have a history of spending large percentages of their revenue on research and using the results to create more competitive products, then a company will have to spend similar amounts just to stay in the industry.

Given the issues noted here, the interpretation of financial statements should encompass a comparison of the research dollars being spent in relation to the product line and the spending of competitors. In some cases, the analyst's main concern may be that a business is spending too *little* in this area.

## Payroll Tax Wage Cap Issues

In a business where employees earn high wages, such as a law firm, consulting firm, or software design establishment, the wages paid to employees may eventually exceed the wage caps that apply to certain types of payroll taxes. For example, the social security tax in 2015 is 6.2% of the first $118,500 earned in the calendar year. The tax does not apply to any wages earned above the $118,500 level. Similarly, the state unemployment tax, which varies considerably by state, has a wage cap that varies from a low of $7,000 to a high of over $40,000. In both cases, this means that the payroll tax expense will tend to decline as the calendar year progresses. The one exception is when a company is continually hiring new employees, in which case it must pay these taxes as of the new employee start dates, which may be later in the year.

## Commission Fluctuations

The commission plans under which sales departments operate can be quite complex, involving splits, overrides, and periodic bonus payments. A common example is the quarterly bonus, where salespeople are paid an additional amount if they meet certain sales goals. If these commission plans exist, expect to see periodic spikes in the commission expense, possibly following the end of each quarter. There may be an especially large expense spike at the end of the year, to reflect year-end bonus payments.

## Non-Cash Operating Expenses

Most of the line items appearing in operating expenses are directly related to actual cash expenditures that have either already been occurred during the reporting period or will be made shortly thereafter. The main exception is depreciation. As described further in the Interpretation of Fixed Assets chapter, depreciation is the gradual write-down of a fixed asset, probably over a period of several years. In this case, cash was only spent when the asset was acquired. Subsequently, the related depreciation expense is a non-cash expense. A similar issue arises with amortization, which is the same as depreciation but is used to reduce the amount of intangible assets over time.

If a company has a major investment in fixed assets, the size of the related depreciation expense can be considerable, and may give a reader the impression that the business is routinely incurring losses. This is not really the case from a cash flow perspective, since the depreciation is not extracting any cash from the company's bank account. Also, if a company has acquired a large amount of intangible assets via an acquisition, it must write them off over a long period of time, which can crush its reported earnings.

Given these issues, the analyst should consider removing the depreciation and amortization figures from the income statement in order to arrive at a net income figure that is more representative of the ongoing earnings that a business is achieving.

## Rent Subleases

Rent arrangements can last for years, perhaps well beyond the point when a company no longer needs the space. If so, it may look for a tenant who is willing to sublease the space. When there is a sublease, look for an immediate and large reduction in the rent expense. However, this decline may not be permanent, since the new tenant may have agreed to lease the space for a relatively short period of time.

## Supplies Expense and the Capitalization Limit

We noted in the sub-section about horizontal analysis that there can be spill-over from the fixed asset accounts into the supplies expense account. This circumstance usually arises when the capitalization limit is set so high that many expenditures do not qualify to be recorded as fixed assets. Instead, they fall into the default classification of the supplies expense. If there is a high capitalization limit, expect the supplies expense to be much higher than would have been the case with a normal capitalization limit, since many lower-cost computers, software packages, and office equipment items will now be charged to expense. There may also be an unusual spike in this expense at the beginning of the budget year, because department managers now have access to funding for these larger expenditures, and will spend the money as soon as they can.

## The Fixed Nature of Compensation in Operating Expenses

There is no direct relationship between sales and the compensation expense recognized in operating expenses. Many of the individuals whose compensation is recorded in this area may never even see a customer – such as the marketing staff, accounting staff, and human resources group. This means that sales can fluctuate a great deal while the amount of compensation expense may remain relatively steady.

The fixed nature of this compensation can be a boon when a company's sales are growing rapidly, for it implies that the overall profit margin of the business will continue to increase, or at least until the point when there is a need for some additional functionality within the operations group, such as more billing clerks to issue invoices to customers. However, this can also have a reverse effect when sales decline, since the compensation will remain, which triggers a gradual decline in the net profit margin. The management team needs to vigorously eliminate positions when there is a sales drop, or else the operations group can act as a drag on the results of the business.

The outside analyst can see these effects at a general level by noting the rate of change in compensation within operating expenses.

**The Public Company Impact on Operating Expenses**

If the management team decides to take a company public, this can have a considerable negative impact on operating expenses. The company must go through much more detailed annual audits, as well as quarterly reviews and periodic control reviews. The accounting software may need to be replaced with a more robust system. It may be necessary to replace the existing board of directors with a more qualified group, which may demand more pay. The cost of directors and officers insurance will increase, probably several times over. In addition, there will be fees for various filings with the Securities and Exchange Commission (SEC), as well as periodic billings from whichever stock exchanges the company uses to list its stock. Also, very expensive securities attorneys will be retained to assist with the writing of an ongoing series of filings with the SEC.

The bulk of these expenses will be incurred by the accounting department. If the operating expenses are classified by the nature of the expense, then look for increases in the compensation, audit and legal fees, and insurance line items.

## Analysis Conclusions

The operating expenses area contains a large number of expense items, which can be difficult to sort through. Where possible, the analyst should attempt to obtain the most detailed income statement possible, which allows for a deeper level of analysis. If this information is available, we suggest the following order of analysis priority:

1. *Conduct horizontal analysis.* A horizontal analysis that covers many prior periods is certainly called for. Look for long-term trends, as well as sudden spikes or drops that can indicate either short-term accounting errors or long-term changes.

2. *Match strategy to operating expenses.* A particular strategic profile will require that certain expenses be incurred. If one can determine the corporate strategy from management comments or the disclosures accompanying the financial statements, this can explain why the expenses are being incurred. Also, if these expenses then change, one can surmise that the corporate strategy may have also changed.

3. *Compare operating expenses to sales.* Operating expenses are relatively fixed within a broad range of sales. It can be useful to compare the expenses to the current sales level, and estimate at what point additional expenses may need to be incurred in the future. This can be useful for modeling the future net profits of a business.

From an analysis perspective, operating expenses can be considered a target-rich environment. The diligent analyst can develop educated guesses about the strategy and expected future performance of a business just by examining every aspect of these expenses.

# Chapter 13
## Interpretation of Other Income,
## Taxes, and Profits

## Introduction

There are a number of residual line items parked at the bottom of the income statement, of which only one – net income – is routinely examined. The others reveal non-operating financial issues that tend to be rather small and so might be considered inconsequential. The income tax expense is also noted here; someone conducting a financial statement review might ignore it, on the assumption that this is calculated as a simple percentage of earnings. They would be wrong – the income tax expense can swing wildly from period to period, based on factors that may not be readily apparent to the casual reader. In this chapter, we cover the presentation of these last remaining income statement line items, as well as the implications of changes in their amounts.

## The Interpretation of Other Income, Taxes, and Profits

The line items related to other income, income taxes, and profitability are located at the bottom of the income statement, along with earnings per share (if the reporting entity is publicly-held). A sample presentation showing where these items are located on the income statement is noted in the following exhibit.

### Sample Presentation of Other Income, Taxes, and Profits

| | |
|---|---|
| Total operating expenses | $520,000 |
| Income from operations | 50,000 |
| | |
| Other income and expense | |
| Dividend and interest income | $8,000 |
| Gains/(losses) on the sale of assets | 2,000 |
| Interest expense | -3,000 |
| Income before income taxes | 59,000 |
| Income taxes | -20,000 |
| Net income | $39,000 |
| | |
| Earnings per share | $0.39 |

The general ledger accounts that are the source of these line items are as follows:
- *Interest income.* Contains the interest income earned from holding debt securities.
- *Dividend income.* Contains the dividend income received from holding equity securities.
- *Gains/(losses) on asset sales.* Contains the net amount of profit or loss derived from the sale of fixed assets. This is the residual after the original asset cost net of accumulated depreciation is subtracted from the asset sale price.
- *Interest expense.* Contains the periodic cost of borrowed funds.
- *Income taxes expense.* Contains the estimated income tax liability associated with the taxable income generated in the reporting period.

There are several issues to be aware of when reviewing these line items, which are covered in the following subsections. We also make note of the several ways to adjust the net income figure to gain a more realistic view of the results of a business.

**Implications of Interest and Dividend Income**

The typical organization reports very little interest and dividend income, for the following reasons:
- *Investment priorities.* It is much more important for them to have highly liquid and safe investments than ones that generate a high return.
- *Capital budgeting.* There are so many investments that can be made in company projects that there is little cash left over for investments.
- *Dividends and buybacks.* If senior management has no other profitable use for funds, it recommends to the board of directors that funds be returned to investors via dividends or stock buyback programs.

If, despite the preceding points, the income statement still reveals a large amount of interest and dividend income, this raises two issues that the analyst could point out to management:
- *Riskiness of investments.* If the return on investment is unusually high, the company may be investing in risky investment vehicles that could cause losses of the invested funds.
- *Excess cash holdings.* The company may simply be holding onto an excessive amount of cash. Management may want to retain excess cash in the event of a business downturn or to acquire another business. Barring these options, it may be possible to convince management to return some part of this excess cash to investors.

## Implications of Gains/Losses on Asset Sales

When the income statement contains gains or losses related to the sale of company assets, the issue is not really the amount of these gains or losses, but rather their presence at all. The following implications may arise from asset sales:

- *Capacity reduction*. The company may be eliminating a portion of its production capacity by selling off equipment. This can be a bad idea when demand tends to spike, since the company will now be limited in its ability to respond to large customer orders.
- *Line of business termination*. If the asset sales are considerable, it can indicate that management is exiting an entire line of business, and so is bent on liquidating all associated assets.
- *Outsourcing*. Management may have decided to terminate an asset-intensive part of the business (such as manufacturing) in order to conserve cash.
- *Orderly shutdown*. Perhaps least likely is a decision to engage in an orderly shutdown of the entire entity, in which case there will be a long series of asset sales that may span many months.

Given these concerns, it makes sense to peruse the disclosures accompanying the financial statements to see if management offers any clues regarding why assets are being eliminated.

## Effects of Interest Expense

The chief element of the other income section of the income statement is usually interest expense. This is considered a financing cost, so it is not included in the operating expenses section of the income statement. The amount of this expense is mainly based on management's decisions regarding how fast to grow the business and whether this growth should be funded with debt. In a high-growth situation, it will be necessary to invest in much more working capital and more fixed assets. If there is an unwillingness to sell more shares, or if lenders are willing to loan money at low rates, the outcome may be a large amount of debt, for which there will be a correspondingly large interest expense.

If a business is a small one, it will be less likely to obtain cheap financing, and will instead have to resort to high-cost lending arrangements, such as the factoring of receivables. Consequently, if the implicit interest rate associated with debt is quite high, one can reasonably infer that management is being forced into very high-cost borrowing arrangements. This is a particular problem when the before-tax profit margin is already low, since a business probably cannot afford the cost of debt.

## Implications of Taxable Income

Taxable income is profit (or loss) upon which the income tax liability is calculated. The composition of taxable income varies by taxation authority, so it will vary depending upon the rules of the governments within which an entity is located or does business. For example, taxes may be reduced if a business is located within an economic development zone, or training credits may be provided to an employee-heavy business, or accelerated depreciation is allowed for certain assets. Given these effects, it is entirely possible that the recognized amount of income tax expense is substantially lower than the standard tax rate that would normally apply to the reported income level.

Another issue to watch for is when the tax rate used to derive the income tax expense is a low one early in the year, and a higher one later in the year. This situation arises because tax rates are usually set by the amount of income reported, with lower tax rates applying to businesses that report little income. The accounting staff should instead use the average tax rate that is expected to be used as of the end of the year, so that the same tax percentage is applied to the reported income level for all interim reporting periods.

A final issue to be aware of is the presence of net operating loss (NOL) carryforwards. These are losses occurring in prior years that can still be used to offset taxable income. NOLs are commonly available to startup companies, which will likely incur losses during their early years, and then use the tax effect of these losses to shield taxable income in later years. The analyst should be aware of the amount of remaining NOLs that can be used, in order to estimate when a business will have to start paying income taxes.

## Effective Tax Rate

A major determinant of the net profit margin just described is the ability of a business to avoid or defer the payment of income taxes. There are a number of strategies available for lowering the statutory tax rate to a level far below what would normally be expected. If a company can successfully engage in a tax reduction or deferral strategy over a long period of time, the result can be a massive increase in net profits, with an attendant increase in cash flows.

To calculate the effective tax rate, divide the aggregate amount of income tax expense stated on the income statement by the amount of before-tax profit reported on the same document.

$$\frac{\text{Recognized tax expense}}{\text{Before-tax profit}}$$

It can be useful to track the effective tax rate over multiple years, to see if a business is capable of maintaining a low tax rate over the long term. A one-year decline in the tax rate is much less indicative of a corporate tax-reduction strategy, since a company may simply have blundered into a tax-reduction scenario without intending to do so.

---

**EXAMPLE**

Clyde Shotguns manufactures extremely high-end shotguns for wealthy collectors around the world. The company has a long-term strategy of building production facilities in multiple countries, each one owned by a separate legal entity. This means that Clyde can utilize

119

favorable transfer pricing to recognize the bulk of the company's income in its Ireland facility, where the tax rate is substantially lower than in other parts of the world where its other subsidiaries operate. The result in the past year was the recognition of $800,000 of tax expense on $5,333,000 of before-tax profit, which is an effective tax rate of 15%.

## Net Profit Margin

The net profit margin is a comparison of after-tax income to net sales. It reveals the remaining income after all costs of production and operations have been deducted from sales, and income taxes recognized. As such, it is a reasonable measure of the overall results of a firm, especially when combined with an evaluation of how well it is using its working capital. The measure is commonly reported on a trend line, to judge performance over time. It is also used to compare the results of a business with its competitors.

The net profit margin is really a short-term measurement, because it does not reveal a company's actions to maintain profitability over the long term, as may be indicated by the level of capital investment or research and development expenditures. Also, a company may delay a variety of discretionary expenses, such as maintenance or training, to make its net profit margin look better than it normally is. Consequently, evaluate this margin alongside an array of other metrics to gain a better picture of a company's ability to continue as a going concern.

Another issue with the net profit margin is that a company may intentionally keep it low through a variety of expense recognition strategies in order to avoid paying taxes. If so, review the statement of cash flows to determine the real cash-generating ability of a business.

To calculate the net profit margin, divide net profits by net sales and then multiply by 100. The formula is:

$$(\text{Net profit} \div \text{Net sales}) \times 100$$

---

**EXAMPLE**

Kelvin Corporation has $1,000,000 of sales in its most recent month, as well as sales returns of $40,000, a cost of goods sold of $550,000, and operating expenses of $360,000. The income tax rate is 35%. The calculation of its net profit margin is:

$1,000,000 Sales - $40,000 Sales returns = $960,000 Net sales

$960,000 Net sales - $550,000 Cost of goods - $360,000 Operating expenses
= $50,000 Income before tax

$50,000 Income before tax × (1 − 0.35) = $32,500 Profit after tax

($32,500 Profit after tax ÷ $960,000 Net Sales) × 100

= 3.4% Net profit margin

---

## Deflated Profit Growth

When a business operates in an inflationary environment, a decline in the value of its home currency can cause the business to report unusually high profits in comparison to prior periods. To gain a better understanding of the underlying profit growth of the business, it is necessary to deflate the profits for the current period and then compare them to the profits reported for the prior period. To calculate deflated profit growth, follow these steps:

1. Divide the price index for the prior reporting period by the price index for the current reporting period.
2. Multiply the result by the net profit figure reported for the current reporting period.
3. Subtract the net profits for the prior reporting period from the result.
4. Divide the result by the net profit figure for the prior reporting period.

The formula is:

$$\frac{\text{Current period net profit} \times \dfrac{\text{Price index for prior period}}{\text{Price index for current period}} - \text{Prior period net profit}}{\text{Prior period net profit}}$$

The use of price indexes only approximates the true impact of inflation on a business. A price index is based on the changes in prices for a mix of common goods and services, which a company may not use in the same proportions built into the index. For example, a price index may have increased primarily because of a jump in the price of oil, but a company may have minimum expenditures for oil. Consequently, there can be differences between the deflated profit growth calculation and the actual impact of inflation on a business.

---

### EXAMPLE

Aphelion Corporation operates telescopes in the Atacama Desert in northern Chile, and uses the Chilean peso as its home currency. The company reported profits of 5,000,000 pesos in the most recent year, and 4,500,000 pesos in the immediately preceding year. The price index for the current year was 127, as opposed to 106 for the preceding year. Based on this information, the deflated profit growth of the company is:

$$\frac{\begin{array}{c}\text{5,000,000 pesos current} \\ \text{period profit}\end{array} \times \dfrac{\text{106 Prior period index}}{\text{127 Current period index}} - \begin{array}{c}\text{4,500,000 pesos prior} \\ \text{period profit}\end{array}}{\text{4,500,000 Prior period net profit}}$$

$$= \frac{\text{4,173,228 Deflated pesos} - \text{4,500,000 Profit prior period}}{\text{4,500,000 Profit prior period}} = -7.3\%$$

121

Thus, when adjusted for inflation, the profits of Aphelion declined by 7.3% in the current reporting period.

## Core Earnings Ratio

There are many ways in which the net profit margin of a business can be skewed by events that have little to do with the core operating capabilities of a business. To get to the root of the issue and concentrate on only the essential operations of a business, Standard & Poor's has promulgated the concept of core earnings, which strips away all non-operational transactions from a company's reported results.

There are a multitude of unrelated transactions that can be eliminated from net profits, some of which are so specific to certain industries that Standard & Poor's probably never thought of them. The most common of these unrelated transactions are:

- Asset impairment charges
- Costs related to merger activities
- Costs related to the issuance of bonds and other forms of financing
- Gains or losses on hedging activities that have not yet been realized
- Gains or losses on the sale of assets
- Gains or losses related to the outcome of litigation
- Profits or losses from pension income
- Recognized cost of stock options issued to employees
- Recognized cost of warrants issued to third parties
- The accrued cost of restructuring operations that have not yet occurred

Many of these special adjustments only occur at long intervals, so a company may find that its core earnings ratio is quite close to its net profit ratio in one year, and substantially different in the next year. The difference tends to be much larger when a company adds complexity to the nature of its operations, so that more factors can impact net profits.

The calculation of the core earnings ratio is to adjust reported net income for as many of the preceding items as are present, and divide by net sales. The formula is:

$$\frac{\text{Net profits} - \text{Core earnings adjustments}}{\text{Net sales}}$$

### EXAMPLE

Subterranean Access, maker of drilling equipment, has reported a fabulous year, with profits of $10,000,000 on sales of $50,000,000. A credit analyst that rates the company's bonds is suspicious of this good fortune, and digs through the company's annual report to derive the core earnings ratio of the business.

She uncovers the following items:

| | |
|---|---|
| Profit from favorable settlement of a lawsuit | $8,000,000 |
| Profit on earnings from pension fund | 500,000 |
| Gain on sale of a subsidiary | 3,500,000 |
| Impairment charge on acquired intangible assets | -1,000,000 |
| Total | $11,000,000 |

When these adjustments are factored out of the company's net profits, it turns out that the core earnings figure is actually a $1,000,000 loss, which results in a core earnings ratio of -2%. Based on this information, the analyst issues a downgrade on the company's debt, on the assumption that the multitude of favorable adjustments will not continue.

---

**Earnings per Share**

Earnings per share (EPS) measures the amount of a company's net income that is theoretically available for payment to the holders of its common stock. A company with a high EPS is capable of generating a significant dividend for investors, or it may plow the funds back into its operations to generate more growth; in either case, a high EPS is presumed to indicate a potentially worthwhile investment, if the market price of the stock is acceptable to the investor.

When researching the performance of a company, EPS is likely to be the first metric found. Despite its prevalence, EPS only yields a snippet of information about the underlying valuation of a company. Consider the following issues:

- *Accrual basis.* EPS information is only reported by publicly-held companies, all of which report their financial statements using the accrual basis of accounting. Because of the accounting rules used for the accrual basis, there can be a significant difference between the cash flows generated and the profits or losses reported. It is quite possible that a company might report skyrocketing profits, and yet have no cash on hand that could be used to pay dividends. This issue can be avoided by focusing instead on the cash information reported in the statement of cash flows.

- *Quarterly basis.* A publicly-held company reports its financial results once every three months, so the focus of EPS is only on the last three months. Given the vagaries of many markets, it is entirely possible that a company's reported EPS will fluctuate over the course of a year, giving investors the impression that earnings are unreliable. This issue can be avoided by only focusing on annual EPS.

- *Dilution.* EPS information is reported by a company in two formats, one of which is fully diluted earnings per share. Diluted EPS incorporates every possible financial instrument issued by a company that might be convertible into common stock. This is an extremely conservative ratio, since many common stock equivalents are never converted into common stock. Consequently, the measurement can report an unusually low EPS number that is not indicative of the actual performance of a business. The issue can at least

123

be mitigated by instead using the basic earnings per share figure, which does not presume dilution from common stock equivalents.

Given these issues, EPS should not be the only measurement used when evaluating a company.

To calculate earnings per share, subtract any dividend payments due to the holders of preferred stock from net income after tax, and divide by the average number of common shares outstanding during the measurement period. The calculation is:

$$\frac{\text{Net income after tax – Preferred stock dividends}}{\text{Average number of common shares outstanding}}$$

---

**EXAMPLE**

Kelvin Corporation has net income after tax of $1,000,000 and also must pay out $200,000 in preferred dividends. The company has both bought back and sold its own stock during the measurement period; the weighted average number of common shares outstanding during the period was 400,000 shares. Kelvin's earnings per share is:

$$\frac{\$1,000,000 \text{ Net income} - \$200,000 \text{ Preferred stock dividends}}{400,000 \text{ Common shares}}$$

$$=\$2.00 \text{ Earnings per share}$$

---

Consider tracking the percentage change in EPS over time, to see if management is improving on the return to investors. To calculate the percentage change, divide the incremental change in EPS by the EPS for the preceding reporting period. The calculation is:

$$\frac{\text{Incremental change in EPS}}{\text{EPS from preceding reporting period}}$$

---

**EXAMPLE**

Kelvin Corporation reported earnings per share of $2.00 in last year's financial results, and has reported $2.10 earnings per share in this year's financial statements. The percentage change in EPS is:

$$\frac{\$2.10 \text{ Latest EPS} - \$2.00 \text{ Preceding EPS}}{\$2.00 \text{ Preceding EPS}}$$

$$= 5\% \text{ Incremental change in EPS}$$

---

The use of a percentage change in EPS calculation focuses attention on the long-term ability of a company to create value by increasing earnings per share. However, it also places pressure on management to do so, sometimes to the extent that they will stretch the accounting rules to continue reporting improved EPS. This issue can only be spotted with an intensive review of a company's financial statements and accompanying disclosures, to see if management is using more aggressive accounting techniques over time. If so, a likely result is a long series of EPS increases, followed by a sudden and significant decline in EPS, when management can no longer use trickery to maintain its reported results.

## Manipulation of Earnings per Share

The amount of earnings reported in the earnings per share figure can trend up or down at a rate that differs from the reported amount of net income. This is because the earnings per share figure is partially derived from the number of shares outstanding. The management of a company can alter this shares figure to improve upon earnings per share in the following ways:

- *Stock buyback*. The board of directors could authorize the repurchase of shares from investors, thereby reducing the amount in the denominator of the EPS calculation.
- *DRIP termination*. A company may have a dividend reinvestment plan (DRIP) in place, whereby investors have their dividend payments converted into additional shares. If the DRIP is cancelled, this curtails a source of new shares (though usually quite a small one).
- *Stock option cancellation*. A company can stop offering stock options to its employees and warrants to outside parties. Doing so eliminates a number of shares that might otherwise be created through the exercise of options and warrants.
- *Conversion features not offered*. If convertible bonds are offered that allow holders to convert their bonds into company shares, the issuer can stop selling these bonds to investors.

The first option actively reduces the number of shares outstanding, while the other options curtail the alternatives under which new shares can be created. The aggregate result of these activities is fewer shares outstanding, which increases earnings per share.

The decision to buy back shares is not always a good one from the perspective of the investor. Companies tend to do this when they are generating lots of excess cash, but this also tends to coincide with their having high stock prices, so they end up spending a large amount of money to retire very few shares. Also, there may be better uses for the cash internally, such as by investing the funds in new product lines or in additional research and development activities.

## Analysis Conclusions

It is in the interests of a company's management team to present the best possible net income figures to the outside world. However, there are numerous ways in which this figure can be modified to present a better outcome than is really the case. In the following analysis steps, we describe a method for improving the odds of discerning the true operational outcome of a business:

1. *Calculate core earnings.* Rather than bothering with the net profit margin at all, use the core earnings formula to strip away a number of areas that are commonly used to modify earnings.
2. *Deflate core earnings.* Use the deflated profit growth calculation to adjust the core earnings for inflation.
3. *Create a trend line.* Run the deflated core earnings figure back in time for several years. This gives the best indication of whether management is actually able to generate improvements in profitability over time.

A trap that the analyst can fall into is assuming that a business showing large profits also has similarly positive cash flows. This may not be the case at all, since there may be a number of expenditures related to working capital and fixed assets that do not appear in the income statement. The result may very well be that a business appears to be highly profitable, and yet is hemorrhaging cash. See the Interpretation of Cash Flows chapter for more information about how to evaluate a company's cash flow situation.

# Chapter 14
## Interpretation of Cash Flows

## Introduction

The statement of cash flows presents the sources and uses of the cash of an organization, and also supplies a derivation of the ending cash balance. This is a valuable document, for it avoids the masking effects of the accrual basis of accounting, which can sometimes report profits even when a company's bank account is being drained. The focus of the document is on the effects of different activities on cash flows. For example, the statement can point out that:

- Buying securities as an investment uses cash
- Cashing in a bond increases cash
- Collecting an account receivable increases cash
- Investing in fixed assets uses cash
- Paying employees uses cash
- Paying for supplies uses cash
- Paying off a loan uses cash
- Receiving a loan increases cash
- Selling company shares increases cash

Cash flows are considered to be positive when the ending cash balance is higher than the beginning cash balance. Cash flows are considered to be negative when the reverse condition exists.

In this chapter, we discuss the different types of information that can be extracted from an analysis of the statement of cash flows.

## The Interpretation of the Statement of Cash Flows

The statement of cash flows is the least used of the primary financial statements, and may not be issued at all, especially during interim reporting periods. Nonetheless, the report can provide valuable information, especially when combined with the other financial statements. In this section, we describe the contents of the report and note a number of methods for analyzing it.

### Overview of the Statement of Cash Flows

The statement of cash flows contains information about the flows of cash into and out of a company; in particular, it shows the extent of those company activities that generate and use cash. The primary activities appearing in the statement are:

- *Operating activities.* These are an entity's primary revenue-producing activities. Examples of operating activities are cash receipts from the sale of goods and services, as well as from royalties and commissions, amounts received or paid to settle lawsuits, fines, payments to employees and suppliers, cash payments to lenders for interest, and contributions to charity.

- *Investing activities*. These involve the acquisition and disposal of long-term assets. Examples of investing activities are cash receipts from the sale of property, the sale of the debt or equity instruments of other entities, the repayment of loans made to other entities, and proceeds from insurance settlements related to damaged fixed assets. Examples of cash payments that are investment activities include the acquisition of fixed assets, as well as the purchase of the debt or equity of other entities.
- *Financing activities*. These are the activities resulting in alterations to the amount of contributed equity and the entity's borrowings. Examples of financing activities include cash receipts from the sale of the entity's own equity instruments or from issuing debt and cash payments to buy back shares, pay dividends, and pay off outstanding debt.

The direct method or the indirect method can be used to present the statement of cash flows. These methods are described next.

**The Direct Method**

The direct method of presenting the statement of cash flows presents the specific cash flows associated with items that affect cash flow. Items that typically do so include:

- Cash collected from customers
- Interest and dividends received
- Cash paid to employees
- Cash paid to suppliers
- Interest paid
- Income taxes paid

The format of the direct method appears in the following example.

| Cash flows from operating activities | | |
|---|---|---|
| Cash receipts from customers | $45,800,000 | |
| Cash paid to suppliers | -29,800,000 | |
| Cash paid to employees | -11,200,000 | |
| Cash generated from operations | 4,800,000 | |
| | | |
| Interest paid | -310,000 | |
| Income taxes paid | -1,700,000 | |
| Net cash from operating activities | | $2,790,000 |
| | | |
| Cash flows from investing activities | | |
| Purchase of fixed assets | -580,000 | |
| Proceeds from sale of equipment | 110,000 | |
| Net cash used in investing activities | | -470,000 |
| | | |
| Cash flows from financing activities | | |
| Proceeds from issuance of common stock | 1,000,000 | |
| Proceeds from issuance of long-term debt | 500,000 | |
| Principal payments under capital lease obligation | -10,000 | |
| Dividends paid | -450,000 | |
| Net cash from financing activities | | 1,040,000 |
| | | |
| Net increase in cash and cash equivalents | | 3,360,000 |
| Cash and cash equivalents at beginning of period | | 1,640,000 |
| Cash and cash equivalents at end of period | | $5,000,000 |

**Reconciliation of net income to net cash provided by operating activities:**

| Net income | | $2,665,000 |
|---|---|---|
| Adjustments to reconcile net income to net cash provided by operating activities: | | |
| Depreciation and amortization | $125,000 | |
| Provision for losses on accounts receivable | 15,000 | |
| Gain on sale of equipment | -155,000 | |
| Increase in interest and income taxes payable | 32,000 | |
| Increase in deferred taxes | 90,000 | |
| Increase in other liabilities | 18,000 | |
| Total adjustments | | 125,000 |
| Net cash provided by operating activities | | $2,790,000 |

The reconciliation attached to the preceding example is used to provide a bridge between the net income figure reported at the bottom of the income statement and the net cash from operating activities figure provided in this version of the statement of cash flows.

The example also referenced a term called a cash equivalent. This is a highly liquid investment having a maturity of three months or less. An example of a cash equivalent is a money market fund.

The standard-setting bodies encourage the use of the direct method, but it is rarely used, for the excellent reason that the information in it is difficult to assemble; companies simply do not collect and store information in the manner required for this format. Instead, they use the indirect method, which is described next.

## The Indirect Method

Under the indirect method of presenting the statement of cash flows, the presentation begins with net income or loss, with subsequent additions to or deductions from that amount for non-cash revenue and expense items, resulting in net income provided by operating activities. The format of the indirect method appears in the following example.

| Cash flows from operating activities | | |
|---|---|---|
| Net income | | $3,000,000 |
| Adjustments for: | | |
| Depreciation and amortization | $125,000 | |
| Provision for losses on accounts receivable | 20,000 | |
| Gain on sale of facility | -65,000 | |
| | | 80,000 |
| Increase in trade receivables | -250,000 | |
| Decrease in inventories | 325,000 | |
| Decrease in trade payables | -50,000 | |
| | | 25,000 |
| Cash generated from operations | | 3,105,000 |
| | | |
| **Cash flows from investing activities** | | |
| Purchase of fixed assets | -500,000 | |
| Proceeds from sale of equipment | 35,000 | |
| Net cash used in investing activities | | -465,000 |
| | | |
| **Cash flows from financing activities** | | |
| Proceeds from issuance of common stock | 150,000 | |
| Proceeds from issuance of long-term debt | 175,000 | |
| Dividends paid | -45,000 | |
| Cash generated from financing activities | | 280,000 |
| | | |
| Net increase in cash and cash equivalents | | 2,920,000 |
| Cash and cash equivalents at beginning of period | | 2,080,000 |
| Cash and cash equivalents at end of period | | $5,000,000 |

The reason for the "adjustments" in the cash flows from operating activities section may not initially be clear. In essence, these adjustments relate to non-cash components of the income statement (from which the initial net income figure was derived). These non-cash gains and losses must be added back to the net income figure to obtain the amount of cash generated from operations. Similarly, changes in working capital (see the Other Analysis Topics chapter) have an impact on cash, and so are noted as separate line items that also adjust the net income figure.

No matter which of the two methods is used to present cash flow information, they tie back to the beginning and ending cash balances stated in the balance sheet. This linkage applies to the "cash and cash equivalents at beginning of period" and "cash and cash equivalents at end of period" at the bottom of the statement.

## Examination of Cash Flows from Operating Activities

An issue with the cash flows from operating activities section – using either of the presentation methods – is that the information is summarized at quite a high level. This means it can be difficult to extract information from it. Nonetheless, here are several areas to examine:

- *Cash generated from operations.* The single easiest item to monitor is the total cash generated from operations. Monitor this item on a trend line to see if there are consistently positive cash flows. Also, put in an adjacent trend line the reported operating profit of the business. Operating profit is the gross profit minus all operating expenses, but before the effects of other income and taxes. If there is a large and ongoing disparity between the two trend lines, a deeper investigation may be warranted, as noted in the following example.

---

**EXAMPLE**

An analyst is reviewing the financial statements of Geodetic International. The company has two divisions. One consistently generates profits from the hourly billing of the federal government for the conversion of wildfire information into maps. The other division is developing an internal software package that will automatically convert satellite imagery into soil maps. A selection of Geodetic's reported financial information is as follows:

| (000s) | Year 1 | Year 2 | Year 3 | Year 4 |
|---|---|---|---|---|
| Operating profit | $1,000 | $1,200 | $1,700 | $2,000 |
| Cash generated from operations | -200 | -300 | -300 | -300 |
| Disparity | -1,200 | -1,500 | -2,000 | -2,300 |
| | | | | |
| Cash balance | 500 | -- | -- | -- |
| Change in fixed assets | +1,400 | +1,700 | +2,200 | +2,500 |
| Change in short-term loans | +900 | +1,700 | +2,200 | +2,500 |

The evidence strongly indicates that Geodetic's management is capitalizing the software development cost associated with its new satellite imagery software. The full amount of the disparity between the reported operating profit and the cash generated from operations is being shifted into the fixed assets line item in the balance sheet and being funded with short-term debt. The result is a highly misleading income statement, as well as a dangerous increase in short-term debt, which is subject to short-term interest rate fluctuations.

---

- *Change in working capital elements.* A good place to view changes in the various elements of working capital (see the Other Analysis Topics chapter) is in this section when using the indirect method of reporting. The specific changes in trade receivables, inventories, and payables are noted. When individually tracked on a trend line, it is possible to see where a business is investing its working capital funds.

---

**EXAMPLE**

The management of Ninja Cutlery is engaged in a rapid expansion of its ceramic knife business from the professional chef market to home cooks. The trouble is that reaching home cooks requires distributing through several retail chains, which require long payment terms. The outcome of this new direction for the company appears in the following working capital figures, which were extracted from its statement of cash flows. Sales into the new market began in the second quarter.

| (000s) | Quarter 1 | Quarter 2 | Quarter 3 | Quarter 4 | Total |
|---|---|---|---|---|---|
| Increase in trade receivables | -$10 | -$360 | -$210 | -$50 | -$630 |
| Increase in inventory | -5 | -200 | -105 | -25 | -335 |
| Increase in trade payables | 10 | 320 | 175 | 120 | 625 |
| Net change | -$5 | -$240 | -$140 | $45 | -$340 |

The analysis reveals that Ninja is being forced to take on a large investment as a result of this new initiative, not only in additional accounts receivable, but also in inventory. This has created a bubble of new financing requirements that expanded rapidly in the second and third quarters, and appears to be tapering off in the fourth quarter. The company is clearly attempting to obtain a portion of the required funding by extending its payment terms with suppliers. Perhaps most troubling is the increase in trade payables in the fourth quarter, when there is no apparent need for it. It is possible that the company has been running short of cash at this point, and needs to extract even more money from its suppliers by delaying payments to them.

---

- *Lawsuit settlements.* If there are any funds received or paid out as the result of a lawsuit, these amounts are noted in a separate line item. It can be useful to add back lawsuit payouts from net income or subtract out from net income the effects of incoming lawsuit receipts, to gain a clearer view of the actual operating results of a business.
- *Cash flows for royalties and commissions.* A business may already be breaking out in its income statement any income or expenses related to royalties and commissions. If not, the information can be found here instead, and is useful for determining the extent to which these items play a role in a company's finances.

The items pointed out for further review are those not readily found elsewhere in the financial statements. For example, lawsuit settlements will probably be noted in the income statement, but may be aggregated into another line item, and so will be less identifiable.

## Examination of Cash Flows from Investing Activities

As was the case with the cash flows from operating activities section, the investing activities part of the statement of cash flows suffers from an excessive degree of aggregation. Nonetheless, it is still possible to detect certain general directions in which management may be taking a company, as noted in the following bullet points:

- *Pre-growth build activities.* The total amount of fixed assets purchased is located in the investing activities section. This figure may have little relevance if a business has a pattern of acquiring fixed assets at a steady rate, year after year. However, in an asset-intensive industry, it may be possible to detect the ramp-up of corporate infrastructure leading to the launch of a new product line. This could be an especially interesting finding if there is a history of such asset purchases in the past, from which one might be able to estimate the future launch dates of new products. This interpretational tool would not work if a business outsources its production activities, since there would then be no fixed asset purchases to detect.
- *Outsourcing.* If there is a large sell-off of fixed assets, it can imply that management is planning to outsource certain asset-intensive parts of a business, such as its manufacturing capability. However, it could also mean that a business is simply cash-poor and needs the cash – which can be detected by examining the amount of cash on hand and the trend of debt acquisition.
- *Corporate takeovers.* One of the line items that may be used in the investing activities section is an aggregation of the debt or equity of other entities. While this amount is presented as an aggregated total, it can still be an indicator of the accumulation of the shares of a possible acquisition candidate, especially if the amount invested is unusually high in comparison to prior periods.

## Examination of Cash Flows from Financing Activities

The nature of the line items used in the financing section makes this the most informative part of the statement of cash flows. There is a clear segregation of information among separate line items for dividends, stock sales, debt sales, stock repurchases, and so forth. This information can lead one to investigate the following topics:

- *Dividend trends.* The amount of dividends paid tends to be quite consistent over time. A key item to watch for is spikes in or the cancellation of dividends. A spike likely indicates a one-time special dividend, perhaps to pass through to investors a large gain experienced by the company. A dividend cancellation is a more significant issue to be aware of, since it can have several implications, such as:

- That cash flows have weakened so much that the business can no longer afford to pay dividends
- That a major growth opportunity exists, which will be paid for by retaining the cash that would normally be distributed through dividends

- *Stock repurchases.* When there is a large stock repurchase, it can have several implications. One is that the repurchases are only triggered when a minimum stock price threshold has been reached – therefore, the stock is selling near the low end of its intended range. Another possibility is that a large investor has demanded a stock repurchase at a high price in order to stop threatening the company with a takeover attempt.
- *Stock and debt sales.* For smaller organizations, obtaining cash through the sale of debt or equity instruments is a relatively rare circumstance, which should certainly be noted when it appears in the statement of cash flows. In particular, determine the effect of any new fund raising on the debt-equity ratio of a business, which can be used to determine the riskiness of future debt repayments and whether it is even possible for an entity to raise any further debt funding. Additional debt is especially risky when the cash flows generated from operating activities are in decline, since this means a business is at greater risk of being unable to pay back the debt. A strong indicator of financial weakness is when a business is forced to sell preferred stock, since this usually means that investors want extra protection for their invested funds that gives them a priority over the holders of common stock.
- *Debt payments.* A key issue is whether a business has the financial resources to pay back its outstanding debt. The amount of these repayments is noted in the financial activities section. Watch this line item around the date of a debt maturity, to see if a business actually pays off the debt or instead rolls it forward into a new debt instrument.
- *Total changes.* Review the long-term trend of an organization's financing activities. If there are a continuing series of cash inflows from financing, there is a good chance that the business is in rapid growth mode, and needs cash from all possible sources in order to fund that growth. This is more likely to be the case if there is no evidence of dividends having been issued. Alternatively, if there is a long-term trend of paying off debt and/or buying back shares, it is reasonable to assume that the growth period is over, and the business is now generating excess funds. These are normal trends in the life cycle of a business. However, if sales and profits are declining and a business is still reporting a net inflow of cash from financing sources, this indicates that the business is inherently unprofitable, and perhaps should be shut down.

## Cash Flow Return on Sales

When a business uses the accrual basis of accounting to record its performance, it is entirely possible that various accruals will twist the reported results to such an extent that the net profit ratio (net profit divided by sales) will not accurately reflect the amount of cash generated by each dollar of sales. If there is a disparity between cash flows and the reported net profit, consider using the cash flow return on sales instead. This approach focuses on the amount of cash generated from each dollar of sales, and so provides a more accurate representation of the results of a business.

To calculate the cash flow return on sales, we must first convert the net income figure into an approximation of cash flows by adding back non-cash expenses (though this does not factor in changes in working capital or fixed assets), and divide by net sales for the measurement period. The formula is:

$$\frac{\text{Net profit} + \text{Non-cash expenses}}{\text{Total net sales}}$$

This measurement should be tracked on a trend line to spot long-term tendencies for cash flows to decline. Also, compare this result to the same measurement for competitors, to see how the company performs in relation to a common benchmark.

---

**EXAMPLE**

Grissom Granaries operates grain barges and a tugboat on the Mississippi River, transporting grain on behalf of clients. The new president of Grissom is concerned about the company's low ongoing cash balance, and asks the CFO to calculate the cash flow return on sales for the business. The result shows minimal cash flow. The hefty depreciation charge provides a clue as to where the problem lies. Further investigation reveals that the barges and tugboat are continually running aground, resulting in much faster hull replacement cycles than had been originally anticipated, and therefore excessive investments in fixed assets. The president responds by firing the tugboat captain and installing sonar on the tugboat.

| Net profit | -$1,800,000 |
|---|---|
| Depreciation | $2,000,000 |
| Net sales | $25,000,000 |
| Cash flow return on sales | 0.8% |

---

# Analysis Conclusions

The intent behind requiring a statement of cash flows is excellent, but the format suffers from an excessive level of aggregation, especially for the cash flows from operating activities and investing activities. Nonetheless, there are some analyses that can be conducted. We recommend the following order of priority:

1. *Compare cash from operations to operating profit.* This is the key comparison, for it reveals the extent of any disparity between the profit being reported and the underlying ability of a business to generate cash.
2. *Investigate financing sources.* If the first analysis indicates that a business is running a cash deficit, examine the sources of cash to see how management is financing this deficit. For example, it may involve asset sales, changes in working capital, obtaining more debt, or the sale of stock.

3.  *Investigate special events.* There may be less-common spikes or dips in the amount of cash in or out, which can indicate special activities, such as outsourcing a department, acquiring another business, or settling a lawsuit liability. The statement of cash flows is a good place to initially spot these more unusual activities.

The main problem with the statement of cash flows is that not all entities issue it. Instead, they only issue the income statement and balance sheet. This may be inadvertent, especially in a smaller business where the accounting staff may not have even heard of this report. However, management may also be trying to hide the report in order to mask the presence of negative cash flows. Consequently, always attempt to obtain this report if it is not initially provided.

# Chapter 15
# Other Analysis Topics

## Introduction

The bulk of this book has been concerned with the examination of individual line items in the financial statements, as well as the use of ratio analysis that pertains to specific line items. In addition, the financial statements contain other information that can be of use to the analyst. In the following sections, we describe the different types of work that an outside auditor can perform on an organization's financial statements, the different types of audit opinions, and analyses relating to working capital, breakeven, and dividend performance.

## Financial Statement Audits, Reviews, and Compilations

A financial statement *audit* is the examination of an entity's financial statements and accompanying disclosures by an independent auditor, with the result being a report by the auditor, attesting to the fairness of presentation of the financial statements and related disclosures. The auditor's report must accompany the financial statements when they are issued to the intended recipients.

The purpose of a financial statement audit is to add credibility to the reported financial position and performance of a business. The Securities and Exchange Commission requires that all publicly-held entities must file annual reports with it that are audited. Similarly, lenders typically require an audit of the financial statements of any entity to which they lend funds. Suppliers may also require audited financial statements before they will be willing to extend trade credit (though usually only when the amount of requested credit is substantial).

Audit fees can be quite high, so some organizations instead hire auditors to conduct a financial statement *review*. A review has a much more limited scope than an audit, and so does not provide much assurance that all significant matters have been discovered that would have been noted in an audit. Given its more limited scope, a review is generally not allowed by lenders and creditors, who instead want to see the result of a full audit.

In a review, the auditor performs only those procedures necessary to provide a reasonable basis for obtaining limited assurance that no material changes are needed to bring the financial statements into compliance with the applicable financial reporting framework. These procedures are more heavily concentrated in areas where there are enhanced risks of misstatement. Examples of these procedures are ratio analysis, the investigation of unusual or complex accounting transactions, and the investigation of significant journal entries.

Audit firms may provide a financial statement *compilation* service. In a compilation, the auditors engage in no activities to obtain assurance that any material modifications to the financial statements are needed. Thus, auditors do not use inquiries, analytical procedures, or review procedures, nor do they need to obtain an understanding of internal controls or engage in other audit procedures. Lenders and creditors are most unlikely to give any credence to financial statements created through a compilation service.

## Audit Opinions

After an auditor has completed a financial statement audit, he or she can issue several types of audit opinions. These opinions are contained within a highly standardized audit report. An audit report is a written opinion of an auditor regarding whether an entity's financial statements are fairly presented. This is written in a standard format, as mandated by generally accepted auditing standards (GAAS). The normal format of this report is called an unqualified opinion, and means that the auditor is satisfied that the financial statements represent fairly the financial position and results of operations of the entity. A sample of the essential text of an unqualified opinion is:

> In our opinion, the consolidated financial statements referred to above present fairly, in all material respects, the financial position of [company name] as of December 31, 20X3 and 20X2, and the results of its operations and cash flows for each of the years in the three-year period ended December 31, 20X3, in conformity with U.S. generally accepted accounting principles.

GAAS requires or allows certain variations in the report, depending on the circumstances of the audit work that the auditor engaged in. For example, the report may include a qualified opinion, depending on the existence of any scope limitations that were imposed on the auditor's work. There may also be qualifications if there was a lack of conformity with the accounting standards, the accompanying disclosures are inadequate, there are uncertainties in the estimates used to develop the financial statements, or if the statement of cash flows has been omitted. An extract from the text of a qualified opinion is:

> ...our audit opinion was qualified for the matter described below.

> In 20X1, management recorded impairment losses pertaining to certain fixed assets amounting to $10,000,000. This impairment loss was determined based on management's projections which assumed that the company will generate significant revenue from exports to a certain market under a proposed agreement currently under active negotiation for which the terms and conditions have not been agreed as of the date of this audit report. We have not obtained sufficient appropriate audit evidence to support the inclusion of the cash flows from these exports. Had management excluded these cash flows from its projections, the company would have recognized an additional impairment loss of $7,000,000. The impact of this adjustment would reduce the carrying amount of fixed assets and shareholders' equity by $7,000,000.

Someone analyzing financial statements should pay close attention to the text of any accompanying audit opinion qualification, to see if the qualification represents a major change to the financial statements. The preceding example contained a major qualification that might represent a sharp drop in the equity of the reporting business.

If an auditor issues an adverse opinion or elects to report no opinion at all, this is a strong indication of problems with the financial statements of a business.

## Working Capital Analysis

In the various balance sheet chapters, we addressed the characteristics of each individual line item, but did not back away from this level of detail to address the overall liquidity of the entity. In particular, it is useful to be aware of the *working capital* position of a business.

Working capital is current assets minus current liabilities. As such, it comprises the amount of short-term cash tied up in an organization to ensure that it can conduct operations. An adequate amount of working capital is needed to extend credit to customers and maintain a sufficient amount of inventory. Offsetting these cash requirements is the amount of credit extended to the business by its suppliers, which takes the form of accounts payable. When interpreting financial statements, the key question is whether a business has a sufficient amount of working capital.

There are numerous indicators of a business having an insufficient amount of working capital, including the following:

- *Late payments*. A business is unable to pay its bills in a timely manner.
- *Late deliveries*. An organization cannot maintain sufficient stocks of inventory, and so must order items from suppliers only after receiving orders for them from customers.
- *Short credit*. An entity is unable to offer generous credit to its customers, instead requiring limited payment terms, or even cash in advance.

Conversely, there are multiple indicators of a business that has adequate working capital, including the following:

- *Early payments*. Its payables turnover is persistently short or at least matches estimated supplier credit terms.
- *No short-term debt*. There may be a line of credit, but it is rarely used.
- *High cash balance*. The business maintains a reasonably high cash balance and may have additional funds parked in short-term investments.
- *Ability to grow*. A business is able to expand its operations without the need for additional funding.

The amount of working capital that an organization needs depends on its business model, in which the differing elements of working capital can play a role in how an organization positions itself with customers. Here are several examples:

- A computer manufacturer takes credit card payments from customers, builds computers only when there is a firm order in hand, and pays its suppliers in 30 days. This entity may require no working capital at all.
- A tractor manufacturer sells directly to small farmers that cannot afford to pay on a timely basis. To be competitive, the manufacturer must offer multi-month credit terms, resulting in massive amounts of accounts receivable.
- A supermarket takes payment from customers in cash, and specializes in turning over its inventory once every few weeks. The business requires a reduced level of working capital.
- A small neighborhood hardware store requires payment in cash, but the service it offers requires it to maintain stocks of rarely-used inventory items, sometimes for many months. In this case, the large inventory investment dominates its working capital needs.

In short, there is no ideal amount of working capital that a business needs to maintain – it depends on the circumstances. Nonetheless, the following two ratios can be used to obtain an indication of whether the amount of working capital is sufficient.

## Quick Ratio

The quick ratio formula matches the most easily liquidated portions of current assets with current liabilities. The intent of this ratio is to see if a business has sufficient assets that are immediately convertible to cash to pay its bills. The key elements of current assets that are included in the quick ratio are cash, marketable securities, and accounts receivable. Inventory is not included in the quick ratio, since it can be quite difficult to sell off in the short term.

To calculate the quick ratio, summarize cash, marketable securities and trade receivables, and divide by current liabilities. Do not include in the numerator any excessively old receivables that are unlikely to be paid. The formula is:

$$\frac{\text{Cash} + \text{Marketable securities} + \text{Accounts receivable}}{\text{Current liabilities}}$$

Despite the absence of inventory from the calculation, the quick ratio may still not yield a good view of immediate liquidity, if current liabilities are payable right now, while receipts from receivables are not expected for several more weeks.

## EXAMPLE

The balance sheet of Rapunzel Hair Products reveals that current assets exceed current liabilities by a ratio of four to one. The breakdown of the ratio components is:

| Item | Amount |
|---|---|
| Cash | $100,000 |
| Marketable securities | 50,000 |
| Accounts receivable | 420,000 |
| Inventory | 3,430,000 |
| Current liabilities | 1,000,000 |
| | |
| Quick ratio | 0.57:1 |

The component breakdown reveals that nearly all of Rapunzel's current assets are in the inventory area, where short-term liquidity is questionable. This issue is only visible when the quick ratio is calculated.

## Working Capital Productivity

The working capital productivity measurement compares sales to working capital. The intent is to measure whether a business has invested in a sufficient amount of working capital to support its sales. From a financing perspective, management wants to maintain low working capital levels in order to keep from having to raise more cash to operate the business. This can be achieved by such techniques as issuing less credit to customers, implementing just-in-time systems to avoid investing in inventory, and lengthening payment terms to suppliers.

Conversely, if the ratio indicates that a business has a large amount of receivables and inventory, this means that the organization is investing too much capital in return for the amount of sales that it is generating.

To decide whether the working capital productivity ratio is reasonable, compare a company's results to those of competitors or benchmark businesses.

To derive working capital productivity, divide annual revenues by the total amount of working capital. The formula is:

$$\frac{\text{Annual revenues}}{\text{Total working capital}}$$

When using this measurement, consider including the annualized quarterly sales in order to gain a better short-term understanding of the relationship between working capital and sales. Also, the measurement can be misleading if calculated during a seasonal spike in sales, since the formula will match high sales with a depleted inventory level to produce an unusually high ratio.

**EXAMPLE**

A lender is concerned that Pianoforte International does not have sufficient financing to support its sales. The lender obtains Pianoforte's financial statements, which contain the following information:

| | |
|---|---|
| Annual revenues | $7,800,000 |
| Cash | 200,000 |
| Accounts receivable | 800,000 |
| Inventory | 2,000,000 |
| Accounts payable | 400,000 |

With this information, the lender derives the working capital productivity measurement as follows:

$$\frac{\$7,800,000 \text{ Annual revenues}}{\$200,000 \text{ Cash} + \$800,000 \text{ Receivables} + \$2,000,000 \text{ Inventory} - \$400,000 \text{ Payables}}$$

$$= 3:1 \text{ Working capital productivity}$$

This ratio is lower than the industry average of 4:1, which indicates poor management of the company's receivables and inventory. The lender should investigate further to see if the receivable and inventory figures may contain large amounts of overdue or obsolete items, respectively.

## Breakeven and the Margin of Safety

A key concern for the analyst is the ability of a business to generate enough sales volume to earn a profit. The foundation of this analysis is the *breakeven* concept. The breakeven point is the sales volume at which a business earns exactly no money, where all contribution margin (sales minus variable expenses) is needed to pay for the company's fixed costs.

The concept is most easily illustrated in the following chart, where fixed costs occupy a block of expense at the bottom of the table, irrespective of any sales being generated. Variable costs are incurred in concert with the sales level. Once the contribution margin on each sale cumulatively matches the total amount of fixed costs, the breakeven point has been reached. All sales above that level directly contribute to profits.

**Breakeven Table**

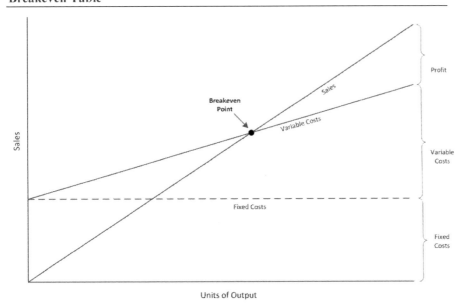

From the perspective of the outside analyst, the breakeven point is useful for determining the sales level below which a business will begin to sustain losses if there is a sales downturn.

In addition, the concept is useful for establishing the overall ability of a company to generate a profit. When the breakeven point is near the maximum sales level of a business, this means it is nearly impossible to earn a profit even under the best of circumstances.

To calculate the breakeven point, divide total fixed expenses by the contribution margin. The formula is:

$$\frac{\text{Total fixed expenses}}{\text{Contribution margin percentage}}$$

A more refined approach is to eliminate all non-cash expenses (such as depreciation) from the numerator, so that the calculation focuses on the breakeven cash flow level. The formula is:

$$\frac{\text{Total fixed expenses} - \text{Depreciation} - \text{Amortization}}{\text{Contribution margin percentage}}$$

**EXAMPLE**

The management of Ninja Cutlery is interested in buying a competitor that makes ceramic knives. The company's due diligence team wants to know if the competitor's breakeven point is too high to allow for a reasonable profit, and if there are any overhead cost opportunities that may reduce the breakeven point. The following information is available:

| | |
|---|---|
| Maximum sales capacity | $5,000,000 |
| Current average sales | $4,750,000 |
| Contribution margin percentage | 35% |
| Total operating expenses | $1,750,000 |
| Breakeven point | $5,000,000 |
| | |
| Operating expense reductions | $375,000 |
| Revised breakeven level | $3,929,000 |
| Maximum profits with revised breakeven point | $375,000 |

The analysis shows that the competitor has an inordinately high breakeven point that allows for little profit, if any. However, there are several operating expense reductions that can trigger a steep decline in the breakeven point. The management of Ninja Cutlery makes an offer to the owners of the competitor, based on the cash flows that can be gained from the reduced breakeven level.

**EXAMPLE**

Milford Sound sells a broad range of audio products. An analyst is concerned that the average contribution margin of these products has been slipping over the past few years, as customers have been switching to personal audio devices. The current average contribution margin is 38%, but the declining trend indicates that the margin could be 30% within two years. The analyst uses this information to construct the following breakeven analysis for the company:

| | Current Case | Projected Case |
|---|---|---|
| Total fixed costs | $20,000,000 | $20,000,000 |
| ÷ Contribution margin | 38% | 30% |
| = Breakeven sales | $52,632,000 | $66,667,000 |

The calculation shows that the breakeven point will increase by $14 million over the next two years. Since Milford's current sales level is $58,000,000, this means that the company faces the alternatives of driving a massive sales increase, fixed cost reductions, or margin improvements in order to remain profitable.

---

The *margin of safety* is the reduction in sales that can occur before the breakeven point of a business is reached. The amount of this buffer is expressed as a percentage.

The margin of safety concept is especially useful when a significant proportion of sales are at risk of decline or elimination, as may be the case when a sales contract is coming to an end. By knowing the amount of the margin of safety, one can gain a better understanding of the risk of loss to which a business is subjected by changes in sales. The opposite situation may also arise, where the margin of safety is so large that a business is well-protected from sales variations.

To calculate the margin of safety, subtract the current breakeven point from sales, and divide the result by sales. The breakeven point is calculated by dividing the contribution margin into total fixed expenses. The formula is:

$$\frac{\text{Total current sales} - \text{Breakeven point}}{\text{Total current sales}}$$

---

**EXAMPLE**

Mulligan Imports is currently reporting sales of $10,000,000. The company has a contribution margin of 32% and fixed costs of $3,000,000. Based on this information, its margin of safety is:

$$\frac{\$10,000,000 \text{ Current sales} - (\$3,000,000 \text{ Fixed costs} \div 32\% \text{ Contribution margin})}{\$10,000,000 \text{ Current sales}}$$

$$=$$

$$\frac{(\$10,000,000 \text{ Current sales} - \$9,375,000 \text{ Breakeven point})}{\$10,000,000 \text{ Current sales}}$$

$$= 6 \tfrac{1}{4}\%$$

Thus, the sales of Mulligan can decline by 6 ¼% before its breakeven point is reached.

---

The resulting percentage may not be entirely accurate, for many businesses will cut back on their baseline expense levels as they approach breakeven, thereby giving themselves a higher margin of safety.

## Dividend Performance

When an investor is inclined to buy the shares of a company that issues dividends, this person or entity is called an *income investor*. An income investor values the stock based on the ability of the issuer to reliably pay out a predictable dividend on an ongoing basis. This type of investor is likely to use the dividend payout ratio to determine the proportion of company income being paid out in the form of dividends, to see if the dividends are sufficiently large, and if they can be sustained. Investors also use the dividend yield ratio to calculate the return on their investment, based on a comparison of dividends paid and the market price of the stock. Both ratios are described in this section.

The dividend payout information used in these ratios is not necessarily contained within the financial statements. Nonetheless, dividend performance is so commonly calculated by analysts that it is necessary to include the following ratios in the interpretation of financial statements.

**Dividend Payout Ratio**

Investors who want a dividend will evaluate a company based on its dividend payout ratio. This ratio is the percentage of a company's earnings paid out to its shareholders in the form of dividends. There are two ways to calculate the dividend payout ratio; each one results in the same outcome. One version is to divide total dividends paid by net income. The calculation is:

$$\frac{\text{Total dividends paid}}{\text{Net income}}$$

The alternative version essentially calculates the same information, but at the individual share level. The formula is to divide total dividend payments over the course of a year on a per-share basis by earnings per share for the same period. The calculation is:

$$\frac{\text{Annual dividend paid per share}}{\text{Earnings per share}}$$

---

**EXAMPLE**

The Conemaugh Cell Phone Company paid out $1,000,000 in dividends to its common shareholders in the last year. In the same time period, the company earned $2,500,000 in net income. The dividend payout ratio is:

$$\frac{\$1,000,000 \text{ Dividends paid}}{\$2,500,000 \text{ Net income}}$$

$$= 40\% \text{ Dividend payout ratio}$$

---

Investors interested in the long-term viability of a series of dividend payments will likely track the dividend payout ratio on a trend line, to see if a business is generating enough income to support its dividend payments over a number of years. If not, they may sell off their shares, thereby driving down the stock price. If an investor sees that the payout ratio is nearly 100% or greater than that amount, then the current dividend level is probably not sustainable. Conversely, if the ratio is quite low, investors will consider the risk of a dividend cutback to also be low, and so will be more inclined to buy the stock, thereby driving up its price.

Investors may also look at the reverse of the dividend payout ratio to see how much of earnings are being retained within a business. If the retention amount is declining, this indicates that the company does not see a sufficient return on investment to be worthy of plowing additional cash back into the business. From this perspective, a declining retention rate will drive away those growth-oriented investors who rely on an increasing share price.

In short, investors rely on ratio analysis on a trend line to determine whether a business is issuing an appropriate amount of dividends, and may alter their stock holdings based on the outcome of this analysis.

From the perspective of a company that is issuing dividends, the main concern is whether the business is capable of issuing a certain dividend amount on a sustained basis. If cash flows have a history of being quite variable, then it will make more sense to set a dividend that can be paid even when the company is suffering through a low point in its business cycle. Conversely, if cash flows are quite stable, then a higher dividend can likely be sustained over time. An additional concern is whether there are internal uses for cash that will generate greater returns for investors over the long term than an immediate dividend. If so, the company's board of directors must weigh the two alternatives and decide how the cash should be used.

## Dividend Yield Ratio

The dividend yield ratio reveals the amount of dividends that a company pays to its investors in comparison to the market price of its stock. Thus, the ratio is the return on investment if an investor were to have bought shares at the market price on the measurement date.

To calculate the ratio, divide the annual dividends paid per share by the market price of the stock at the end of the measurement period. Since the stock price is measured on a single date, and that measurement may not be representative of the stock price over the measurement period, consider using an average stock price instead. The calculation is:

$$\frac{\text{Annual dividends paid per share}}{\text{Market price of the stock}}$$

---

**EXAMPLE**

Horton Corporation pays dividends of $4.50 and $5.50 per share to its investors in the current fiscal year. At the end of the fiscal year, the market price of its stock is $80.00, which is a representative value for its shares over the entire year. Horton's dividend yield ratio is:

$$\frac{\$10 \text{ Dividends paid}}{\$80 \text{ Share price}}$$

$$= 12.5\% \text{ Dividend yield ratio}$$

---

When deriving and using this measurement, be aware of the following issues:

- *Consistent dividend measurement.* The calculation should be based only on dividends paid, not on dividends declared but not yet paid. Otherwise, there is a risk of double-counting, where dividends declared are included in the measurement for one period, and then included again in the measurement for the next period when the dividends are actually paid.

- *Consistent share price measurement.* If you elect to use an average market price for the stock that spans a number of days or months, use the same averaging technique for all measured periods. Otherwise, a likely result is inconsistent measurements that reveal little about the actual yield being generated. This is a particular problem when a company's share price is highly variable.

## Analysis Conclusions

Despite being "miscellaneous" topics, the subjects in this chapter can be quite important elements of a comprehensive analysis of financial statements. Several key points are:

- A full audit of a company's financial statements, accompanied by an unqualified opinion, gives considerable credence to the accuracy of the presented information. Conversely, no audit or a highly qualified opinion casts doubt upon whether financial statements can be relied upon.
- The working capital productivity measure is a reliable indicator of the amount of working capital that a company needs to operate. Any future deviation from this historical proportion can indicate issues with maintaining a sufficient level of liquidity to operate a business.
- Always calculate the breakeven point of a business. If this point happens to coincide with the maximum sales that a business can achieve, then the entity will likely fail. Conversely, a low breakeven point is a strong indicator of the ability of a business to weather serious downturns in its sales. Continue to calculate the breakeven point shortly after a business rolls out a new product line or adds a subsidiary, to see if these changes have altered the breakeven point in any way.

# Chapter 16
# Additional Public Company Information

## Introduction

If a business is publicly-held, the amount of information available for the analyst is vastly greater than just the financial statements that we have been describing in the preceding chapters. In addition, the Securities and Exchange Commission (SEC) requires a massive amount of additional reporting. This chapter covers the SEC's reporting requires for all of the major reporting areas within the Form 10-K, which must be issued by each publicly-held company following the end of its fiscal year, along with sample disclosures that were modified from actual SEC filings. We also make suggestions at the end of the chapter regarding key analyses that can be extracted from the report.

The Form 10-K is the traditional "mother lode" that most analysts will access as part of the research into a company's financial statements. However, this is not the only report issued by public companies. Other reports include:

- *Form 10-Q.* This is the quarterly version of the Form 10-K. Its filing requirements are somewhat reduced from those of the Form 10-K. Its greatest value is in providing more current information than what can be found in the Form 10-K.
- Form 8-K. This form is used to disclose a broad range of material events that impact a business, and must be filed within four business days of the triggering event. Many of these reports may be filed each year, and provide the best source of immediate information about a business.
- *Forms 3, 4, and 5.* These forms are used to disclose the holdings of corporate insiders in the reporting entity, and any changes in that ownership. The information can be interpreted as indications of how insiders feel about the financial prospects of a business.
- *Form S-1.* A company that wants to sell registered stock must file a registration statement with the SEC. This Form S-1 is an extremely detailed document that describes a company's financial and operational condition, as well as other matters.

All of these reports are available for downloading at the SEC website, which is www.sec.gov.

## The Form 10-K

A publicly-held company is required to issue the Form 10-K to report the results of its fiscal year. The Form 10-K includes not just the financial statements, but also a number of additional disclosures. The following table itemizes the more common disclosures. Examples of these disclosures are noted in the following sub-sections.

**Selection of Form 10-K Disclosures**

| Item Header | Description |
|---|---|
| **Item 1.** Business | Provide a description of the company's purpose, history, operating segments, customers, suppliers, sales and marketing operations, customer support, intellectual property, competition, and employees. It should tell readers what the company does and describe its business environment. |
| **Item 1A.** Risk factors | A thorough listing of all risks that the company may experience. It warns investors of what could reduce the value of their investments in the company. |
| **Item 1B.** Unresolved staff comments | Disclose all unresolved comments received from the SEC if they are material. |
| **Item 2.** Properties | Describe the leased or owned facilities of the business, including square footage, lease termination dates, and lease amounts paid per month. |
| **Item 3.** Legal proceedings | Describe any legal proceedings currently involving the company, and its estimate of the likely outcome of those proceedings. |
| **Item 4.** Mine safety disclosures | If applicable, discuss mine safety laws, and the types of warnings and penalties that occurred during the reporting period. |
| **Item 5.** Market for company stock | Describe where the company's stock trades and the number of holders of record, as well as the high and low closing prices per share, by quarter. |
| **Item 6.** Selected financial data | For the last five years, state selected information from the company's income statement and balance sheet (should be in tabular comparative format). |
| **Item 7.** Management's discussion and analysis (MD&A) | Describe opportunities, challenges, risks, trends, future plans, and key performance indicators, as well as changes in revenues, the cost of goods sold, other expenses, assets, and liabilities. |
| **Item 7A.** Quantitative and qualitative disclosures about market risk | Quantify the market risk at the end of the last fiscal year for the company's market risk-sensitive instruments. |

| Item Header | Description |
| --- | --- |
| **Item 8.** Financial statements and supplementary data | Make all disclosures required by GAAP, including descriptions of:<br>• Accrued liabilities<br>• Acquisitions<br>• Discontinued operations<br>• Fixed assets<br>• Income taxes<br>• Related party transactions<br>• Segment information<br>• Stock options |
| **Item 9.** Changes in and disagreements with accountants on accounting and financial disclosure | Describe any disagreements with the auditors when management elects to account for or disclose transactions in a manner different from what the auditors want. |
| **Item 9A.** Controls and procedures | Generally describe the system of internal controls, testing of controls, changes in controls, and management's conclusions regarding the effectiveness of those controls. |
| **Item 10.** Directors, executive officers and corporate governance | Identify the executive officers, directors, promoters, and individuals classified as control persons. |
| **Item 11.** Executive compensation | Itemize the types of compensation paid to company executives. |
| **Item 12.** Security ownership of certain beneficial owners and management and related stockholder matters | State the number of shares of all types owned or controlled by certain individuals classified as beneficial owners and/or members of management. |
| **Item 13.** Certain relationships and related transactions, and director independence | If there were transactions with related parties during the past fiscal year, and the amounts involved exceeded $120,000, describe the transactions. |

| Item Header | Description |
|---|---|
| **Item 14.** Principal accountant fees and services | State the aggregate amount of any fees billed in each of the last two fiscal years for professional services rendered by the company's auditors for:<br>• Reviews and audits;<br>• Audit-related activities;<br>• Taxation work; and<br>• All other fees. |
| **Item 15.** Exhibits and financial statement schedules | Item 601 of Regulation S-K requires that a business attach a number of exhibits to the Form 10-K, including (but not limited to):<br>• Code of ethics<br>• Material contracts<br>• Articles of incorporation<br>• Bylaws<br>• Acquisition purchase agreements |

The following sub-sections contain examples of the items just noted for the Form 10-K.

## Item 1. Business

The description of the business that is required by the SEC can be quite extensive. A summarized version of the SEC's requirements in this area is as follows:

- Describe the general development of the business during the past five years. Note the year of organization, and the form of organization, the nature and results of any bankruptcy proceedings, and the nature and results of any material mergers or consolidations.
- Report revenues, profit or loss, and assets for each business segment for each of the last three fiscal years. This presentation may be cross-referenced to the financial statements.
- Describe the business done by the company, and what it intends to do, focusing on the dominant segment or each reportable segment. This includes the company's principal products and services, and methods by which they are distributed. Also note the following:
  - For each of the last three years, the amount or percentage of total revenue contributed by each class of products or services which account for 10 percent or more of revenues.
  - The status of new products or services, without revealing information that would interfere with the competitive stance of the business.
  - The sources and availability of raw materials.

- o The duration and effect on the business of the patents, trademarks, licenses, concessions, and so forth that the organization holds.
- o The extent to which the business is seasonal.
- o The need for working capital within the industry, and by the company, such as to offer long credit terms to customers.
- o The dependence of the business on one or a few customers. Disclose the names of these customers if the amount sold to each one equals or exceeds 10 percent of the company's revenues.
- o The dollar amount of firm customer orders on backlog, as compared to a similar period in the preceding year. Also note any seasonal or other material aspects of the backlog.
- o Any material portion of the business that may be subject to renegotiation of profits, or in which contracts can be terminated by the government.
- o The competitive conditions in the industry, including an estimate of the number of competitors and the competitive position of the company within the industry. Dominant competitors should be identified. Note the principal methods of competition, such as by price, service level, or product performance.
- o The amount spent in each of the past three years on research and development activities.
- o The material effects that compliance with government regulations concerning the discharge of materials into the environment has had upon capital expenditures, earnings, and the company's competitive position.
- o The number of persons employed by the company.
- Describe the following financial information about the geographic areas in which the company did business for each of the last three fiscal years:
  - o Revenues from customers attributed to the company's home country, all foreign countries in total, and any individual foreign country, if material.
  - o Long-lived assets located in the company's home country, all foreign countries in total, and any individual foreign country, if material.
- Describe any risks related to the foreign operations and any dependence of the company's segments on its foreign operations.

This section of the Form 10-K can be massive. A much abbreviated example of Item 1 follows:

The mission of Ninja Cutlery is to be the premier provider of knives to commercial chefs, worldwide. The company was incorporated in New York in 19X5 by four partners, all professional chefs and amateur knife makers. All four partners remain with the company today in various senior management roles. Ninja began offering knife products in 19X5, and has continued to expand its product line since then.

Ninja has two operating segments. One follows the original mission of the company, manufacturing and distributing cutlery to commercial chefs. Distribution is through independent retailers and mailed catalogs. Only high-end knife products are sold, including carbon-steel blades and ceramic self-sharpening knives. The other segment serves the backwoods survival market with low-cost plastic-and-steel multi-purpose blades that are intended for abbreviated use. This segment sells direct to consumers through an on-line store, as well as through Army-Navy stores.

Ninja has a diverse customer base that includes many of the largest restaurant chains in the ten countries where Ninja products are sold. In 20X3, our largest customer was Lethal Sushi, which generated 8% of total sales for the commercial knife division. The Sharper Edge retail chain is the largest retail purchaser of the division's products, comprising 11% of the segment's sales in 20X3.

Ninja obtains the metal for its knife blades from Artisanal Metal Products, and its ceramic blades from Ferro-Cast Corporation. Knife handles are cast in-house, using commodity-grade rubber and plastic beads obtained from several suppliers.

Sales and marketing operations are conducted by an in-house direct sales staff for all sales in the United States. A locally-based sales staff is used to solicit sales in all other countries where Ninja sells its products. The survival market is serviced through an on-line store, as well as a separate in-house sales staff that maintains relations with Army-Navy stores. Marketing efforts include a well-maintained web site, a quarterly e-newsletter to selected retailers and restaurant chains, attendance at trade shows, participation in selected trade associations and an assortment of collateral materials.

Sales cycles are quite short. Customers place orders for standard products, and orders typically ship within two business days. We do not provide custom products, so there is no need for a produce-to-order system. Instead, goods are produced to stock and then shipped as needed.

We maintain a customer service department in our New York location, which is open during regular business hours to assist customers. All customer contacts handled through the customer service desk are tracked using a customer relationship database. We have posted training manuals on the company website that discuss the proper use and maintenance of all of our knife products.

The carbon blade knives used by the commercial chef segment rely heavily on intellectual property, since the blades use a patented technology developed by the company. Ferro-Cast Corporation is the only licensed user of this technology, and Ferro-Cast is only allowed to produce blades for Ninja. We regard our intellectual property as a valuable asset and use intellectual property laws, as well as confidentiality agreements with our employees and others to protect our rights. In addition, we exercise reasonable measures to protect our intellectual property rights and enforce these rights when we become aware of any potential or actual violation or misuse.

The dominant player in the knife marketplace is Universal Blades, which primarily sells knives for use in the residential kitchen. There is little direct competition with

Universal, since the price points at which we sell our products are much too high for the typical home cook. Other competitors include The Point Brothers, Scissor Results, Carvers, Inc., and Chop Knives. These other companies occupy competitive positions with lower price points and product quality levels than Ninja's and so tend to compete more directly with Universal than with Ninja.

As of December 31, 20X3, we employed 240 employees, of which 10 were part time employees, and all of whom are located within the United States. The sales staff that sells in other countries is also based in the United States. None of the employees are represented by a collective bargaining agreement, and employee relations are considered to be good.

## Item 1A. Risk Factors

The SEC insists on comprehensive statements regarding every possible risk factor to which a business may be subjected. More specifically, the SEC offers the following advice regarding the disclosure of risks:

- State the most significant risk factors that make the company's shares speculative or risky.
- Explain how the risk affects the company.
- The risk factors may include:
    o The lack of an operating history
    o The lack of profitable operations in recent periods
    o The financial position of the business
    o The business or proposed business

Corporate counsel also wants to include all possible risks, on the grounds that doing so gives investors reduced grounds for initiating lawsuits if they were already warned of risks. This typically results in long lists of risks, of which the following sample provides an overview:

> You should carefully consider the following risks and all of the other information set forth in this report. If any of the events or developments described below actually occurs, our business, financial condition, and results of operations may suffer. In that case, the trading price of our common stock may decline and you could lose all or part of your investment.

Some of the risks related to the business include:

- *Affiliate control*. Members of Ninja's Board of Directors and its executive officers, together with their affiliates, own a significant number of shares of Ninja outstanding common stock. Accordingly, these stockholders, if they act together, can have significant control over matters requiring approval of company stockholders, including the election of directors and approval of significant corporate transactions. The concentration of ownership, which could result in a continued concentration of representation on the Board of Directors, may delay, prevent or deter a change in control and could deprive stockholders of an opportunity to receive a premium for their common stock as part of a sale of our assets. Ninja's directors, executive officers and other affiliates will continue to exert significant control over the company's future direction, which could reduce its future sale value.

- *Customer concentrations.* In the commercial chef market, sales to large restaurant chains comprise a significant proportion of total company sales. The termination of sales to Ninja's five largest restaurant chain customers would eliminate 35% of that segment's total sales. The company cannot be certain that current customers will continue to purchase from it.

- *Dividends.* The company has never declared or paid any cash dividends or distributions on its common stock and intends to retain future earnings, if any, to support operations and to finance expansion. Therefore, the company does not anticipate paying any cash dividends on the common stock in the foreseeable future.

- *Funding availability.* Given the state of the current credit markets, it may be difficult to obtain funds for either operational needs or prospective acquisitions. Ninja currently has $3 million of debt funding available through a previously authorized loan through Fourth National Bank. The company's next-year budget projects sufficient cash requirements to use all but $500,000 of the available debt funding.

- *Growth strategy.* Ninja's growth strategy involves expanding into additional foreign markets. The company's ability to do so may be negatively impacted by the need to work with foreign partners, as well as to sell into markets where there may be currency restrictions. There may also be cases in which vigorous local competition from existing businesses could impede Ninja's ability to gain any significant market share.

- *Industry trends.* The company derives a large part of its revenue from customers in the commercial restaurant business. As a result, Ninja's business, financial condition, and results of operations depend upon the conditions and trends affecting this industry. For example, a decline in consumer spending could lead restaurant chains to reduce their spending on kitchen supplies, which would reduce Ninja's sales.

- *Patent protection.* The patent protecting the company's use of carbon blade knives will expire in 20X9. At that time, competitors may use the same technology to create their own knife blades, which could result in extensive price competition. If so, the company's margins on the sale of this product will likely decline.

- *Personnel loss.* The future success of the company depends in part on the continued service of the executive officers and other key management, sales, and operations personnel, and on the company's ability to continue to attract, motivate, and retain additional highly qualified employees. The loss of the services of one or more of these people, or the company's inability to recruit replacements for them or to otherwise attract, motivate, or retain qualified personnel could have an adverse effect on the business, its operating results, and financial condition.

- *Stock sales.* Sales of substantial amounts of Ninja common stock in the public market, or the perception that such sales could occur, could adversely affect the market price of its shares. Any sales of common stock by Ninja or its principal stockholders, or the perception that such sales might occur, could have a material adverse effect on the price of Ninja shares.

- *Stock price volatility.* The company's share price is likely to fluctuate in the future because of the volatility of the stock market in general and a variety of factors, many of which are beyond the control of the company, including:
  - o Quarterly variations in actual or anticipated results of operations;
  - o Changes in financial estimates by securities analysts;
  - o Actions or announcements by the company or its competitors;
  - o Regulatory actions;
  - o Litigation;
  - o Loss or gain of major customers;
  - o Additions or departures of key personnel; and
  - o Future sales of the company's common stock.

These fluctuations may result in an immediate and significant decline in the trading price of Ninja's common stock, which could cause a decline in the value of an investor's investment.

## Item 1B. Unresolved Staff Comments

Certain types of companies are required to make note of any unresolved SEC staff comments regarding their reports. In these situations, disclose the substance of the unresolved comments that the company considers to be material. The company may also note its position regarding these comments. The following is a sample disclosure related to unresolved staff comments:

The company received a comment letter from the SEC dated November 10, 20X3 regarding its quarterly report on Form 10-Q for the quarter ended September 30, 20X3. These comments are unresolved as of March 2, 20X4. We have filed with the SEC a response to the comment letter. Additionally, we have incorporated into our subsequent periodic filings with the SEC additional disclosures that we believe are responsive to the SEC's comments.

In general, the unresolved staff comments relate to the methodologies used to determine a reserve for obsolete inventory, and how evenly those methodologies are applied across our various product lines. We believe that the ultimate resolution of these comments will not have a material impact on our consolidated financial statements and/or related footnotes.

## Item 2. Properties

This section should contain descriptions of the leased or owned facilities of the business, as enumerated by the SEC:

- State the location and character of the principal plants, mines and other materially important physical properties of the company. In addition, identify the business segments that use the properties described. If any property is not held in fee or is held subject to a major encumbrance, describe the situation.

- In the case of an extractive business that does not involve oil and gas producing activities, describe production, reserves, locations, development, and the nature of the company's interest. If individual properties are of major significance to an industry segment, supply more detailed information and disclose the locations of these properties.
- In the case of extractive reserves other than oil and gas reserves, do not disclose estimates other than proven or probable reserves.

If there are a number of facilities, consider providing the information in a tabular format. Consider the following example text:

The company's principal locations, their purposes and the expiration dates for the leases on facilities at those locations as of June 30, 20X3 are shown in the table below. Ninja has renewal options on several of its leases.

| Location | Purpose | Approximate Square Feet | Principal Lease Expiration Dates |
|---|---|---|---|
| Corning, New York | Corporate headquarters | 30,000 | Owned |
| Little Falls, New York | Main assembly facility | 45,000 | 20X9 |
| Port Jervis, New York | Knife handle production facility | 52,000 | 20X8 |

Ninja owns its headquarters building, comprising approximately 30,000 square feet, as noted in the preceding table. The table excludes approximately 12,000 square feet for a storage facility that the company has classified as a discontinued operation. Ninja also leases facilities for its sales staff in each country where it conducts sales activities, including the United Kingdom, Italy, and France. The company believes its facilities are suitable and adequate for its current and near-term needs, and that it will be able to locate additional facilities as needed.

## Item 3. Legal Proceedings

The legal proceedings of a business are extensively described in the Form 10-K. The SEC gives the following instructions:

- Describe any material pending legal proceedings, other than ordinary routine litigation incidental to the business, to which the company is a party. Include the name of the court or agency in which the proceedings are pending, the date instituted, the principal parties, the factual basis alleged to underlie the proceeding and the relief sought.
- Do not include information about lawsuits that involve a claim for damages if the amount involved does not exceed 10 percent of the current assets of the company.
- Describe any material bankruptcy, receivership, or similar proceeding.
- Describe any material proceedings to which any director, officer or affiliate of the company, any owner of record or beneficially of more than five per-

cent of any class of voting securities of the company, or security holder is a party adverse to the company.

- Describe any administrative or judicial proceeding arising under any government provisions regulating the discharge of materials into the environment or for the purpose of protecting the environment, if material to the business.

For example:

In August 20X2, Outdoor Devices (OD) brought suit against Ninja, seeking monetary damages and injunctive relief based on Ninja's alleged infringement of certain patents held by OD. Specifically, OD identified the company's FlipBlade product as infringing the patents OD is asserting. On the company's motion, the case was transferred to the United States District Court for New York. In October 20X2, OD voluntarily dismissed its claims asserted against the FlipBlade. In November 20X2, the court entered a final judgment in this case, dismissing OD's claim. The time for filing an appeal of the decision has now passed, and neither party filed an appeal.

From time to time, the company has received notices from third parties alleging infringement of such parties' patent or other intellectual property rights by the company's products. In such cases it is the company's policy to defend the claims, or if considered appropriate, negotiate licenses on commercially reasonable terms. However, no assurance can be given that the company will be able to negotiate necessary licenses on commercially reasonable terms, or at all, or that any litigation resulting from such claims would not have a material adverse effect on the company's consolidated financial position, liquidity, operating results, or consolidated financial statements taken as a whole.

## Item 4. Mine Safety Disclosures

The discussion of mine safety issues only applies to a minority of situations, and in all other cases can be tagged as not applicable. Where such disclosures *do* apply, make note of the following information:

- For each coal or other mine of which the company is an operator, identify the mine and disclose:
  - The total number of violations of mandatory health or safety standards that could significantly contribute to the cause and effect of a coal or other mine safety or health hazard for which the operator received a citation from the Mine Safety and Health Administration (MSHA)
  - The total number of orders issued by MSHA
  - The total number of citations and orders for unwarranted failure of the mine operator to comply with mandatory health or safety standards by MSHA
  - The total number of flagrant violations
  - The total number of imminent danger orders issued

- o The total dollar value of proposed assessments from MSHA
- o The total number of mining-related fatalities
- A list of the coal or other mines, of which the company is an operator, that receive written notice from MSHA of:
  - o A pattern of violations of mandatory health or safety standards that are of such nature as could have significantly contributed to the cause and effect of coal or other mine health or safety hazards
  - o The potential to have such a pattern
- Any pending legal action before the Federal Mine Safety and Health Review Commission involving such coal or other mine.

For example:

The following disclosures are provided pursuant to the Dodd-Frank Wall Street Reform and Consumer Protection Act and Item 104 of Regulation S-K, which requires certain disclosures by companies required to file periodic reports under the Exchange Act that operate mines regulated under the Federal Mine Safety and Health Act of 1988. Whenever the Federal Mine Safety and Health Administration MSHA) believes a violation of the Mine Act, any health or safety standard or any regulation has occurred, it may issue a citation which describes the alleged violation and fixes a time within which the operator must abate the alleged violation. In some situations, such as when MSHA believes that conditions pose a hazard to miners, MSHA may issue an order removing miners from the area of the mine affected by the condition until the alleged hazards are corrected.

When the MSHA issues a citation or order, it generally proposes a civil penalty, or fine, as a result of the alleged violation, that the operator is ordered to pay. Citations and orders can be contested and appealed, and as part of that process, are often reduced in severity and amount, and are sometimes dismissed. The following table reflects citations and orders issued to the company by MSHA during the year ended December 31, 20X3.

|  | Total Number of Significant and Substantial Violations | Total Number of Citations and Orders Issued | Total Number of Imminent Danger Orders | Total Amount of Proposed Assessments from MSHA |
|---|---|---|---|---|
| Meager Mine | 4 | 1 | 1 | $29,540 |

## Item 5. Market for Company Stock

The SEC wants investors to understand the markets in which a company's stock is sold, the prices at which its shares have traded recently, who holds the stock, the amount of dividends paid out, and similar information. More specifically, the SEC mandates that the following information be disclosed:

- The principal United States market in which each class of the company's common stock is traded, or note if there is no established market for the stock. Also state the high and low sales prices for the stock for each full quarterly period within the two most recent fiscal years and any subsequent interim period.

- The approximate number of holders of each class of common stock of the company as of the latest practicable date.
- The frequency and amount of any cash dividends declared on each class of the company's common stock for the two most recent fiscal years and any subsequent interim period. Describe any restrictions on the ability of the company to pay dividends. If there is no intent to pay cash dividends in the foreseeable future, state that point. If an entity has a history of paying cash dividends, indicate whether there is an expectation to continue doing so in the future; if not, state the nature of the change in the amount or rate of cash dividend payments.
- For any equity compensation plans approved or not approved by shareholders, state the number of securities to be issued upon the exercise of outstanding options and similar instruments, the weighted-average price of these instruments, and the number of securities remaining available for future issuance under the plans. Also describe the material features of these plans.
- A line graph that compares the yearly percentage change in the company's cumulative total shareholder return on each class of registered common stock, alongside both of the following for comparison purposes:
  - The cumulative total return of the broad equity market index that includes companies whose equity securities are traded on the same exchange or are of comparable market capitalization
  - The cumulative total return of a published industry index, or a peer entity, or issuers with similar market capitalizations

For example:

Since February 15, 19X8, the company's stock has traded on the NASDAQ Capital Market under the trading symbol "NINJ". The following table sets forth the quarterly high and low selling prices for the company's stock as reported on the NASDAQ since January 1, 20X2.

|  | Common Stock | |
| --- | --- | --- |
|  | High | Low |
| **Fiscal Year Ended December 31, 20X2** | $15.50 | $14.00 |
| Fiscal quarter ended March 31, 20X2 | $15.53 | $13.91 |
| Fiscal quarter ended June 30, 20X2 | $15.10 | $13.01 |
| Fiscal quarter ended September 30, 20X2 | $13.49 | $12.81 |
| Fiscal quarter ended December 31, 20X2 |  |  |
|  |  |  |
| **Fiscal Year Ended December 31, 20X3** |  |  |
| Fiscal quarter ended March 31, 20X3 | $13.58 | $12.77 |
| Fiscal quarter ended June 30, 20X3 | $13.08 | $12.20 |
| Fiscal quarter ended September 30, 20X3 | $12.34 | $11.68 |
| Fiscal quarter ended December 31, 20X3 | $10.19 | $10.00 |

As of February 4, 20X4, there were 1,512 holders of record of Ninja's common stock, and the closing stock price was $10.15.

The annual changes for the five-year period shown in the following graph are based on the assumption that $100 had been invested in Ninja stock, the Standard & Poor's 500 Stock Index (S&P 500) and the Dow Jones Industrial Average (DJIA) on December 31, 20X8, and that all quarterly dividends were reinvested. The total cumulative dollar returns shown on the graph represent the value that such investments would have had on December 31, 20X3.

**Five-Year Financial Performance Graph**

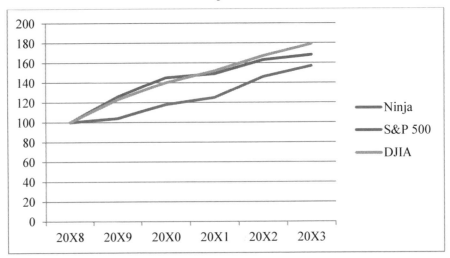

|  | 20X8 | 20X9 | 20X0 | 20X1 | 20X2 | 20X3 |
|---|---|---|---|---|---|---|
| Ninja | 100 | 104 | 118 | 125 | 146 | 157 |
| S&P 500 | 100 | 126 | 145 | 149 | 163 | 168 |
| DJIA | 100 | 123 | 140 | 152 | 167 | 179 |

Following is a summary of dividends declared per common share during the fiscal year 20X3 (in thousands, except per share amounts):

| Date of Declaration | Dividend per Common Share | Date of Record | Date of Payment | Total Amount |
|---|---|---|---|---|
| December 8, 20X2 | $0.15 | January 10, 20X3 | January 20, 20X3 | $450 |
| February 27, 20X3 | 0.15 | April 12, 20X3 | April 22, 20X3 | 525 |
| June 7, 20X3 | 0.15 | June 24, 20X3 | July 5, 20X3 | 570 |
| September 8, 20X3 | 0.20 | September 19, 20X3 | September 29, 20X3 | 590 |

The company will pay future dividends at the discretion of the board of directors. The continuation of these payments, the amount of such dividends, and the form in which the dividends are paid (cash or stock) depend on many factors, including the results of operations and the financial condition of the company. Subject to these qualifications, the company currently expects to pay dividends on a quarterly basis.

162

## Item 6. Selected Financial Data

The SEC mandates that financial data be provided by the company that gives readers a view of performance levels over time. This information is to be provided in columnar format, and should include the following items for each of the last five years:

- Net sales or operating revenues
- Income or loss from continuing operations
- Income or loss from continuing operations per common share
- Total assets
- Long-term obligations and redeemable preferred stock
- Cash dividends declared per common share

Additional items may be included if doing so would enhance the understanding of the reader. Also note factors such as accounting changes, or business combinations or dispositions that materially affect the comparability of the information appearing in the selected financial data. Finally, discuss any material uncertainties where these issues might cause the data stated in this section to not be indicative of the company's future financial condition or its results of operations. A sample disclosure that follows these instructions is:

The following selected data are derived from the company's consolidated financial statements and should be read in conjunction with "Item 7. Management's Discussion and Analysis of Financial Condition and Results of Operations" and "Item 8. Financial Statements and Supplementary Data". All financial information presented in the following table is in thousands, except per share amounts.

| | December 31, 20X3 | December 31, 20X2 | December 31, 20X1 | December 31, 20X0 | December 31, 20X9 |
|---|---|---|---|---|---|
| Sales | $61,700 | $43,000 | $38,200 | $33,500 | $29,000 |
| Cost of goods sold | 24,700 | 17,200 | 15,300 | 13,400 | 11,600 |
| Gross profit | 37,000 | 25,800 | 22,900 | 20,100 | 17,400 |
| Administrative expenses | 26,400 | 20,900 | 18,300 | 16,600 | 15,000 |
| Operating income | 10,600 | $4,900 | $4,600 | $3,500 | $2,400 |
| Interest expense | 3,600 | 300 | -- | -- | -- |
| Provision for income taxes | 2,400 | 1,600 | 1,600 | 1,200 | 800 |
| Net income | $4,600 | $3,000 | $3,000 | $2,300 | $1,600 |
| | | | | | |
| Operating income per share | $5.30 | $2.45 | $2.30 | $1.75 | $1.20 |
| Dividends declared per share | $1.37 | $1.20 | -- | -- | -- |
| | | | | | |
| Total assets | $17,020 | $11,860 | $10,540 | $9,250 | $8,000 |
| Long-term debt | $32,000 | $5,000 | -- | -- | -- |

## Item 7. Management's Discussion and Analysis of Financial Condition and Results of Operation (MD&A)

This section of the Form 10-K traditionally receives the most attention from the analyst, since it is used to explain the information appearing in the financial statements. It is an area that also receives a detailed perusal from the SEC, and which may trigger occasional comment letters from the SEC. Pertinent topics include:

- Discuss the company's financial condition, changes in financial condition and results of operations for the years presented, which shall include the following items:
  - o Identify trends, demands, commitments, events, or uncertainties that can reasonably result in material changes in the liquidity of the entity; if there is a material deficiency, note the course of action that has been or will be taken. Also describe the company's internal and external sources of liquidity, and discuss any material unused sources of liquid assets.
  - o Describe the company's material commitments for capital expenditures; indicate their purpose, and the source of funds to fulfill these commitments. Also note any material trends in the company's capital resources. Further, describe any expected material changes in the mix and relative cost of these resources.
  - o Describe any infrequent or unusual events or transactions or significant economic changes that materially affected the amount of reported income, and the extent to which income was affected.
  - o Discuss other significant components of revenues and expenses that should be addressed in order to understand the company's results of operations.
  - o Describe any trends or uncertainties that have had or that the company reasonably expects will have a material impact on net sales or income from operations.
  - o Discuss the reasons for material increases in net sales, such as the impact of price or unit volume increases, or the introduction of new products.
  - o Address the concept of inflation and changing prices on the company's net sales and income from operations.
  - o Discuss any off-balance sheet arrangements that have had or will have a material effect on the company's financial statements. Also note the nature and purpose of these arrangements, and their importance to the company. Further, state the amounts of revenues, expenses and cash flows of the company arising from these arrangements, the nature and amounts of any interests retained, securities issued and other indebtedness incurred by the company in connection with these arrangements. In addition, note any other obligations of the company arising from these arrangements that could be-

come material, as well as the triggering events that could cause them to arise.

- ○ Describe any known event, demand, commitment, trend or uncertainty that will likely result in the termination or material reduction in availability to the company of those off-balance sheet arrangements that provide material benefits to it, and the course of action the company has taken or can take in response to these circumstances.

- ○ Provide a summary of the company's contractual obligations in tabular format, showing payments due in total, in less than one year, in 1-3 years, in 3-5 years, and in more than 5 years, for the major classes of obligations. These classes may include long-term debt obligations, capital lease obligations, operating lease obligations, and so forth.

- If interim period financial statements are included, this section shall give sufficient information for the reader to assess material changes in financial condition and the results of operations. Note any seasonal aspects of the business which have had a material effect on the financial condition or results of operation of the entity.

The MD&A sections of company filings can be extensive; the following example presents a compressed and non-inclusive set of statements taken from the MD&A language of an assortment of public companies:

The following discussion of our consolidated results of operations and financial condition should be read together with the other financial information and consolidated financial statements included in this Form 10-K. This discussion contains forward-looking statements that involve risks and uncertainties. Our actual results could differ materially from the results anticipated in the forward-looking statements as a result of a variety of factors, including those discussed in "Item 1A. Risk Factors" and elsewhere in this report.

The company's revenue has increased substantially over the past three years, primarily due to our ability to expand the existing product line into new foreign markets, and also the introduction of our new line of ceramic chef knives. Given that sales organizations have only been installed in ten countries, we believe there is a possibility of substantial new growth by continuing to add new markets.

*Net revenue.* The company derives its revenue from limited manufacturing services and product sales. Net revenue increased $18.7 million from the prior year, to $61.7 million in 20X3. The introduction of the company's products in five new foreign markets contributed to approximately $10 million of this amount. $6 million of the remaining increase was attributable to the rollout of a new line of ceramic knives.

*Gross profit.* The company's gross profit increased $11.2 million from the prior year, to $37.0 million in 20X3. The gross profit percentage was the same as the preceding year, indicating that the company was able to apply its standard product pricing in the new geographic regions into which it introduced the full suite of products.

*Administrative expenses.* Selling, general and administrative expenses increased $5.5 million from the prior year, to $26.4 million in 20X3. This represented a reduced proportion of total net revenue, which was caused by the use of more streamlined selling organizations in the new territories into which sales were introduced.

*Interest expense.* Interest expense increased $3.3 million from the prior year, to $3.6 million in 20X3. This was due to a $27 million increase in company debt, which was needed to fund the additional inventory and receivables required to support the new foreign sales regions. Of this amount of debt, $19 million was used to fund additional inventory, and $8 million was used to fund an increase in accounts receivable. The interest rate charged on the company debt increased from 6.0 percent at the end of 20X2 to 7.4% at the end of 20X3.

*Income taxes.* The $2.4 million 20X3 income tax provision consists of current tax expense of $2.7 million and a deferred tax benefit of $0.3 million.

The Company's credit facility provides potential total availability of up of $40 million. Loans made under the credit facility will mature and the commitments thereunder will terminate in May 20X8. Actual borrowing availability under the credit facility is determined by a monthly borrowing base collateral calculation that is based on specified percentages of the value of eligible accounts receivable and inventory. Based on that calculation, as of December 31, 20X3, we had actual total borrowing availability under the credit facility of $34.1 million, of which we had drawn down $29.8 million, leaving $4.3 million available for borrowing. Along with an unrestricted cash balance of $2.1 million, we had total cash and available borrowing capacity of $6.4 million as of December 31, 20X3.

The credit facility contains a number of covenants that limit or restrict our ability to dispose of assets, incur additional indebtedness, incur guarantee obligations, prepay other indebtedness, and pay dividends. Our ability to service our indebtedness will require a significant amount of cash. Our ability to generate this cash will depend largely on future operations. Based on our current level of operations and our current business plan, we expect to be able to meet the financial covenants of our credit facility for at least the next twelve months. However, changing business, regulatory and economic conditions may mean that actual results will vary from our forecasts.

We do not have any material off-balance sheet arrangements that have or are reasonably likely to have a current or future effect on our financial condition, changes in financial condition, revenues or expenses, results of operations, liquidity, capital expenditures or capital resources as of December 31, 20X3.

## Item 7A. Quantitative and Qualitative Disclosures about Market Risk

This classification of disclosure is intended to reveal the extent to which the results of a business can be impacted by changes in such factors as interest rates, exchange rates, and commodity prices. The SEC has exceptionally detailed reporting requirements in this area, for which only the general requirements are noted in the following bullet points:

- Provide quantitative information about market risk as of the end of the latest fiscal year, subdividing information by instruments entered into for trading purposes and instruments entered into for purposes other than trading. Within these categories, present information for each market risk exposure category, such as for interest rate risk, foreign currency exchange rate risk, commodity price risk, and other relevant market risks. This information may be presented using any one of the following three disclosure alternatives:
  - A tabular presentation, from which a reader can determine future cash flows.
  - A sensitivity analysis that discloses the potential loss in future earnings, fair values, or cash flows based on hypothetical changes in interest rates, foreign currency exchange rates, commodity prices, and so forth over time.
  - A value at risk disclosure that expresses the potential loss in future earnings, fair values, or cash flows of market risk sensitive instruments over a period of time, with a likelihood of occurrence, from changes in interest rates, foreign currency exchange rates, commodity prices, and other relevant market rates or prices. For each category for which value at risk disclosures are made, provide either:
    - The average, high and low amounts, or the distribution of the value at risk amounts for the reporting period; or
    - The average, high and low amounts, or the distribution of actual changes in fair values, earnings, or cash flows from the market risk sensitive instruments occurring during the reporting period; or
    - The percentage or number of times the actual changes in fair values, earnings, or cash flows from the market risk sensitive instruments exceeded the value at risk amounts during the reporting period
- Describe the company's primary market exposures, how these exposures are managed (noting objectives, strategies, and any instruments used), and changes in the company's primary market risk exposures.

For example:

In the normal course of business and consistent with established policies and procedures, we employ a variety of financial instruments to manage exposure to fluctuations in the value of foreign currencies and interest rates. It is our policy to utilize these financial instruments only where necessary to finance our business and manage such exposures; we do not enter into these transactions for trading or speculative purposes.

We are exposed to foreign currency fluctuations, primarily as a result of our international sales, product sourcing and funding activities. Our foreign exchange risk management program is intended to lessen both the positive and negative effects of currency fluctuations on our consolidated results of operations, financial position and cash flows. We use forward exchange contracts and options to hedge certain anticipated but not yet firmly committed transactions as well as certain firm commitments and the related receivables and payables, including third-party and intercompany transactions. We have, and may in the future, also use forward contracts to hedge our investment in the net assets of certain international subsidiaries to offset foreign currency translation adjustments related to our net investment in those subsidiaries. Where exposures are hedged, our program has the effect of delaying the impact of exchange rate movements on our consolidated financial statements.

The timing for hedging exposures, as well as the type and duration of the hedge instruments employed, are guided by our hedging policies and determined based upon the nature of the exposure and prevailing market conditions. Generally, hedged transactions are expected to be recognized within 12 to 18 months. Hedged transactions are principally denominated in Euros, British Pounds and Japanese Yen.

Our earnings are also exposed to movements in short- and long-term market interest rates. Our objective in managing this interest rate exposure is to limit the impact of interest rate changes on earnings and cash flows and to reduce overall borrowing costs. To achieve these objectives, we maintain a mix of bank loans and fixed rate debt of varying maturities and have entered into interest rate swaps for a portion of our fixed rate debt.

We monitor foreign exchange risk, interest rate risk and related derivatives using a variety of techniques including a review of market value, sensitivity analysis, and value-at-risk (VaR). Our market-sensitive derivative and other financial instruments are foreign currency forward contracts, foreign currency option contracts, interest rate swaps, fixed interest rate U.S. Dollar denominated debt, and fixed interest rate Japanese Yen denominated debt.

We use VaR to monitor the foreign exchange risk of our foreign currency forward and foreign currency option derivative instruments only. The VaR determines the maximum potential one-day loss in the fair value of these foreign exchange rate-sensitive financial instruments. The VaR model estimates assume normal market conditions and a 95% confidence level. There are various modeling techniques that can be used in the VaR computation. Our computations are based on interrelationships between currencies and interest rates. These interrelationships are a function of foreign exchange currency market changes and interest rate changes over the preceding one year period. The value of foreign currency options does not change on a one-to-one basis with changes in the underlying currency rate.

The VaR model is a risk analysis tool and does not purport to represent actual losses in fair value that we will incur, nor does it consider the potential effect of favorable changes in market rates. It also does not represent the full extent of the possible loss that may occur. Actual future gains and losses will differ from those estimated because of changes or differences in market rates and interrelationships, hedging instruments and hedge percentages, timing and other factors.

The estimated maximum one-day loss in fair value on our foreign currency sensitive derivative financial instruments, derived using the VaR model, was $0.9 million and $0.5 million at December 31, 20X3 and 20X2, respectively. The VaR increased year-over-year as a result of an increase in the total notional value of our foreign currency derivative portfolio combined with a longer average duration on our outstanding trades at December 31, 20X3. Such a hypothetical loss in the fair value of our derivatives would be offset by increases in the value of the underlying transactions being hedged.

Details of third-party debt and interest rate swaps are provided in the following table. The table presents principal cash flows and related weighted average interest rates by expected maturity dates.

| (Dollars in millions) | Expected Maturity Date | | | | | | |
|---|---|---|---|---|---|---|---|
| | 20X3 | 20X4 | 20X5 | 20X6 | 20X7 | Thereafter | Total |
| **Foreign Exchange Risk** | | | | | | | |
| Japanese Yen debt – Fixed rate | | | | | | | |
| Principal payments | $0.2 | $0.3 | $0.3 | $0.3 | $0.5 | $1.2 | $2.8 |
| Average interest rate | 3.5% | 4.8% | 4.8% | 5.0% | 5.0% | 5.0% | |
| | | | | | | | |
| **Interest Rate Risk** | | | | | | | |
| Japanese Yen debt – Fixed rate | | | | | | | |
| Principal payments | $0.2 | $0.3 | $0.3 | $0.3 | $0.5 | $1.2 | $2.8 |
| Average interest rate | 3.5% | 4.8% | 4.8% | 5.0% | 5.0% | 5.0% | |
| U.S. Dollar debt – Fixed rate | | | | | | | |
| Principal payments | $1.0 | $0.8 | $0.8 | $0.7 | $0.7 | $2.3 | $6.3 |
| Average interest rate | 4.5% | 6.0% | 6.2% | 6.5% | 6.7% | 5.9% | |

## Item 8. Financial Statements and Supplementary Data

Item 8 may be considered the core of the Form 10-K, since it includes the financial statements and the notes related to those statements, as well as the report of the public accounting firm that examined the financial statements. The requirements for the production of financial statements and their related footnotes go well beyond the scope of this book (see the latest annual edition of the author's *GAAP Guidebook* for comprehensive coverage of this topic). In the following bullet points, we make note of several presentation issues related to the financial statements:

- The balance sheet shall be presented as of the end of each of the last two fiscal years
- The income statement shall be presented for each of the last three years
- The statement of cash flows shall be presented for each of the last three years
- The statement of retained earnings shall be presented for each of the last three years

## Item 9. Changes in and Disagreements with Accountants on Accounting and Financial Disclosure

A clear area of concern for the reader of a company's financial statements is when the company switches its auditors. The change could be triggered by a disagreement over the presentation of information in the financial statements, which could mean that company management wants to take an unusually aggressive approach to certain topics. The SEC ensures that these matters are illuminated by requiring the following presentation of information:

- If the independent accountant resigned or was dismissed during the two most recent fiscal years, disclose the following information:
  - Whether the accountant resigned, declined to stand for re-election or was dismissed, as well as the date of this occurrence.
  - Whether the accountant's report on the financial statements for either of the past two years contained an adverse opinion or a disclaimer of opinion, or was qualified or modified as to uncertainty, audit scope, or accounting principles, and also note the nature of each adverse opinion, disclaimer of opinion, modification, or qualification.
  - Whether the decision to change accountants was recommended or approved by the audit committee or the board of directors.
  - Whether there were disagreements with the former accountant on any matter of accounting principles or practices, financial statement disclosure, or auditing scope or procedure. If so, describe these disagreements, whether the board or audit committee discussed the matter with the accountant, and whether the company has authorized the accountant to respond fully to the inquiries of the successor accountant concerning the subject matter of the disagreements; if not, note the nature of and reason for any limitations.
- If a new independent accountant has been engaged, identify the new accountant and note the date of the engagement. Also disclose the following information:
  - If the company consulted the newly engaged accountant regarding the application of accounting principles to a specific transaction, or the type of audit opinion that might be rendered, or there was a matter that was the subject of a disagreement, then:
    - Identify the issues
    - Describe the views of the new accountant
    - State whether the former accountant was consulted regarding these issues, and if so, provide a summary of the former accountant's views

There are additional non-reporting requirements under which the new accountant is requested to provide a letter, stating whether it agrees with the statements made by the company, and any issues over which it does not agree.

## Item 9A. Controls and Procedures

The SEC requires that a company disclose the conclusions of its principal executive and principal financial officers regarding the effectiveness of the company's disclosure controls and procedures. There should be an accompanying report that contains the following:

- A statement of management's responsibility for establishing and maintaining adequate internal control over the financial reporting of the company.
- A statement identifying the framework used by management to evaluate the effectiveness of the company's internal control over financial reporting.
- Management's assessment of the effectiveness of the company's internal control over financial reporting, including a statement as to whether the internal control over financial reporting is effective (disclosures of material weaknesses in the company's internal control over financial reporting must be disclosed).
- The registered public accounting firm's attestation report on the company's internal control over financial reporting, if the company is an accelerated filer or a large accelerated fiier.
- Any change in the company's internal control over financial reporting that occurred during the company's last fiscal quarter that has materially affected, or is reasonably likely to materially affect, the company's internal control over financial reporting.

The following example contains several elements of the preceding SEC requirements:

The company maintains a set of disclosure controls and procedures, designed to ensure that information required to be disclosed by the company in reports that it files or submits under the Exchange Act is recorded, processed, summarized or reported within the time periods specified in SEC rules and regulations. Management necessarily applies its judgment in assessing the costs and benefits of such controls and procedures, which, by their nature, can provide only reasonable assurance regarding management's control objectives. The company's management, including the chief executive officer and the chief financial officer, does not expect that our disclosure controls and procedures can prevent all possible errors or fraud. A control system, no matter how well conceived and operated, can provide only reasonable, not absolute, assurance that misstatements due to error or fraud will not occur or that all control issues and instances of fraud, if any, within the company have been detected. Judgments in decision making can be faulty and breakdowns can occur because of simple errors or mistakes. Additionally, controls can be circumvented by the individual acts of one or more persons. The design of any system of controls is based in part upon certain assumptions about the likelihood of future events, and while our disclosure controls and procedures are designed to be effective under circumstances where they should reasonably be expected to operate effectively, there can be no assurance that any design will succeed in achieving its stated goals under all potential future conditions. Because of the inherent limitations in any control system, misstatements due to possible errors or fraud may occur and not be detected.

The company's management, with the participation of the chief executive officer and chief financial officer, has evaluated the effectiveness of the company's disclosure controls and procedures as of December 31, 20X3. Based on that evaluation, the company's chief executive officer and chief financial officer concluded that the company's disclosure controls and procedures were effective as of December 31, 20X3.

The company's independent registered public accounting firm, Ernst & Young LLP, is appointed by the audit committee. Ernst & Young LLP has audited and reported on the consolidated financial statements of Ninja Cutlery and the company's internal control over financial reporting, each as contained in this Form 10-K.

During the year ended December 31, 20X3, including the quarter ended December 31, 20X3, our management completed corrective actions to remediate the material weakness identified in our 20X2 Form 10-K. Specifically, the following actions were taken with respect to the following identified material weakness: The company did not maintain sufficient resources in the corporate tax function to provide for adequate and timely preparation and review of various income tax calculations, reconciliations, and related supporting documentation. To resolve this issue, we implemented the following improvements:

- Hired two additional tax managers
- Changed the reporting of the tax function to the corporate controller
- Installed new tax management software and provided training in its use to the tax staff
- Formalized policies and procedures for the main reporting tasks

## Item 10. Directors, Executive Officers and Corporate Governance

The disclosure of background information about the directors and executive officers of an organization is extensive. The SEC requires that the following information be provided in regard to the directors and executive officers of an organization, as well as certain corporate governance issues:

- List the names and ages of all company directors and all persons nominated to become directors. Also indicate all positions and offices with the company held by each of these people. List each person's term of office as a director, and any periods during which he or she has already served in this role. Also note any arrangement under which the person is or was to be selected as a director or nominee.
- List the names and ages of all executive officers of the company and all persons chosen to become executive officers. Note all company positions held by these persons. List each person's term of office as an officer, and the period during which each individual has served in this role. Also note any arrangement under which the person is or was to be selected as an officer.
- Identify all significant employees, such as production managers or research scientists, who are expected to make significant contributions to the busi-

ness. Also note their backgrounds to the same extent as the executive officers.

- State the nature of any family relationship between any director, executive officer, or person nominated to become a director or executive officer.
- Note the business experience during the past five years of each of the preceding individuals, including their principal occupations and employment, the name and principal business of any entity in which such work was carried on, and whether these entities were a parent, subsidiary or other affiliate of the company. Also describe the specific experience, qualifications, or other attributes that led to a person serving as a director of the company. Also for directors, indicate other directorships held.
- Describe any of the following events that occurred during the past ten years and that are material to an evaluation of the ability or integrity of any director or executive officer:
  - o Bankruptcy by the individual or a business of which the person was an executive officer
  - o A criminal conviction or a named subject of a pending criminal proceeding, other than minor offenses
  - o Any court orders enjoining a person from participating in the securities industry in various roles, or violations of federal securities or commodities laws, or mail or wire fraud
- Identify each person who was a director, officer, beneficial owner of more than 10 percent of any class of the company's equity securities that failed to file a Form 3, 4, or 5 on a timely basis. For these individuals, state the number of late reports, the number of transactions not reported on a timely basis, and any known failure to file a form.
- Disclose whether the company has adopted a code of ethics that applies to the entity's principal executive officer, principal financial officer, and principal accounting officer. If not, explain why there is no applicable code of ethics.
- Describe any material changes to the procedures by which shareholders can recommend nominees to the board of directors.
- State whether the company has a separately-designated standing audit committee, and identify each committee member. If the entire board of directors is acting as the audit committee, reveal this situation.
- Disclose that there is at least one financial expert serving on the audit committee, or that there is no such person on the committee, and why no such person is on the committee. If so, disclose the name of the financial expert and whether the person is independent.

The following is a condensed example of several of the preceding disclosure requirements:

The names, ages, year first elected and current titles of each of the executive officers of the company as of December 31, 20X3 are set forth below:

| Name | Age | Year First Elected Executive Officer | Title |
|------|-----|--------------------------------------|-------|
| Gerald Evans | 62 | 19X8 | Chief executive officer |
| Bruce Nolan | 59 | 19X8 | President |
| Allison Vincent | 43 | 20X9 | Chief financial officer |
| Robert Tomberlin | 59 | 19X8 | Chief operating officer |
| Robert Miller | 38 | 20X1 | Senior vice president |
| Stephanie Honor | 31 | 20X7 | Chief product designer |

Additional information regarding the backgrounds of the executive officers is as follows:

Gerald Evans was elected chief executive officer of the company in October 19X8. He was previously the chief product manager at Sharper Products from 19X0 to 19X8.

Bruce Nolan was elected president of the company in October 19X8. He was previously employed as the vice president of marketing at Sharper Products from 19X0 to 19X8.

Allison Vincent was elected chief financial officer in 20X9. She was previously a senior manager at Ernst & Young from 19X4 to 20X5, and previously served as the controller of Ninja from 20X6 to 20X8.

Robert Tomberlin was elected the chief operating officer in 19X8. He was previously the production manager at Sharper Products from 19X2 to 19X8.

Robert Miller was elected to the senior vice president position in 20X1. He was previously the sales manager at the Lethal Sushi restaurant chain from 19X8 to 20X0.

Stephanie Honor was appointed to the chief product designer position in 20X1. She was previously the chief metallurgist at Katana Blades from 20X3 to 20X7.

There is no family relationship between any of the above-named persons, or between any of such persons and any of the directors of the company.

The Company has adopted a Code of Conduct that applies to its principal executive officer, principal financial officer and controller, among others.

## Item 11. Executive Compensation

The amount of disclosure required for executive compensation has grown substantially in recent years, having now reached the point where this can be the second-largest disclosure area outside of the management's discussion and analysis of financial condition and results of operation. The SEC mandates the following disclosures:

- Discuss the compensation of the executive officers, including the objectives of their compensation plans, what the programs are designed to reward, each element of compensation, the reasons for paying each element, how the amount of each element is determined, how the elements fit into the company's overall compensation objectives, and whether the company has considered the results of the most recent shareholder advisory vote on executive compensation.
- Provide a summary compensation table that shows all elements of the compensation of the named executive officers of the company for each of the last three years. The table should include the following columns:
  - Name and principal position of each person listed
  - The applicable fiscal year
  - The dollar value of the base salary
  - The dollar value of the cash and non-cash bonus earned
  - The aggregate grant date fair value for awards of stock
  - The aggregate grant date fair value of option awards
  - Non-equity incentive plan compensation
  - The change in pension value and non-qualified deferred compensation
  - All other compensation, such as perquisites
- Provide a summary of grants of plan-based awards in a table that shows each grant of an award made to an executive officer in the last fiscal year. The table should include the following columns:
  - Name of the executive officer
  - The grant date for equity-based awards
  - The dollar value of the estimated future payout
  - The number of shares of stock to be paid out
  - The number of shares of stock granted that were not required to be disclosed in the preceding columns
  - The number of securities underlying options that were not required to be disclosed in the preceding columns
  - The per-share exercise price of the options granted in the fiscal year
  - If the preceding exercise price was below the market price on the grant date, list in another column the closing market price on the date of the grant
  - The grant date fair value of each equity award
- Provide a narrative description of any material factors needed to understand the information disclosed in the preceding tables. This may include, for example, terms of employment agreements and the nature of any option repricing.

175

- Provide a summary of outstanding equity awards as of the end of the last fiscal year. The table should include the following columns:
  - Name of the executive officer
  - The number of securities underlying unexercised options that are exercisable
  - The number of securities underlying unexercised options that are unexercisable
  - The number of shares underlying unexercised options awarded under an equity incentive plan that have not been earned
  - The applicable exercise or base price for the preceding items
  - The expiration date for each of the preceding items
  - The total number of shares that have not vested
  - The aggregate market value of shares that have not vested
  - The total number of shares awarded under any equity incentive plan that have not vested and that have not been earned, and the number of shares underlying each such unit
  - The aggregate market or payout value of the shares under any equity incentive plan that have not vested and that have not been earned
- Provide a summary table containing option exercises and similar instruments, and each vesting of stock during the last fiscal year for the executive officers. The table should include the following columns:
  - Name of the executive officer
  - The number of securities for which the options were exercised
  - The aggregate dollar value realized upon exercise of the options or similar instruments
  - The number of shares of stock that have vested
  - The aggregate dollar value realized upon the vesting of stock or such similar transaction
- Provide a summary table containing pension benefits. The table should contain the following columns:
  - Name of the executive officer
  - Name of the plan
  - The number of years of service credited to the executive officer under the plan
  - The actuarial present value of the executive officer's accumulated benefit under the plan
  - The dollar amount of any payments and benefits paid to the executive officer during the last fiscal year
- Provide a summary table containing nonqualified defined contribution and other nonqualified deferred compensation plans. The table should contain columns for the following information:
  - Name of the executive officer
  - The dollar amount of aggregate executive contributions during the last fiscal year

- o The dollar amount of aggregate company contributions during the last fiscal year
- o The dollar amount of aggregate interest or other earnings accrued during the last fiscal year
- o The aggregate dollar amount of all withdrawals by and distributions to the executive during the last fiscal year
- o The dollar amount of the total balance in the executive's account at the end of the fiscal year
- For each contract, agreement, or plan that provides for payments to an executive officer as part of a termination or change in control of the business, provide the following information:
  - o The circumstances under which a payment or other benefit would be triggered
  - o A quantification and description of the estimated payments and benefits that would be provided in each circumstance, and who would provide these items
  - o The determination of payments and benefits under the different circumstances
  - o The conditions or obligations applicable to the receipt of payments or benefits, such as the use of non-compete agreements, and the duration and provisions of these agreements
  - o Other material factors regarding each contract, agreement, or plan
- Provide a summary table containing the compensation of the directors for the last fiscal year. The table should contain columns for the following information:
  - o The name of each director
  - o The aggregate dollar amount of all fees earned as a director
  - o The aggregate grant date fair value for awards of stock
  - o The aggregate grant date fair value for awards of options
  - o The dollar value of all earnings for services performed during the fiscal year pursuant to non-equity incentive plans, and all earnings on any outstanding awards
  - o The aggregate change in the actuarial present value of the director's accumulated benefit under all defined benefit and actuarial pension plans, and the above-market or preferential earnings on compensation that is deferred on a basis that is not tax-qualified
  - o All other compensation for the fiscal year that could not be reported in any other columns, such as perquisites, discounted stock purchases, insurance premiums, and consulting fees.
  - o The dollar value of total compensation for the covered fiscal year.

> **Note:** Executive officers are considered to be the principal executive officer, principal financial officer, and the three most highly compensated individuals after the principal executive officer and financial officer.

In the interests of brevity, a substantially reduced example of these disclosures follows:

The company's named executive officers (NEOs) are: Gerald Evans, Chief Executive Officer (CEO); Bruce Nolan, President; Allison Vincent, Chief Financial Officer (CFO); Robert Tomberlin, Chief Operating Officer (COO); and Robert Miller, Senior Vice President (SVP).

The compensation committee adopted and implemented a new executive compensation program design for the NEOs in 20X3. The primary objective of the new design was to increase the amount that an executive's compensation is specifically tied to the operational and financial performance of the company. The following changes incorporate this new objective:

- The CEO was granted long-term equity incentives of which 80% are performance-based restricted stock units (RSUs) and 20% are time-based restricted stock units. The performance units only vest if threshold levels of certain operational and financial metrics are met during a three-year performance measurement period;
- All other NEOs were granted similar long-term equity incentives, using a 50/50 ratio of performance-based to time-based restricted stock units; and
- A new formulaic annual incentive cash bonus program was established based on the levels of achievement of three operational and financial metrics.

The company believes the changes made to its annual incentive cash bonus and long-term equity incentive programs for 20X3 represent a significant step toward enhancing its executive pay structure and further aligning its NEOs' pay opportunities with the interests of its long-term shareholders.

The company's executive compensation program is designed to reward its officers, including the NEOs, for creating long-term value for Ninja's shareholders. This approach allows the company to incentivize its executives for delivering value to shareholders while reducing or eliminating certain compensation if performance goals are not achieved. Ninja competes for the same talent against all companies in the New York area, and, therefore, a primary objective of its compensation program is to attract, retain and challenge executive talent.

The company's compensation program is comprised of elements common in the industry and each individual element serves an important purpose toward the total compensation package.

The primary elements of the 20X3 executive compensation package are base salary, annual incentive cash bonus, and long-term equity incentives, as noted in the following table:

| Component | Type of Payment/Benefit | Purpose |
|---|---|---|
| Base salary | Fixed cash payment with NEO generally available for annual increase | Attract and retain talent; designed to be competitive with comparable companies |
| Annual incentive cash bonus | Annual cash payments based on performance | Pay for performance tied to success in achieving annual revenue increase, total return on assets, and net profits after tax |
| Long-term equity incentives | 3-year cliff vested performance RSUs | Align NEO compensation with that of long-term shareholders; performance RSUs vest at levels corresponding to the achievement of the three-year total shareholder return |

Base salary provides our NEOs with a base level of income and is based on an individual's responsibility, performance assessment, and career experience. We have historically set base salaries for our officers within the third quartile of the competitive market to attract and retain the best talent, and base salary adjustments are made from time to time as a result of our review of market data.

The following table shows the percentage increase in base salaries for our NEOs, along with the actual base salaries of our NEOs for 20X2 and 20X3.

| Named Executive Officer | 20X2 Salary | 20X2 Percentage of Salary Increase | 20X3 Salary | 20X3 Percentage of Salary Increase |
|---|---|---|---|---|
| Gerald Evans, CEO | $820,000 | 3% | $845,000 | 3% |
| Bruce Nolan, President | 600,000 | 3% | 618,000 | 3% |
| Allison Vincent, CFO | 550,000 | 3% | 567,000 | 3% |
| Robert Tomberlin, COO | 460,000 | 3% | 474,000 | 3% |
| Robert Miller, SVP | 400,000 | 3% | 412,000 | 3% |

The 20X3 annual cash incentive bonus program is based on our pay for performance philosophy. For 20X3, the annual target cash bonus is stated as a percentage of base salary. The target award levels were set, in part, based on discussions with an independent compensation consultant regarding industry trends and competitive compensation data for similar executive positions of our peers.

The following table displays for each NEO their target bonus opportunity and the calculation of their potential annual cash bonus, incorporating an actual achievement rate of 38% of the targeted performance levels.

| Named Executive Officer | 20X3 Target as Percentage of Base Salary | 20X3 Annual Target Bonus | 20X3 Annual Cash Bonus Potential Based on 20X3 Performance (38% of Target) |
|---|---|---|---|
| Gerald Evans, CEO | 100% | $845,000 | $321,000 |
| Bruce Nolan, President | 80% | 494,000 | 188,000 |
| Allison Vincent, CFO | 60% | 340,000 | 129,000 |
| Robert Tomberlin, COO | 60% | 284,000 | 108,000 |
| Robert Miller, SVP | 60% | 247,000 | 94,000 |

Long-term equity incentive awards are a critical element in our executive compensation design and are the largest component of an executive's potential compensation. To set the target level amount of long-term equity incentives, our compensation committee utilized position-specific marketplace data, comparing our 20X2 long-term incentive target for our NEOs to the market median provided by an independent compensation consultant. This marketplace data identified that the 20X2 long-term incentive targets for our NEOs were lower than the median of our peer group and led the compensation committee to increase the target for long-term incentives by 20% for each NEO. The following summarizes the 20X3 long-term incentive targets as a percentage of the NEO's base salary:

| Named Executive Officer | Approved 20X3 Long-Term Incentive Target as a Percentage of Base Salary |
|---|---|
| Gerald Evans, CEO | 400% |
| Bruce Nolan, President | 300% |
| Allison Vincent, CFO | 200% |
| Robert Tomberlin, COO | 200% |
| Robert Miller, SVP | 200% |

The new performance RSUs granted to our NEOs will measure performance over a three-year performance period. Each NEO's performance RSU award payout opportunity ranges from zero to 200% of target depending on the level of performance, with performance levels above target intended to reward for overachievement. The compensation committee approved the following table of weightings and performance levels:

| Metric | Threshold Performance (50% of Target) | Target Performance (100% of Target) | Challenge Performance (200% of Target) |
|---|---|---|---|
| 3-year total shareholder return | > 25th Percentile | > 50th Percentile | > 75th Percentile |

To determine payout levels, at the end of the three-year performance period, the performance metric will be compared to actual performance to determine the number of shares earned by each NEO. Performance below the threshold level will result in no credit awarded. Performance at or above the threshold level will result in computing the pro rata percentage points achieved. The compensation committee will certify the performance results.

The following table sets forth certain summary information regarding compensation paid or accrued by the company to or on behalf of the company's CEO, CFO, and each of the three most highly compensated executive officers of the company other than the CEO and CFO, who were serving as an executive officer at the end of the last fiscal year, for the fiscal years ended December 31 of 20X1, 20X2, and 20X3.

| Name and Position | Year | Salary | Bonus | Stock Awards | All Other Compensation | Total |
|---|---|---|---|---|---|---|
| Gerald Evans, CEO | 20X3 | $845,000 | $321,000 | $-- | $25,000 | $1,191,000 |
| | 20X2 | 820,000 | 279,000 | 410,000 | 25,000 | 1,534,000 |
| | 20X1 | 795,000 | 318,000 | 795,000 | 20,000 | 1,928,000 |
| Bruce Nolan, President | 20X3 | 618,000 | 188,000 | -- | 43,000 | 849,000 |
| | 20X2 | 600,000 | 162,000 | 300,000 | 38,000 | 1,100,000 |
| | 20X1 | 582,000 | 204,000 | 582,000 | 12,000 | 1,380,000 |
| Allison Vincent, CFO | 20X3 | 567,000 | 129,000 | -- | 21,000 | 717,000 |
| | 20X2 | 550,000 | 110,000 | 275,000 | 18,000 | 953,000 |
| | 20X1 | 534,000 | 155,000 | 534,000 | -- | 1,223,000 |
| Robert Tomberlin, COO | 20X3 | 474,000 | 108,000 | -- | 72,000 | 654,000 |
| | 20X2 | 460,000 | 92,000 | 230,000 | 60,000 | 842,000 |
| | 20X1 | 446,000 | 129,000 | 446,000 | 49,000 | 1,070,000 |
| Robert Miller, SVP | 20X3 | 412,000 | 94,000 | -- | -- | 506,000 |
| | 20X2 | 400,000 | 80,000 | 200,000 | -- | 680,000 |
| | 20X1 | 388,000 | 113,000 | 388,000 | 20,000 | 909,000 |

The table below and the discussion that follows reflect the amount of compensation payable to each NEO upon the occurrence of the different circumstances of change of control, termination without good cause, or termination for good reason under each NEO's employment agreement and the company's change of control severance plan. The amounts shown assume that such termination was effective December 31, 20X3.

The actual amounts to be paid out can only be determined at the time of each executive's separation from the company.

| Named Executive Officer | Cash Payments | Benefit Cost | RSU Equity Acceleration | Total |
|---|---|---|---|---|
| Gerald Evans, CEO | | | | |
| Change of control | $2,535,000 | $30,000 | $1,205,000 | $3,770,000 |
| Termination for good reason | 845,000 | 10,000 | 1,205,000 | 2,060,000 |
| Termination without good cause | 1,690,000 | 30,000 | 1,205,000 | 2,925,000 |
| | | | | |
| Bruce Nolan, President | | | | |
| Change of control | 1,854,000 | 30,000 | 882,000 | 2,766,000 |
| Termination for good reason | 618,000 | 10,000 | 882,000 | 1,510,000 |
| Termination without good cause | 1,236,000 | 30,000 | 882,000 | 2,148,000 |
| | | | | |
| Allison Vincent, CFO | | | | |
| Change of control | 1,701,000 | 30,000 | 809,000 | 2,540,000 |
| Termination for good reason | 567,000 | 10,000 | 809,000 | 1,386,000 |
| Termination without good cause | 1,134,000 | 30,000 | 809,000 | 1,973,000 |
| | | | | |
| Robert Tomberlin, COO | | | | |
| Change of control | 1,422,000 | 30,000 | 676,000 | 2,128,000 |
| Termination for good reason | 474,000 | 10,000 | 676,000 | 1,160,000 |
| Termination without good cause | 948,000 | 30,000 | 676,000 | 1,654,000 |
| | | | | |
| Robert Miller, SVP | | | | |
| Change of control | 1,236,000 | 30,000 | 588,000 | 1,854,000 |
| Termination for good reason | 412,000 | 10,000 | 588,000 | 1,010,000 |
| Termination without good cause | 824,000 | 30,000 | 588,000 | 1,442,000 |

When calculating the compensation payable under all three of the preceding scenarios, the same formula applies to each NEO, which is:
- Upon a change of control, the individual is paid three times his or her ending annual salary, plus one year of medical insurance coverage, and all outstanding RSUs are immediately vested.
- Upon a termination for good reason, the individual is paid his or her ending annual salary, plus four months of medical insurance coverage, and all outstanding RSUs are immediately vested.
- Upon a termination without good cause, the individual is paid two times his or her ending annual salary, plus one year of medical insurance coverage, and all outstanding RSUs are immediately vested.

## Item 12. Security Ownership of Certain Beneficial Owners and Management and Related Stockholder Matters

The SEC wants the shareholders of a business to know the share ownership of the executive officers and directors of a business, as well as the identities of the principal shareholders. The reporting requirements are:
- For any shareholders of more than 5% of any class of the company's voting securities, reveal the following information in tabular format:
  - Class of securities held

- ○ Name and address of owner
- ○ Amount and nature of ownership
- ○ Percent ownership of class of securities
- For any directors and executive officers, reveal the following information in tabular format:
  - ○ Class of securities held
  - ○ Name of owner
  - ○ Amount and nature of ownership
  - ○ Percent of ownership of class of securities

Also describe any arrangements that may subsequently result in a change in control of the company.

The following is an abbreviated example of the type of reporting that the SEC expects to see:

The following tables give information concerning the beneficial ownership of Ninja's common stock as of January 20, 20X4 by all directors, director nominees, all directors and executive officers as a group, and the persons who are known to Ninja to be the owners of more than five percent of the outstanding common stock of Ninja Cutlery.

**Executive Officer and Directors**

| Name | Shares Owned Sole Voting and Investment Power | Shared Voting and Investment Power | Shares Subject to Options Exercisable within 60 Days | Shares Underlying Restricted Stock Units | Total Beneficial Ownership |
|---|---|---|---|---|---|
| Albert Cowling | 40,000 | -- | -- | 45,000 | 85,000 |
| Bronson Davis | 120,000 | -- | 40,000 | | 160,000 |
| Ephraim Foss | 78,000 | 5,000 | -- | 72,000 | 155,000 |
| Garland Hill | 12,000 | -- | 20,000 | | 32,000 |
| Ichabod James | 400,000 | 200,000 | -- | | 600,000 |
| Kevin Land | 200,000 | 13,000 | -- | 10,000 | 223,000 |
| All as a group | 850,000 | 218,000 | 60,000 | 127,000 | 1,255,000 |

**Principal Stockholders**

| Name and Address | Amount and Nature of Beneficial Ownership | Percent of Class |
|---|---|---|
| Mango Farms Trust 111 Main Street, Milpitas CA | 8,000,000 (1) | 20.00% |
| Nederland Family Trust 45 Brook Lane, Newbury MA | 6,500,000 (1) | 16.25% |
| Orehouse Mining Development Trust 300 Central Ave., Elko NV | 4,000,000 (1) | 10.00% |

(1) Based on Schedule 13G filings with the Securities and Exchange Commission. These entities have sole voting and dispositive power of the shares owned by them.

## Item 13. Certain Relationships and Related Transactions, and Director Independence

If there have been any transactions with related parties, they are to be disclosed. The SEC provides the following supporting commentary in regard to the level of detail that should be disclosed:

- Make note of any transaction since the beginning of the last fiscal year, or currently proposed, in which the company is or shall be a participant, and the amount involved is at least $120,000, and where a related person has a direct or indirect material interest. The following information is to be disclosed:
  - The name of the related person and the basis of the relationship
  - The related person's interest in the transaction, including the person's position or relationship with the entities involved in the transaction
  - The dollar value of the transaction
  - The dollar value of the amount of the related person's interest in the transaction
  - If there is indebtedness, the largest aggregate amount of principal outstanding during the disclosure period, the ending balance on the last practicable date, the principal paid and interest paid during the disclosure period, and the interest rate
  - Other information related to the transaction or person that is material to investors
- Describe the company's policies and procedures for the review, approval, or ratification of any related party transaction, as well as any transactions not requiring such review, or where a review was not followed.

For example:

The board of directors has adopted a written policy for the review of transactions involving more than $120,000 in any fiscal year in which the company is a participant and in which any director, executive officer, holder of more than 5% of Ninja's outstanding shares or any immediate family member of any of these persons has a direct or indirect material interest. Directors, 5% shareholders and executive officers are required to inform the company of any such transaction promptly after they become aware of it, and the company collects information from directors and executive officers about their affiliations and the affiliations of their family members so the company can search its records for any such transactions. Transactions are presented to the board for approval before they are entered into or, if this is not possible, for ratification after the transaction has been entered into. The board approves or ratifies a transaction if it determines that the transaction is consistent with the best interests of the company, including whether the transaction impairs the independence of a director.

The policy does not require review of the following transactions:

- Employment of executive officers approved by the compensation committee

- Charitable contributions to entities where a director is an executive officer of the entity, if the amount is less than $250,000 and less than 5% of the annual contributions received by the entity

- Compensation of directors approved by the board
- Transactions in which all shareholders receive benefits proportional to their shareholdings

- Ordinary banking transactions identified in the policy

- Transactions with entities where the related party's sole interest is as a non-executive officer, employee, or trustee of the entity.

During fiscal year 20X3, there were no transactions requiring disclosure with related parties of the company.

## Item 14. Principal Accountant Fees and Services

It is necessary to disclose the amounts paid to the company's auditors for their audit and other services. The SEC defines these disclosures as follows:

- Under the *audit fees* caption, the aggregate fees billed for each of the last two years for professional services rendered by the principal accountant for the audit of the company's annual financial statements and review of its quarterly Form 10-Q.
- Under the *audit-related fees* caption, the aggregate fees billed for each of the last two years for assurance and related services by the principal accountant that are reasonably related to the performance of the audit or review of the company's financial statements. Describe the nature of these services.
- Under the *tax fees* caption, the aggregate fees billed for each of the last two years for professional services rendered by the principal accountant for tax compliance, tax advice, and tax planning. Describe the nature of these services.
- Under the *all other fees* caption, the aggregate fees billed for each of the last two years for products and services provided by the principal accountant. Describe the nature of these products and services.

For example:

The following table presents fees paid for professional services rendered for the audit of the company's annual financial statements for 20X3 and 20X2 and fees paid for other services provided by our independent auditor in those years:

|  | 20X3 | 20X2 |
|---|---|---|
| Audit fees (1) | $287,000 | $272,000 |
| Audit-related fees (2) | 43,000 | 56,000 |
| Tax fees (3) | 91,000 | 87,000 |
| All other fees (4) | 20,000 | 15,000 |
| Totals | $441,000 | $430,000 |

(1) Fees for services associated with the annual audit (including internal control reporting), reviews of quarterly reports on Form 10-Q and accounting consultations.
(2) Fees for employee benefit plan audits and certain attestation services not required by statute or regulation.
(3) Primarily fees for tax compliance in various international markets.
(4) Fees for miscellaneous advisory services.

## Analysis Conclusions

The Form 10-K is a rich source of information that the analyst can spend hours perusing. The result can be insights into many aspects of the operations and financial results of a business. In the following bullet points, we note certain areas within the Form 10-K where especially useful nuggets of information may be located:

- *Item 1 – Business.* Review the segment and product information on a trend line to determine which parts of the business are changing in size and profitability. Also compare the company's descriptions of its business plans with those of prior years, to see if there are any changes. Note any changes in the names of those customers whose business comprises more than 10% of revenues. Also, plot the reported backlog on a trend line to see if the rate of backlog growth is changing. Finally, note any changes in the amount of research and development spending as a percentage of sales. In short, the intent of this analysis is to review financial results and reported intentions over a period of time.
- *Item 1A – Risk factors.* Note changes in the risks presented from one year to the next. Look in particular for additions to the list, which can indicate new concerns for the analyst to be aware of.
- *Item 1B – Unresolved staff comments.* It is quite rare for there to be any unresolved staff comments. When there is a disclosure in this area, review it quite carefully, for it may relate to a significant point of accounting that the SEC is disputing.
- *Item 2 – Properties.* Note the lease expiration dates in this section, which can be used to estimate reductions in rental costs in future periods. This

information can also be used to estimate the amount of property at risk in countries having political difficulties or which are threatening expropriation.

- *Item 3 – Legal proceedings.* Legal issues can threaten the life of a business or at least drain its bank account, so peruse all disclosures in this area in detail. Environmental liabilities can be particularly damaging.
- *Item 4 – Mine safety disclosures.* A large number of incidents can indicate a possible shutdown, future expenditures for safety equipment, or employee lawsuits.
- *Item 5 – Market for company stock.* The discussion of dividend payments can be used to estimate the timing and amount of future dividends. Also note the number of stock options and their features, to estimate their impact on the number of shares outstanding.
- *Item 6 – Selected Financial Data.* This section is not especially useful to the analyst, who has access to more detailed information in the accompanying financial statements.
- *Item 7 – MD&A.* This can be a rich source of information, but only if the company controller is feeling expansive about discussing the indicated topics. Many organizations provide the bare minimum required by the SEC, so the amount of information to be gleaned will vary greatly by company. Among the better topics in this section are the discussions of uncertainties, unusual events, the introduction of new products, and off-balance sheet arrangements – in short, any indicators of future changes in financial results.
- *Item 7A- Market Risk.* This can be a useful section, depending on the risks to which a company is exposed. Look for large exposure levels relating to interest rates, foreign exchange holdings, and commodity prices, and the offsetting risk management strategies being used.
- *Item 9 – Changes in and Disagreements with Accountants.* The dismissal of the company's auditors can be a major event, indicating the use of aggressive accounting that the auditors were opposed to. A perusal of the reasons for a change in accountant can be illuminating.
- *Item 9A – Controls and Procedures.* Though the intention behind the disclosure of controls was good, the result has been boilerplate reporting that reveals little about the actual control situation within a company. If there is a discussion of control weaknesses, compare it to the disclosures in prior years to see if the situation has changed.
- *Item 10 – Governance.* Review this section in detail to see if any of the people managing a business have criminal convictions or are subject to court orders. The presence of these individuals is a major warning flag to steer clear of a company. The existence of related parties is not necessarily bad, since they may be willing to provide funding to the entity.
- *Items 11 and 12 – Executive compensation and security ownership.* When reviewing executive compensation and share ownership, the main point is to discern whether the aggregate amount paid out is egregious, to the point

where managers are clearly not looking out for the best interests of investors.

- *Item 13 – Certain relationships.* Related party transactions can be quite revealing, in terms of special deals. This can be a cause for concern if there is a long-running history of favoritism toward related parties.
- *Item 14 – Principal accountant fees and services.* Though it may be mildly interesting to know the fees charged by the company's outside accountants, this is usually not a key analysis issue, unless the fees are egregious.

# Glossary

## A

*Accounts receivable.* Short-term amounts due from buyers to a seller who have purchased goods or services from the seller on credit.

*Accrual basis of accounting.* A method of recording accounting transactions for revenue when earned and expenses when incurred.

*Amortization.* The gradual charging to expense of an intangible asset's cost over its useful life.

*Audit.* The examination of an entity's financial statements by an independent auditor.

*Audit opinion.* A statement by an auditor regarding whether the information in a company's financial statements is fairly presented.

## B

*Bad debt.* An account receivable that cannot be collected.

*Balance sheet.* A summary of the financial position of a business as of a specific point in time.

*Book value.* The original cost of an asset, less any subsequent depreciation.

*Breakeven.* The sales level at which a business earns zero profit.

*Burn rate.* The amount of cash being used up per reporting period.

## C

*Capitalization.* The recordation of an expenditure as an asset.

*Capitalization limit.* The cost threshold below which an expenditure is not capitalized.

*Cash.* Bills, coins, bank balances, money orders, and checks.

*Compilation.* A presentation of financial statements performed by an outside party, but not accompanied by any verification of the accuracy of the presented information.

*Contra account.* An account used to offset the balance in another, related account with which it is paired.

*Contribution margin.* Sales minus all variable expenses.

*Cost.* The expenditure required to create and sell products and services, or to acquire assets.

*Cost of goods sold.* The cost associated with the sale of goods to customers.

*Covenant.* A promise in a debt agreement that certain measures will be achieved or activities carried out.

*Current liabilities.* Obligations payable within the next 12 months.

*Cycle counting.* The systematic and ongoing comparison of inventory records to on-hand balances.

## D

*Debt.* An amount owed for funds borrowed, for which there is an associated interest payment.

*Depreciation.* The gradual charging to expense of a tangible asset's cost over its useful life.

*Direct method.* The practice of writing off individual invoices when it becomes apparent that they cannot be collected.

## E

*Effective tax rate.* The average income tax rate at which a business is taxed.

*Equity.* The residual value in a business, after liabilities are subtracted from assets.

*Expense.* The reduction in value of an asset as it is used to generate revenue.

## F

*Financial statements.* A collection of reports about an organization's financial results, condition, and cash flows.

*Fixed asset.* An item with a useful life of greater than one reporting period, and which exceeds the capitalization limit.

*Form 10-K.* The annual financial report that the Securities and Exchange Commission requires a publicly-held company to file with it.

## G

*General ledger.* The master set of accounts in which is stored all transactions occurring within a business.

*Goodwill.* The excess amount paid for an acquisition, above the fair values of the assets and liabilities acquired.

*Gross margin.* Sales minus the cost of goods sold; shows the proportion of sales remaining to pay for operating expenses and generate a profit.

## I

*Income investor.* An investor that acquires securities that yield a consistent payout over time.

*Income statement.* A summary of the sales generated and expenses incurred by a business during a reporting period, resulting in a profit or loss.

*Inventory.* That portion of a company's assets that are intended for sale in the ordinary course of business.

*Investments.* The securities of other entities, held with the objective of earning a return.

**L**

*Line of credit.* A commitment from a lender to pay a company whenever it needs cash, up to a pre-set maximum level.

*Liquidity.* The ability of an entity to pay its liabilities in a timely manner, as they come due for payment under their original payment terms.

**M**

*Margin of safety.* The sales decline that can occur before a business reaches its breakeven point.

**N**

*Net income.* Revenues minus all expenses, including income taxes.

**O**

*Order of liquidity.* The presentation of line items in the balance sheet based on the amount of time it should take to convert each item into cash.

**P**

*Periodic system.* A system for deriving the ending inventory balance and the cost of goods sold that depends on a physical inventory count at the end of each reporting period.

*Perpetual system.* A system for maintaining an ongoing and accurate inventory record balance by continually updating the inventory records as transactions occur.

*Prepaid expenses.* Expenditures made for which the related assets will not be consumed until a later period.

**R**

*Retained earnings.* The cumulative earnings of a business, less dividends paid.

*Review.* An examination of financial statements that has a more limited scope than an audit.

**S**

*Sales.* An increase in assets or decrease in liabilities caused by the provision of services or products to customers.

*Sales discount.* A reduction in the price of a product or service that is offered by the seller, in exchange for early payment by the buyer.

*Sales return.* The original sales amount associated with goods returned to the seller by the buyer.

*Statement of cash flows.* One of the financial statements, which aggregates cash inflows and outflows into different classifications.

## T

*Taxable income.* The amount of income to which an income tax rate is applied.

*Trade receivables.* Amounts billed by a business to its customers when it delivers goods or services to them in the ordinary course of business.

*Treasury stock.* Shares repurchased from investors.

## U

*Useful life.* The expected life span of a depreciable asset.

## W

*Working capital.* Current assets minus current liabilities.

# Index

Made in the USA
Middletown, DE
14 July 2016